FROM WAR TO PEACE:
ARAB-ISRAELI RELATIONS
1973–1993

From War to Peace: Arab-Israeli Relations 1973–1993

Edited by

Barry Rubin
Joseph Ginat
Moshe Ma'oz

With an introductory chapter by
Ezer Weizman,
President of Israel

New York University Press
Washington Square, New York

First published in the U.S.A. 1994 by
NEW YORK UNIVERSITY PRESS
Washington Square
New York, N.Y. 10003

Library of Congress Cataloging-in-Publication Data

From war to peace : Arab-Israeli relations, 1973–1993 / edited by
  Barry Rubin, Joseph Ginat, Moshe Ma'oz ; with an introductory
  chapter by Ezer Weizman.
  p.   cm.
  Includes bibliographical references and index.
  ISBN 0–8147–7462–8
  1. Jewish-Arab relations—1973–   2. Israel-Arab conflicts.
3. Middle East—Foreign relations.   4. Israel-Arab War, 1973—
Influence.   5. Israel. Treaties, etc. Munazzamat al-Tahrir al-
Filastiniyah, 1993 Sept. 13. I. Rubin, Barry M.   II. Ginat, J.
III. Ma'oz, Moshe.
DS119.7.F757   1994
956.9405′4—dc20   94-38055
                                                       CIP

Printed and bound in Great Britain by
Biddles Ltd, King's Lynn and Guildford

Contents

Acknowledgments

Joseph Ginat
Moshe Ma'oz

This book is based on the proceedings of a conference, "From War to Peace: 1973–1993," sponsored jointly by the Harry S. Truman Research Institute for the Advancement of Peace and the Leonard Davis Institute for International Relations, both at the Hebrew University of Jerusalem, the Arab-Jewish Center at Haifa University, and the Central Office of Information of the Ministry of Education, Culture and Sport of the State of Israel. The conference began on the 24th of October, 1993 at the Truman Institute and continued the next day at the University of Haifa. The conference also enjoyed the support of the American Cultural Center in Jerusalem.

Several individuals were instrumental in seeing the book to press, including Chaia Beckerman, Director of Publications at the Truman Institute, and Rachel Misrati, Assistant Editor. The conference could not have taken place without the devoted efforts of Tomy Horkany, Director of the Department of Institutions of Higher Education at the Central Office of Information, Idit Avidan and Dan Bitan of the Truman Institute, and Sarah Tamir, Administrator at the Jewish-Arab Center. Prof. Amnon Sella, Chairperson of the Davis Institute, was involved in organizing the conference, as well as backing the creation of the book.

Barry Rubin's willingness to take on the task of editing was the primary factor in ensuring that from a pile of papers and transcripts, a book could in fact take shape.

Last, but by no means least, thanks go to the contributors themselves: Mr. Ezer Weizman, President of the State of Israel, Dr. Yossi Beilin, Deputy Minister of Foreign Affairs, Dr. Joseph Sisco, President of the American University in Washington, and the distinguished scholars who participated from Israel, the West Bank and abroad.

From War to Peace: Arab-Israeli Relations, 1973–1993

Part I

Political Perspectives

Part I, Political Perspectives, takes a broad overview of the lessons of the 1973 War and the two decades of diplomatic effort to resolve the Arab-Israeli conflict which followed. The authors reveal new, first-hand material based on their involvement at a high political level. They have sharply differing perspectives on whether the 1973 War was avoidable through diplomatic efforts or was a necessary precondition for progress in negotiations. There is general agreement, however, that the war was a turning point in the conflict's history, beginning – in some cases more quickly, in others more slowly – an evolution by all the parties in their view of the conflict itself and the way to end the dispute.

In "From War to Peace," Barry Rubin gives an overview of the material covered in the book, examining the main debates, points of consensus, and themes. The Arab states, the Palestinians, Israel, the United States and the U.S.S.R. all underwent major changes in their political stance and their strategic situation between 1973 and 1993, and these were the necessary basis for a final breakthrough to peace.

Israel's President Ezer Weizman, in "Some Lessons Learned," places this era in the context of the conflict's history and draws on his personal experience with the 1973 War and the ensuing political process. He was especially impressed by the personal momentum created when Israelis and Egyptians began meeting face to face, even in dealing with details of the post-war cease-fire.

Former U.S. Under Secretary of State Joseph Sisco, in "The U.S. Role in the Peace Process," focuses on the American role, recounting his own participation in the peace process during the 1970s and the roots of U.S.-Soviet cooperation in the region. Sisco describes how he wrote the UN resolution defining the post-war diplomatic goals while sitting in the Kremlin. The language was sent to both the U.S. and Soviet delegations for their support.

Yossi Beilin, Israel's deputy foreign minister and chief negotiator at the secret talks producing the Israel-PLO agreement, gives his view in "The Opportunity that was not Missed." He stresses that the personal and creative element in diplomacy is often the decisive factor between success and failure. He is highly critical of the fact that Sadat's offer was not heeded before the 1973 War and he talks for the first time, giving examples from his own experience in secret diplomacy, about the handling of several initiatives in more recent years.

1

From War to Peace

Barry Rubin

The September 1993 Israel-PLO agreement marked the greatest advance to peace in the Arab-Israel conflict's history. This was the culmination of a process that began with the October 1973 War, exactly two decades earlier. It may seem terribly ironic that peace in the Middle East began with a war, yet this makes eminent sense given the nature of international affairs and power politics.

For frustration to be transformed into negotiations may require tensions building higher, giving the parties an incentive to solve the problem and making them willing to concede more to settle it peacefully. Indeed, it took still another armed conflict – Iraq's invasion of Kuwait and the ensuing 1991 Gulf War – to put the last elements in place for a diplomatic breakthrough.

This volume deals with the two pivotal events, in 1973 and 1993, leading the Middle East from war to peace, as well as the dramatic changes connecting them over time. It includes the reflections of Israeli, Palestinian, and American scholars and participants in the fighting, diplomacy, and secret contacts which moved toward resolving the world's longest ongoing conflict.

Beyond the Arab-Israeli conflict itself, this transformation has broader implications for the working of politics and decision-making. How can a zero-sum conflict about existence or sovereignty be turned into a more normal, potentially resolvable, state-to-state dispute? How can leaders differentiate between great opportunities to reduce problems and unacceptable risks that might endanger their people's survival?

In these circumstances, diplomacy can be like a complex ballet danced by elephants, who have their own unique grace but find it hard to change course. The burden of responsibility and struggle for political advantage makes it understandable that national leaders act so cautiously. Given the cost for their citizenry, though, it often makes for tragedy as well.

The difficulty of making peace in the Arab-Israeli conflict was a function of the issue's definition. The problem's defining root was that the Arab states and the Palestinian national movement refused to accept Israel's existence and believed that it could be destroyed. (While the Palestinians' plight was an equally fundamental factor, they could still aspire beyond it.) These two aspects – the rejection in principle of Israel and the expectation of total victory – were joined by a third factor: the political impossibility for the Arab side to make peace based on the constraints of ideology, public opinion, maintaining regime stability, and inter-Arab politics.

Only when this stance began shifting toward a reversal of its first two elements did diplomacy enter the picture as anything more than a public relations effort. That is, once Arab states or the PLO concluded that they could not destroy Israel, they began to face the structural problems of peacemaking and to calculate what Israel might offer in exchange for a negotiated compromise settlement. For the Arab states, this meant principally, territory captured by Israel in the 1967 War; for the Palestinians, this meant the chance of achieving their own state.

Naturally, the 1967 War was a necessary precondition for this stage, both in terms of the demonstrative effect of their defeat on the Arabs and Israel's gaining possession of bargaining chips – the Sinai, Golan Heights, West Bank and Gaza – territories the Arab side wanted to regain.

Egypt was the first Arab state to begin this transition. But this phase's onset, in about 1971, did not mean it had reached fruition. The war itself was part of that effort, designed by President Anwar al-Sadat, to draw in the great powers, prepare his people for a new stage, and improve Egypt's bargaining power *vis-à-vis* Israel. After the 1973 War, it became clear that he had embarked on a diplomatic process which – after Sadat's dramatic decision to go to Israel in 1977 – led to the Camp David Accords.

It is impossible to date precisely the point at which other Arab parties began to follow this pattern. King Hussein of Jordan thought along the same lines as Sadat, but because of the third factor – internal and regional opposition – he was unable to act. Syria and the PLO, however, took this path far more slowly and uncertainly. Only by the end of the 1980s had they reached the point attained by

Sadat in the early 1970s; only in the 1990s were they ready to go as far as Sadat did in the late 1970s.[1]

If the Arab position underwent an evolution, Israel's position followed a circle. Israel was already ready for peace with the Arab states. Before 1967, the disposition of the West Bank and Gaza was in Arab hands; after 1967, Israel's Labor party governments – with Yitzhak Rabin and Shimon Peres as prime ministers – saw the captured territories as bargaining chips to be returned in exchange for peace. Given the PLO's hard-line stance, Israel's government preferred to pass the West Bank back to Jordan but at that point, of course, Jordan could introduce any arrangements it wished for meeting Palestinian aspirations there.

By 1977, however, Israeli policy had changed in two respects. First, mistrust of the Arab sides' openly stated positions – plus the PLO strategy of terrorism – had made Israelis skeptical about the possibility or value of such a solution. The start of the movement to create Jewish settlements in the captured territories both reflected and deepened the sense that these lands should be kept, that there was no real peace option. Second, the election of a conservative Likud government headed by Prime Minister Menahem Begin, in 1977, put in place a very different Israeli policy. Begin concluded the Camp David agreement with Sadat, but this was as far as he was willing to go in terms of major concessions.

What happened after the Camp David accords led to a situation of no war, no peace. Both Israel and the Arab states found it undesirable to make war (the PLO lacked the power to generate a war between states) and either undesirable or impossible to make peace. The diplomatic alternative to this deadlock was perceived by all sides as requiring unacceptable and dangerous concessions. Thus, the peace process – often directed by the United States – sought to reach a point at which other Arab forces would be ready to recognize Israel and at which Israel would be ready to concede territory. This effort made possible a gradual advance, but success required independent, self-willed action by the parties themselves.

The main debate over the Arab-Israeli conflict's history now seems to be over whether the progression from war to peace was necessarily a steady, necessary evolution or whether success was detoured and forestalled by missed opportunities. Scholars must be careful not to be like prospectors hunting among events only for gold nuggets, the first glimmerings of what came later. They must weigh all the evidence to understand the preponderant forces and what was possible at any given time. Ideas develop gradually as alternative among several options – in leaders' minds and government policies – well before becoming national priorities.

The Arab-Israeli conflict was no typical international dispute over land or power, easily settled by compromise or some ingenious formula. To outsiders, wrote one scholar, failure to resolve the issue was "as puzzling as the solutions are obvious." It seemed simple for Israelis and Palestinians to recognize each other and divide the territory to give a national homeland to both peoples. Arab governments could recognize Israel, security guarantees could be formulated, and a golden age of peace and prosperity could begin.[2]

Rationally, such an approach seems obvious – though it was never so apparent to many Arabs, Israelis, or others who followed the conflict as politicians, officials, or scholars. Still, this does not mean such an outcome was actually available at any time in history as long as the conflict's framework was an existential struggle, or other conditions – U.S.-Soviet conflict, Arab politics, Palestinian goals, Israeli perceptions – were inimical.

Each objective fact was mediated through a particular leadership and political spectrum. Things which seemed rational – and were logical in the abstract – did not necessarily fit the rationality of international, regional, and domestic circumstances.

The 1973 War and the immediately preceding diplomacy make a superb case study of this problem.[3] Aside from the material situation, events were driven by the two statesmen who had strategies for change: Sadat and U.S. National Security Advisor and Secretary of State Henry Kissinger. Their two approaches interlocked, though differing on the crucial element of timing. Sadat, viewing the deadlock as threatening Egypt's economic stability, was ready to launch a limited war to make diplomatic progress possible by drawing in the superpowers and altering the balance of power. Before doing so, however, he made some hints and proposals for advancing the peace process. These offers were not taken up by the United States and were rejected by Israel.[4] Kissinger's strategy was to achieve détente with the U.S.S.R. by avoiding friction between the superpowers and discouraging Moscow from fomenting regional instability. His Middle East policy aimed to show the radical Arab regimes that they could gain nothing through war, extremism, or Soviet patronage. They would then have to come to the United States and the bargaining table, presenting reasonable proposals.

Kissinger's concept predicted what would come after the 1973 War. While Sadat was already thinking in that direction before the hostilities, he was far from being ready or able to transform Egypt's policy. Of course, when so many lives and resources are lost in a battle, it is hard not to think seriously – even with anguish – about whether things could have been different.

The situation is summarized by Professor Amnon Sella in his chapter: "When we take into consideration that the U.S. and the U.S.S.R. at the time were engaged in an effort to reach a global agreement, we can understand how Israel's over-confidence joined Egypt's need 'to regain by force what had been taken away by force' to produce a war in order to make peace." In other words, the United States and U.S.S.R. did not want their cooperation effort endangered either by a Middle East war or by the inevitable stresses between them – and between them and their allies – that a serious, probably abortive, peace effort would bring. Nor did they trust each other much.

Israel, feeling both haughty and insecure, believed itself able to handle the existing status quo but did not trust the Arabs to make peace. With good reason, Israel's leaders expected that a peace process would bring U.S. and international pressure for unilateral concessions. Egypt wanted to regain the Sinai, but the weight of its political system – despite Sadat's effort to change it – favored maximal aims, Arab cooperation, and no concessions. Indeed, even after the 1973 War it took five more years to reach an Egypt-Israel treaty.

Whether or not something might have come from Sadat's pre-1973 initiative, the war's aftermath opened a process that did lead to diplomatic progress. The war's high cost and limited result in military terms showed the futility of that method. On the Arab side, it produced renewed pride but also a sense of limits. Egypt, acting as a nation-state, regained the Sinai and built an alliance with the United States. For Israel, the war gave both a greater incentive for change to defuse the crisis and avoid more fighting, and a belief that the conflict could be ended. Yet even then this process – except in the Egypt-Israel case – took 20 years to bear fruit.

The years between 1973 and 1993 saw all the parties evolve in their view of the conflict and approach to a negotiated settlement. In general, the status quo was manageable enough to avoid another full-scale war: Israel held the territories and was generally at peace (except with Lebanon in 1982–83); the Arab states knew they could not defeat Israel or enjoy full Soviet support, while being distracted by the long Iran-Iraq war.

The Palestinians suffered most from the status quo but they were also the party most locked into an intransigent stance, explicitly preferring deadlock to a solution requiring any real compromise.[5] The PLO's basic strategy was in line with Abu Iyad's 1971 statement that the PLO had "no right" to negotiate a settlement. Rather, the highest duty was to struggle on, preserving the option to regain all Palestine "even if they cannot liberate a single inch." Otherwise, the Arabs would lose Palestine forever.[6]

There were many factors that gradually broke this deadlock.

In Israel, for example, these included the *intifada*'s cost, the election of a Labor government in 1992, and the fact that Arafat finally met Israel's old conditions in 1993. For the PLO, key factors included a long chain of defeats, the growing weight of West Bank/Gaza Palestinians brought about by the *intifada*, Saddam Hussein's failure in 1991, and the loss of Soviet and Arab state support. Among Arab states, a growing sense of the conflict's futility and wastefulness, stronger individual states willing to seek their own interests, the decline of Pan-Arab nationalist ideology, the need for America's favor, the loss of Soviet support, and fear of Iraq and Iran must be counted.

By 1989, Egyptian President Hosni Mubarak could argue persuasively, "God has granted us a mind with which to think. We fought for many years, but where did we get?" The Arabs had lost much money and many martyrs in the struggle and their situation was still terrible. "I am therefore not ready to take more risks," Mubarak continued. "Moreover, wars have generally not solved any problem. Regardless of the difficulties or obstacles surrounding the present peace process," it was the only way out.[7] The Cold War's end in a U.S. victory and Iraq's defeat were victories of moderation over radicalism which put the final piece in place.

The cumulative effect of events and the failure of alternative routes involving maximal demands were the key factors producing the 1993 breakthrough.[8] Once it believed that the Arabs were ready and willing to make a compromise peace, Israel was ready to make territorial concessions and negotiate with the PLO. Once the PLO had redefined its goal as obtaining a West Bank/Gaza state rather than destroying Israel, knowing that its bigger aim was impossible, it was ready to negotiate with Israel, subject to being convinced that the more modest objective was possible.

There are fascinating parallels between Sadat's change in the 1971–79 era and that of the other Arabs in the 1988–93 period. A lack of choice was coupled with a single Arab leader being ready to recognize the situation, gradually strengthening his signals of this change to the point where it was clear to the United States but most of all to Israel. For the Palestinians, the *intifada* played a function parallel to that of the 1973 War.

While these two events put pressure on Israel to agree to change the status quo, even more important was a diplomatic offer persuading them that change was both possible and preferable.

The Arabs had long refused to make peace with Israel; knowing this, Israel had refused to make major concessions. The Arab stance had to change and it took time both to execute this shift and for Israel to recognize its occurrence. The outcome shows how states and movements can totally reverse their most deeply held beliefs and policies; test and perceive change; build mutual confidence; and blend caution and risk-taking at the highest political level.

Notes

1. These issues are extensively analyzed in Parts I and II of this book.
2. Janice Stein, "The Alchemy of Peacemaking," *International Journal*, Vol. 38 (Autumn 1983), p. 1.
3. The author's view on the course of Arab politics in this era is presented in Barry Rubin, *Cauldron of Turmoil: America in the Middle East* (New York, 1992), especially pp. 112–133.
4. The chapter by Professor Shimon Shamir describes the two sides of the historical debate over Sadat's initiative.
5. The author discusses the PLO's evolving position in Barry Rubin, *Revolution until Victory? The Politics and History of the PLO* (Cambridge, Mass., 1994).
6. Abu Iyad, 9 January 1971, *International Documents on Palestine 1971* (Beirut, 1972), p. 352. Arafat used almost precisely the same words in December 1977 – *IDOP 1977*, p. 458 – and again in 1988, "Knowing the Enemy," *Time*, 11 November 1988, pp. 47–48.
7. Interview, Middle East News Agency, 24 January 1989 (*FBIS*, 25 January 1989, p. 15).
8. The position of Israel and the PLO and the consequences of their agreement are discussed in Parts III and IV of this book.

2

Some Lessons Learned

Ezer Weizman

The past twenty years, from 1973 to 1993 – a period that has brought us from war to negotiations for peace – must be seen as part of the long conflict between us and the Arab world in this area.

Our forefathers, inspired by their prayers to live "next year in Jerusalem," began to return and settle here, taking the first steps toward the Jewish state. This process was begun about 120 years ago by Old City residents of Jerusalem and new immigrants. They founded Rosh Pina, Rehovot, Nes Ziona, Rishon Lezion and other settlements, which in many respects were the cornerstone of the new state. Later, in the first half of the twentieth century, there came the Second and the Third Aliyah – Jews coming to Israel for historical reasons to live a different way of life from their ancestors, to shape their own destiny in their own environment.

The settlers encountered diseases, difficult weather conditions, and problematic relations with the Arab population. The malaria, typhoid and dysentery which took so many lives can now be controlled by medicine; and we have also learned to control, or at least mitigate, drought by new systems of irrigation. But the relationship between us and the Arabs cannot be controlled by computers, by physics, by advances in science. It can only be achieved by profound thinking and feeling, and most of all by strength. The strength I am talking about is not military, political or social domination, but the will to live together without the impact of the sword.

Ever since we set foot here, we have encountered problems. My generation grew up preparing to fight. I don't think that the Egyptian youngsters in those days felt the same way. It was not until 1948 that they began to think in terms of war with us. We, on the other hand, knew that we had to wield the plough with one hand, the rifle with the other: that was not just a picturesque saying but the basic reality of our education and life. We had to face attacks in 1921, 1929 and 1936.

Parallel to this our country was being built up – the Technion in Haifa, the Herzliah Gymnasia, the Reali School in Haifa and the Weizmann Institute, established in 1933. Notwithstanding the Zionist efforts of the last 100 years, the conflict was far from solution. The British Mandatory authorities set up the Peel Commission, the Anglo-American Commission. All efforts at conflict resolution testified to the grave existence of the Jewish problem and the Arab problem. Could we live together, or not? A British expert once said: "There is no room to swing a cat in Palestine." That was in the early thirties, but since then we have swung tigers and lions here.

Eventually, after the terrible days of World War II (when many Jews served in the British Army) and the savage Holocaust that consumed so many millions of Jewish lives, the proposal to create a Jewish State and an Arab State was accepted at the United Nations, in November 1947. No sooner was this decided than battle began, the War of Independence, which was the most severe battle we have ever had to fight. The Yom Kippur War was difficult, but it was short. The real battle was in '48 where we fought for our lives. At that time we were only 600,000 here. Thank God, we are 4.2 million now. I wish I could be sure that we will be 6 million in the foreseeable future. To bring Jews here is our hope and aim: we want it *per se*, not only *vis-à-vis* the 200 million Arabs in the region.

After the 1948 war our forces found themselves at what is known today as the Green Line. We had not succeeded in taking Jerusalem or Latrun or remaining in Gush Etzion. We wanted to – if anyone tells you we didn't want to reach the Jordan, send him to me. We did not achieve our aims, partly because of lack of capability in those days and partly for lack of preparation. Ours was only half a victory and all those who took part will, I think, agree with me that it was our wish to do more in '48, but we simply did not have the resources.

So we consolidated our efforts within the Green Line and created the State of Israel, continuing to bring in new immigrants. The battle, however, did not subside. Unfortunately, we began to be more at loggerheads with the neighboring Arab nations than with the local population – with Egypt, with Syria, with Lebanon, with Jordan, and with parts of the Palestinian population. In their view – and I cannot argue with them – the Palestinian problem was an Arab problem. Then we had another battle, the so-called Suez Campaign of '56. Subsequently, many years later (in 1978) a good friend of mine, General Gamasi, at the beginning of our talks with the Arab world, said to me: "I can understand your concern in '67 when you thought that we had so many tanks in the Sinai, but why did you go with the British and French imperialists to take the Suez Canal from us in '56?" When he said this, I was shocked. And here was a lesson for me: you can read intelligence reports, you can read books about the other side, but nothing can be the same as meeting face-to-face with people who have been on the other side of the fence.

In 1967 – despite misgivings, and knowing that we had enemies on all sides – we took decisive action to engage our forces. The result is history.

We thought that this was the end of the story. We thought that '67 was the beginning of a new era. We thought '67 was the final battle. And then came Yom Kippur 1973. The media continues to ponder where blame is to be laid. But twenty years later this issue is not relevant to the peace treaty at hand. A more important chapter has opened up for us.

It is ironic, but it is true, that had it not been for the 1973 Yom Kippur War the Egyptians would not have talked to us. That is another important lesson for us. We always talk about our own pride, our Jewish pride. But we must be sensitive to the pride of the other side, too. The unfortunate surprise we suffered was, from a military point of view, from a professional point of view, a great achievement: the "pride situation" was reversed in that attack, which came on both sides, north and south, at the same time, at the same hour, without our taking the necessary steps or even properly assessing that this would happen. After the Yom Kippur attack both sides were able to reassess their enemy.

The late Anwar Sadat, the brains and motive power behind the Yom Kippur attack, realized about a year and a half before that battle that he wanted to break away from the Soviet Union. He saw it as his task to take Egypt along a constructive path, one that would serve a growing population, increasing at a rate of 1.2–1.3 million a year. When we began talks with the Egyptians in 1977 there were about 38 million Egyptians; now there are close to 60 million.

I learned from Sadat that his primary concern was the well-being of the Egyptian people. If you have been to Egypt then you know of the problems of food, the problems of housing, and even the problems of lack of mosques – most religious Egyptians pray in the streets.

Back to '73. A year before, Sadat had told the Russians to leave Egypt. He was very proud of his decision. From his point of view, the 1973 conflict between Egypt and us and Syria was a great achievement because he initiated it without Russia. As he pointed out, after regaining honor in war, and breaking the status quo, he wanted to see what America could do for Egypt. And remember, this was at a time when the Soviet Union was always a major factor in Israel's deliberations. If we get to the Suez Canal, what will the Russians say? If we get closer to Damascus, what will the Russians say? If we bomb here or there, what will the Russians say? Most of our analysis in GHQ (General Headquarters), and especially in Dayan's case, dealt with the effect of this or that action on the Russians. As a matter of fact, in 1967 it was not a major government decision to get to the Suez Canal, but rather the impetus and swing of the army. But the battlefield move brought with it a major concern about the Russians' reaction. As we all know, we eventually negotiated a disengagement agreement. General Yariv was the first to meet an Egyptian general – General Gamasi – at 101 km. He reported back that this is a man one can talk to.

To cut a long story short, a very important period in our relationship with the Arab world began here – meeting, getting to know and to understand some of the people on the other side of the fence. The rest is history – Dayan's trip to Morocco; Camp David; and the signing of the peace treaty in March 1979.

At the time people used to ask why we were signing a peace treaty with one man. If he disappears, what will happen to the peace treaty? For the last twelve years Egypt has been led by Hosni Mubarak, a man dedicated to his country's welfare and to the preservation of the bilateral relationship between Egypt and us and the whole Arab world. He has been faithful to the agreement struck by his predecessor. You have to be very brave to carry through such a commitment. And so, from this conference, I send him my *salaams* and greetings.

In the first encounters with the Egyptians we were forced to redefine the issues of our defense, our security. The issues involved in giving up Sinai were very complicated. But the same situation, from a military angle, provided the key for both sides: defense, as seen at Camp David, is more than military considerations, it includes understanding and neighborly relations. Cromwell's dictum "Trust the Lord and keep your powder dry" helped us evolve a perception of how to proceed. Both sides agreed to peace, to commerce, to relations, but both sides kept arms – smaller, bigger, the size is irrelevant. The problem of defense and security is a problem which we are going to encounter in the future. In the case of Egypt, we solved it in a certain way. Not everyone was happy with the arrangement. As in a battle, you have to take a certain risk.

Camp David was the initial framework. We negotiated a peace agreement only with Egypt, and Egypt took it upon itself to decide on a proposal for initiating a solution of the Palestinian problem, an interim arrangement for autonomy. This was done without consulting the Palestinians or Jordan, at least not formally. I remember Sadat telling me: "I just talked to the King." Sadat was trying to persuade King Hussein of Jordan to join the peace process. The King has made a few mistakes in the past, but I hope he does not make mistakes in the future. The ultimate aim is a comprehensive peace.

Now a warning: one battle does not resemble another. Any general who fights a future war as he fought the last war is bound to lose. This has happened many times and it happened here. The same principle applies in politics and perhaps in other fields of life. Despite the fact that I took part in past arguments and agreements, I always warn myself: Don't treat Camp David as a model. Don't say "This is what we did and said"; today's situation is completely different.

In November sixteen years ago Sadat made his historic visit to Israel. Sixteen years is a long time in a fast-moving world with its technological changes and its ups and downs in political life. In Sadat we had an Egyptian leader who was confident, who was satisfied with his achievements, and who knew what he wanted. He took the risk of being isolated from the Arab world, in spite of the fact that he always used to say that the other countries would come back – which they did after his lifetime. Sometimes he used to talk angrily about the Arab world. He was furious that they turned their backs on him. But he had the courage to see his commitment through, though he gave his life for it.

I personally wanted all along to move toward direct negotiations with Egypt. I wanted to see whether we could solve the differences between them and us. It did not work: perhaps it could not work. And the fact is that we ended up at Camp David, asking the United States to help finish the job, in September 1978. I believe that we are now approaching a comprehensive situation, a situation that is a beginning. It is not a stopover but neither is it a solution. People were wrong fifteen years ago when they thought that the autonomy proposed by the Israeli government was a permanent status resolution. At the time of Camp David we were worried about calling it the final solution. In the end it turned out to be an interim arrangement toward a solution; there was an understanding, from which the recent agreement took its genesis.

Sixteen years ago, when Egypt signed the peace treaty, the Palestinians were worried that they were being neglected. Now the Palestinians have come forward and Syria is afraid that she is being neglected. There is a peculiar similarity between the two situations. Just as the Palestinians were not sold down the river, for eventually the Israeli leadership entered into direct talks with the PLO, so I believe the same sequence of negotiations will occur with the party that is now afraid of being left on the sidelines.

I am neither optimistic nor pessimistic: I'm realistic. And because I'm realistic, I think it will take us a long time to reach a situation where there is a genuine mutual recognition of Palestinians and Israelis. There will be pitfalls and landmines, ups and downs. But what has been started – a good start to solving a host of problems – will provide a catalyst, a momentum, toward mutual co-existence. One can argue that we should have started with the Syrians years ago, but the fact is that we did not. The current process will not finish as Camp David did, limiting our relations for fifteen years to only one country. Even if it takes ten years, I believe we will end up talking to everybody. In the history of nations, and especially in the history of the Middle East, the time scale is not the issue. Our respective governments will have to decide what they mean by security and by defense. Arab governments will have to come to terms with Zionism and the wishes and wills of the Israelis: we and they will have to come to terms with the wishes and wills of the Palestinians.

A conflict that goes back 100 years cannot be easy to come to terms with. All sides will have to make painful decisions as to who gives up what, who doesn't give up, who fights for what, and who stands for what. And as I stated before, this is only the beginning. The peace process in the Middle East will be pushed forward by our respective perceptions of a dramatically changing world. We will no longer be able to rely on the United States to act as intermediary. The U.S. is beset by its own problems – the economy, ethnic groups, crime. The

President wants to see life in America change and get better, and it is inevitable that efforts and resources will be directed toward the U.S. internal scene rather than to the Middle East, which will be quite capable of solving its own political and economic problems, if only we can compromise.

The point of this diversion is that we have to study what goes on in the world outside of the Middle East. We cannot isolate ourselves and our problems. Wherever one looks in the world, and especially in the United States, one sees dramatic economic change. We cannot forget the current world political turmoil as we approach the twenty-first century: the collapse of Communism; Western capitalism in crisis; the advent of China as a major economic power.

It is a truism that the world is becoming a smaller place. No sooner than it happens, we know about an event on the other side of the world. But that does not mean that we, as a world community, make the right decisions: the U.S. getting mixed up in Somalia; Yugoslavia neglected because there's no oil there; 700,000 troops going to Kuwait because of oil. These events, and many others, impinge on us. Just as the Europeans wanted a different world after the Second World War and we wanted a different world after the '67 and '73 wars, our neighbors now harbor hopes which we must recognize. We must be open-minded, we have to talk to the other side; and to study it so that lack of knowledge does not hinder our progress. Above all, we have to respect the other side. Instead of acting like extremely knowledgeable Israelis, we should advance timidly, knowing that we are good, knowing that we have knowledge, knowing that we have ability, but wanting to learn. We must be careful not to attempt to be the teachers of the Arab world.

I shall share with you a painful example of my own lack of caution. A certain gentleman in Egypt used to attend meetings with his wife. A little later in our association, I commented that I had not seen her recently, and he told me that she was very sick in hospital. So I, like a fool, said: "Why don't you send her to Israel? We have some good doctors." He looked at me and said slowly: "We have very good doctors in Egypt." This is what we have to be careful about. We have to learn to be companions, to be partners, not teachers. We have to remember that we have much to learn from the Arab world.

Israelis who have been in contact with Egypt over the last fifteen years know that my attitude toward this Egyptian gentleman is a pitfall to avoid. But, despite such misunderstandings, I believe that we are going in the right direction, albeit sometimes not on the right path. Though accidents, unfortunately, are bound to occur, our actions and experiences in the last fifteen years, and the recognition by all parties in this conflict of the future problems the region faces, indicate that a comprehensive peace situation in the Middle East is unfolding. There will be great difficulties for all sides. It may take four years, five years, six years, but the process is inevitable.

I have not dwelt here on the problems we face in making Israel a better Israel, a well lived-in Israel, a defensible Israel, an Israel that lives in partnership with its neighbors. Jewish tradition says: *"Tov shachen karov me'ach rachok"* (better a close neighbor than a distant brother). The same saying exists in Arabic. So you see, we have many things in common. I love my Jewish brothers and sisters abroad, and I wish they would all come here. But I have to live with my Arab neighbors, and that means learning to live with ourselves. The Jewish State, the Israeli State, has to take account of solutions for the future. I think we have the necessary resources and will. I think it can be done. But, as you must have noticed, I haven't provided solutions. Hopefully this book will go some way toward rectifying this.

3

The U.S. Role in the Peace Process

Joseph Sisco

Like hundreds of others, I sat on the South Lawn of the White House viewing and hearing the unbelievable and the unthinkable. In my mind, it matched, if not outstripped, a similar dramatic occasion I witnessed at the White House a decade previously – President Jimmy Carter between Begin and Sadat. I too had never dreamed in my lifetime that I would witness such a momentous occasion, nor did I ever expect to witness the crumbling of the Berlin Wall. For Arabs and Jews, people of long histories and time immemorial, the unfolding events of recent days may not yet have closed the vicious circle of bloodshed, but it is to be hoped that this could soon become a beginning toward a real peace.

This breakthrough is primarily because of the parties themselves. And I hope that there is no one who believes that the United States feels in any way slighted simply because of the fact that the preparatory discussions went on secretly in Oslo. No country has been more strongly committed to the concept of direct negotiations than the United States.

It is very exhilarating to be a witness to history; it's more fun, and sometimes more painful, to be a participant. For decades I've had an abiding belief that, whatever the U.S. role, the parties to the peace must be the parties to the negotiations, which is what my very dear friend, Yitzhak Rabin, used to tell me daily when he was the Israeli Ambassador to the United States and I was the Assistant Secretary of State for the Middle East.

There are two possible outcomes for the Middle East and the Gulf. In one, the region is dominated by extremist forces, weapons of mass destruction, and terrorism, with prospects of another Arab-Israeli or an Arab-Arab war. The alternative is, as a result of the Israeli-PLO accord – to borrow a phrase from John Maynard Keynes – "a peace of coal, of iron, and bread," in which both sides have a vested interest and in which the near-limitless resources of this area bring a better life day by day to all of the peoples.

Of course, whatever vision prevails can be affected but not determined by the power of the United States. We have undertaken over the years a very active, largely unilateral, peacemaking role. How did this singular diplomatic role come about? The United States obviously has vital strategic interests in this area. Diplomatic passivism for the United States is not a feasible policy, for it is only a short step from passivism to disengagement.

How did this come about? The story goes something like this: Nixon took over as president in 1969. Kissinger was assigned the world; Rogers was assigned the Middle East. And as was common knowledge, the competition between these two individuals was very keen indeed. Unfortunately, the competition became intertwined in policy, as is inevitable in any government, or even corporate, structure. In 1969, at my first meeting with Nixon, who saw this area largely within the framework of U.S.-U.S.S.R. geopolitical terms, he said to me, "I want a test of the Soviets in the Middle East. Do they want peace or do they want to pursue tactical opportunism and maintain the area in turmoil and in tension?" He named me as his envoy and, for 8 months in 1969, I negotiated with Dobrynin, Vinogradov and Gromyko.

From this was born the Rogers Plan. We had developed, with the Soviets, a substantive proposal with much of the wording that now embraces the Egyptian-Israeli treaty, but nobody was ready to move ahead and, I believe, for very good reasons. The Rogers Plan was premature. Nasser was still pursuing his pan-Arab policy. There was an understandable deep suspicion of him in Israel. While the Soviets may have mildly encouraged Nasser toward accommodation, Moscow refused to take a position on substance that went beyond the Egyptian position – nothing less than: total Israeli withdrawal to the international border; a proposal closer to non-aggression pact than to full peace; and Cairo's unwillingness to engage Israel in direct negotiations on the security arrangements.

From this episode, Nixon drew one hard conclusion, from which he never deviated. He told me: "We're going ahead alone diplomatically in the Middle East. No more trying to work with the Soviets. They may not want war and confrontation over the Middle

East with us, but they do not want peace and stability in the region as we do."

During the entire shuttle diplomacy, the Russians were kept on the sidelines, primarily by us, but this was reinforced by the fact that fundamentally neither the Arabs nor the Israelis – and when I say neither the Arabs, I include President Hafiz el-Assad of Syria – wanted any shared brokering with the Soviets. But I don't want to be misunderstood. America viewed the Soviet Union then, and Russia now, as an important Middle Eastern power. It cannot, and should not, be excluded. The cooperation between us as co-sponsors of the Madrid framework, the parallel interests in defeating and containing Saddam Hussein, the parallel interest in stability in the area (particularly along the Iranian border, as militant Islam asserts itself) and the need to prevent proliferation of weapons of mass destruction – all underscore the need for full cooperation between Russia and the United States.

Looking ahead to the next decade, we may be somewhat less suited to play the singular mediating role that we played in the 1970s and 1980s. In the era ahead, as both Presidents Bush and Clinton have said, we have to play a role in the peace process, but there are others, too. The best demonstration of this new reality is the current process of multilateral working groups. So a number of countries have to be involved.

Now, one inescapable result of being a superpower is that we're going to have to be, in one way or another, the security guarantor of any agreement achieved. In the United States there is a debate about the use of force, as a result of Bosnia, Haiti and Somalia. Defining the role of the Congress and the executive branch is an argument that started at the beginning of our republic 200 years ago. Every president has won this battle, and I have no doubt that President Clinton likewise will win this battle because the American government works best when there is strong presidential leadership. Foreign policy cannot be pursued by 535 members of Congress, all of whom are would-be secretaries of state. Moreover, the strong bipartisan understanding of the past as to our vital interests in the Middle East remains strong.

If we should get to the point at which the decisive factor becomes how any peace between Syria and Israel will be monitored, the debate in the United States, is not likely to prevent the U.S., with or without a United Nations umbrella, from sending American peacekeeping forces to the Golan and policing any such agreements.

The disengagement agreement between Syria and Israel that we negotiated in 1975 during the shuttle diplomacy has been carried out impeccably by both sides. Assad respects Israeli power. He did not and cannot achieve strategic parity with Israel. Now that he has lost his Soviet patron, there is only one power left, namely, the United States.

Let me give you an example. In 1974 we were in about the 20th day of the negotiations between Israel and Syria during the Syrian–Israeli disengagement talks. I said to Henry Kissinger: "We are not really getting very far. A secretary of state can't continue to be here. You are beginning to look like a fool. I will write two sentences on a piece of paper announcing the suspension of the talks. If after four, or five, or six hours we have come to the conclusion that there is not much more we can do, I'm going to pull this piece of paper out."

So that is the way it went in the meeting. At that point I pulled that piece of paper out and gave it to Kissinger who read it to Assad. He said: "Well, President Assad, here are a couple of sentences which would announce the suspension, which we want you to review."

Henry was about to hand it to Assad, and Assad said: "Wait a minute." And we got the map out again, and we restarted the negotiations, and he gave more concessions. This is what I mean by brinkmanship. But he is a realist. He fears and he respects Israeli power.

Peace in this area is a strategic necessity for the United States. I can't underscore that enough. But it will not be kept by unilateral action alone. It is not that we want to disregard or keep the Russians out of the picture. Russia is a Middle Eastern power. It cooperated in the Madrid framework. It has to cooperate in the future. Other nations in this area have to make a contribution through money and investment. Moreover, we have always favored direct negotiations between the parties. We are not in a position to resolve the issues here, but that does not mean that we should be on the sideline. Active American diplomacy is essential in protecting our overall interest here.

Yes, we are in favor of multilateralism, and trying collective action, and getting others to share the burdens and the responsibilities. But this does not mean that this administration has given up its right to act individually, if we feel our interests are threatened. Objective geopolitical interests don't change from administration to administration. The United States is going to continue to contain

Iraq and Saddam Hussein. It is going to try to maintain the broad coalition, but if that broad coalition is fractionized, I think that you will find, if we feel the security situation requires it, that the United States is prepared to act unilaterally if necessary.

We are going to try to continue to contain Iran in its quest to obtain weapons of mass destruction and its support of international terrorism. The Iranians have a legitimate interest in the Gulf, but if they threaten Saudi Arabia and the energy and oil resources of the region, we will act. But we have also said to the Iranians, if you want to work out a practical working relationship with the United States, we are ready. They are not ready.

The United States is not going to disengage, albeit that it will have to engage itself with admittedly more limited resources than in the past. I have no doubt that we can play the role as necessary.

4

The Opportunity that was not Missed

Yossi Beilin

In 1984 a meeting took place between Israel's Prime Minister Shimon Peres, and Secretary of State George Schultz. We had, in the past, prepared many plans for peace with the Arab states and Palestinians and we came with the whole file to the Secretary of State. He advocated "CBMs" – confidence-building measures. This meant, for example, increasing the sum of money permitted to be taken across the bridges between Jordan and the West Bank from 1,000 dinars to 5,000 dinars. He had a very long and boring list. I thought to myself, he has all these ideas about CBMs and we want peace.

Now, ten years later, I ask myself who was wrong. It has been said that there is no price or almost no price for CBMs. But there is in fact one price: time. Usually, it means a process of building confidence, a psychological process, which is not something that takes place over a month or two, or in one meeting on the White House lawn. And the length of the process is a big price which may eventually create a situation of missed opportunities.

I would like to talk about missing opportunities, the subject I love most. I think that one of the reasons why opportunities were missed is that people believed that time was on their side. You need the process, and the process is long, and time is there and you can do something today, something else tomorrow, then something else next week, and eventually something will happen. Nowadays I am a great believer in CBMs.

The Helsinki process which eased East-West tensions in Europe did not happen in the Middle East. Helsinki was for recognized states which had diplomatic relations with each other. In the Middle East we were speaking about a state of war.

Consider the tautological explanation: it was impossible to make peace earlier because the time was not ripe. This can be used to explain almost every missed opportunity. The reality is that many times an opportunity is missed because of some kind of misunderstanding or because somebody wasn't in the right place at the right time. Sometimes a totally unimportant factor can create circumstances whereby an achievement on the road to peace is taken two steps backwards instead of one step forward.

For example, in 1987 we were involved with beginning a relationship with the Soviet Union. It had been a dream for Israel for many years. The Soviets spoke about the assets of the White Church in Jerusalem as a means for them to launch a process toward some kind of new relationship between us. There was an important meeting in Helsinki, but nothing happened there. They had some demands; we had some demands. Our delegation went to Helsinki guided by the view that there should be reciprocity. Then the talks moved to Washington and we negotiated between our respective ambassadors. Eventually our ambassador, Meir Rosenne, told me that he was almost sure that nothing would happen. On the question of reciprocity the Soviets said, "You do not have any kind of church in Moscow."

I talked to the Prime Minister, who said: "The future is the future and I want something now. We need reciprocity, because if they are coming to Israel we want to be able to send a delegation to Moscow. [This would] create a situation that would be perpetuated; they will come to Tel Aviv, but we will never get to Moscow. We have to do something now." I replied: "Maybe we will say the following, since it was a written agreement: 'We are inviting a Soviet delegation to visit Israel in order to deal with the assets of the White Church, assuming that the same kind of delegation will go from Israel to Moscow in due course.'"

At first the Soviets said, "How can you impose conditions?" But eventually they understood that it wasn't a condition, it was us unilaterally assuming that in due course we could send a delegation.

Eventually, there was a Soviet delegation, which became a permanent one in Israel. The White Church was just a pretext. We sent our delegation and it became a permanent one. And later still we had full diplomatic relations. But it would have been so easy to have missed this opportunity. Under the circumstances it would have been quite reasonable for somebody in our party to have said, "If there is no reciprocity, nothing will happen." Even under those circumstances I'm sure that eventually we would have determined a working relationship without this funny delegation. But the fact that by 1987 there was already such a beginning made it much easier for us to establish full relations four years later.

That story is just one example of why I am very careful about missing opportunities. It is not just a coincidence that three of us who are currently Foreign Ministry officials – Ambassador to Washington Itamar Rabinovich, UN Ambassador Gad Yaacobi and myself – have published books about missing opportunities in the Middle East. Rabinovich concerned himself with the affair with Syrian leader Hosni Zaim in 1949. Gad Yaakobi wrote about the idea of an interim solution in 1971, by a partial Israeli withdrawal from the Suez Canal. And my input was to discuss the Jarring plan of February 1971.[1]

All three of us were so involved in reading materials from the archives and participating in seminars on these subjects that it created for us a feeling that we could not repeat the mistakes of those who established the State of Israel and who had made such huge mistakes since 1948. Now that last sentence sounds very accusing. But in the context of knowing how easy it is to miss an opportunity, and knowing that we cannot afford to miss the next opportunity, I hope that the accusation will be understood to mean that it is not by chance that we and many others involved in the peace process are aware of missed opportunities. The records and archives show that the record, but behind the faded papers lie the political and human decisions that kept this situation from resolution.

Both Israelis and Arabs are experts on missing opportunities. Perhaps the earliest was in 1947. Had the Palestinians then decided to have their own state, we would have been in a much better situation. Two states, two peoples, some such arrangement. All their dreams which have not been fulfilled – and God knows whether they will be fulfilled – could have been met then in 1947.

Then we missed a chance, too. To use Itamar's example, Hosni Zaim, who was elected in April 1949 and assassinated in August 1949, didn't want our land. The situation was very different from today. When Zaim suggested talks with Ben-Gurion about peace between Syria and Israel in the spring of 1949, Ben-Gurion was not ready to talk to him because Syria was encroaching on our side of the border between Syria and Israel. He demanded that Zaim withdraw to the international border before anything else. Zaim said no, first I would like to talk to you and then I'll consider whatever suggestions you have. Ben-Gurion said no, and sent two very important people, one of them Yigal Yadin. Nothing happened.

Now, who can prove that such a meeting could have brought about a peaceful outcome? It's very difficult to prove such a thing. It's impossible to refute. But one thing is sure: Ben-Gurion, for whatever reasons, did not even try.

Next, we move to 1967. I believe that the story of 1967 has not yet been told. Many theories abound. I belong to the party which believes that the Six Day War was the watershed in modern Jewish history: our biggest victory, but the biggest curse to Israeli society. Immediately after the war we were ready to withdraw, especially from the Sinai Peninsula and the Golan Heights. A famous secret resolution of 19 June 1967, a resolution one week after the war, referred specifically to this idea: that Israel was ready to withdraw, to negotiate with Syria and Egypt on the basis of the international borders and Israel's security needs.

Foreign Minister Abba Eban gave the resolution paper to U.S. Ambassador to the UN Arthur Goldberg, who gave it to the Egyptians and Syrians. As an answer he received the famous No's of Khartoum: no negotiations, no peace, and no recognition of Israel. That was an opportunity totally missed by the Arabs.

Then came 1971. The mistake in 1971 was the mistake of Golda Meir, who could not understand that Sadat was serious about what he called the year of decision. Sadat wanted back the Sinai Peninsula, either by war or by peace. He was serious about it. She was still used to Gamal Abdul Nasser. We all considered Sadat a temporary leader who would be replaced by somebody stronger. But that was a grave mistake. When Gunnar Jarring came, in February 1971, with his idea for a total withdrawal from the Sinai Peninsula in exchange for peace with Israel, Sadat's answer was that a full, just and comprehensive peace would not take place in the Middle East *unless Israel withdrew from all the occupied territories.*

Instead of understanding that Sadat had to say these words, that he was politically compelled to refer to the other fronts too, Golda Meir said, "You see? That was a condition." Her understanding was that Sadat was not content just to get back the Sinai Peninsula – which by itself was a difficult Israeli concession – Dayan had said it was better to have Sharm El-Sheikh in Sinai than to have peace.

Golda said, "Look, he is demanding all the territories, and we are not even holding negotiations with the others. So as a condition to make peace with Egypt we have to give back all the territories? No way." And immediately that was the view we all took.

Nobody told her that there *might* have been another interpretation of Sadat's answer. And that is the real march of folly: not just the mistake of a leader, but the mistake of a leader which is perceived at the time as a consensus. Golda Meir, who I believe can be blamed for the disaster of the Yom Kippur War, did not read the answer. I think that that was perhaps the biggest opportunity missed by Israel since statehood.

But there were still other missed opportunities. In 1987 we could have done something with Jordan. What exactly? Nobody knows. But there was an agreement in London as reported in the press between Shimon Peres and King Hussein. There was a readiness. We spoke about an international conference. The preamble detailed bilateral talks between Israel and the different Arab countries, and between Israel and the Palestinians who denounced terror, and who were prepared to recognize Israel.

But this opportunity was rejected by the Israeli government. By following through on the expressed readiness we could probably have prevented the *intifada* – the *intifada* began on a very ripe soil of frustration, of poverty, of a feeling that occupation would go on forever and something should be done. If in April or May 1987 there could have been an international conference conducive to bilateral talks, the whole atmosphere in the Middle East would have changed. But that was not the case. And it was our mistake, and that of America, not to understand the importance of the moment. Instead of coming to the Middle East to talk to the Jordanians and Israelis, to understand what was behind the secret maneuverings, the Secretary of State did not want to become involved in internal affairs of the Israeli political arena.

It was a mistake of the Reagan Administration not to pursue the Reagan plan, which was shelved to please us. The second mistake was not to send over Secretary Schultz in order to see whether there was really an opportunity behind the so-called London Agreement between Israel and Jordan.

All these missed opportunities left an increasingly loud message: we should not miss the next one. All the partners in the Middle East – the Lebanese, the Syrians, the Jordanians, the Palestinians, the Israelis – are speaking *now* for the first time, all of them, about peace. After so many years, that is an important step. The second step is that they are speaking more or less about the same peace, about the same solution. Despite using other words, other symbols, we know more or less what the solution will be.

Such was the background for the Oslo channel, the Declaration of Principles signed by Israel and the PLO, and the mutual recognition between Israel and the PLO. From personal experience, I can tell you that in such a political process one has to take very seriously the chances, the accidents, the trifles on the way – the things that are usually not considered but eventually become so important to the success of such a process. One wrong word at the wrong time can destroy the process. Recognition of previously missed opportunities heightens the sense of occasion, sometimes to dramatic effect, to a feeling that success hinges on every word spoken.

It is customary, in personal as well as political life, to try to create *after the fact* a theory to explain how events were actually determined from the beginning. But this is not always the case, and even the handshake between Rabin and Arafat, which was the culmination of the whole process, was not pre-planned. We had no CBMs in place before the historic handshake. Arafat was still perceived by Israel's leadership and public opinion as anathema. But we found ourselves there in the heat of September on the lawn of the White House, taking part in a ceremony of mutual recognition between the Jewish national movement and the Palestinian national movement, symbolized and personalized by Rabin and Arafat – a moment that was never planned.

That moment was the culmination of a process, an inevitable process. If you want to have an agreement with the other side, you have to have an agreement with Arafat, for he represents the other side. There is no way that we could deceive ourselves or public opinion.

When two of our soldiers were kidnapped and assassinated in Gaza, the murderers left a note stating that peace would prevail only in the cemeteries. Despite such atrocities, we are committed to continuing the process of peace. Right from the beginning we have known that those extremists, the terrorists, will do whatever they can in order to continue fighting against us, fighting against the pragmatic regimes, fighting against whoever wants peace – because peace is their biggest enemy. We will not serve the terrorist by ending or by slowing this peace process. We will continue the process with the Palestinians. We will enlarge the group of states with whom we are negotiating seriously, including Syria, Lebanon, and Jordan.

For too long there was an unsigned coalition between extremists in the Middle East, because whenever there was somebody in Israel who said something in favor of transfer, in the Arab world they said, "You see? He is not speaking for himself. It is very transparent. He is speaking for all the Israelis. He is speaking for all the Jews. They want us to disappear."

And the same on the other side: when there was anybody who said something in favor of the "salami" tactics – first of all, we will have a separate Palestinian state, then we will push them into the sea, or then we will push them from the sea – there was somebody on our side who would say, "You see? This is the same old Arab. He is not trying to play games with us like many other diplomats. He is saying the real things because he is expressing the views of all the Arabs."

I believe that today we are beginning a new chapter, and that is the chapter of a coalition among the pragmatic forces in the Middle East.

Note

1.   Yossi Beilin, *Israel, A Concise Political History* (New York: St. Martin's Press, 1992, 1993); Itamar Rabinovitch, *The Road Not Taken* (New York: Oxford University Press, 1991); Gad Yaacobi, *A New Course* (Bnei Brak: Steimatzky, 1991).

Part II

The Legacy of the 1973 War

The 1973 War was a turning point for the modern Middle East and in permitting the start of an Arab-Israeli peace process. From a standpoint of two decades later, the war can now be put in historical perspective. This section analyzes the war and its consequences.

The key issue of contention is whether the war could have been avoided by prior diplomatic efforts – especially Egyptian President Anwar al-Sadat's 1971 initiative – or whether the fighting was a necessary precondition for a shift in the regional political situation and the attitude of the chief powers.

Shimon Shamir, in "The Yom Kippur War as a Factor in the Peace Process," presents both scenarios. He concludes that the peace offer was sincere but that this does not mean it would have succeeded. Amnon Sella, in "Policy and Back Channels: 1970–1973," shows the complex motives of the powers involved, focussing especially on the superpowers' Cold War strategies. Zeev Maoz's "Decision-Making and Bargaining in the Arab-Israeli Conflict" takes a close look at Egypt's options in deciding to attack and Israel's potential responses, showing how misperceptions and goals became entangled.

Yoram Meital, in "Drums of War and Bells of Peace: Egypt's Perspective on the 1973 War," demonstrates how Egypt's strategy was organized around its twin goals of rebuilding national morale and breaking the frozen status quo. Gabriel Ben-Dor, in "Confidence-Building and the Peace Process," discusses the preconditions for establishing a basis of mutual trust sufficient for negotiations and applies this model to the 1973 War.

Moshe Shemesh, in "The PLO: From Armed Struggle to Political Solution," examines how Sadat pushed the PLO toward change and that organization's taking a first step in the direction of accepting a diplomatic settlement of the conflict. Finally, Joseph Ginat considers "Changes in Egyptian Society Since 1973," discussing the psychological, economic, and political trends in that country growing out of the situation created by the war.

5

The Yom Kippur War as a Factor in the Peace Process

Shimon Shamir

In studying the transformation to peace in Egypt, the main facts are well known. There are two versions on this question, both of them by now quite famous. There is the version of February 1971 and the version of October 1973.

The first version points to the fact that on 4 February 1971 President Sadat addressed *majlis al-uomma*, as it was called at the time, and suggested prolonging the cease-fire, and clearing and reopening the Suez Canal. Israel would withdraw to a certain distance from the Canal, and all this would take place within the framework of some timetable for implementing Security Council resolutions.

Eleven days later, on 15 February, as is well known, when he was asked about Egypt's conditions for peace, President Sadat wrote in his answer to Jarring that Egypt was ready for a peace agreement with Israel. This was the first time in the history of Egyptian-Israeli relations that an Egyptian leader put on paper the words "peace agreement with Israel" – and then he went on to list the conditions of this peace. These were actually a repetition of what is included in Resolution 242, the reference to the problem of refugees in general, with no mention of the Palestinian problem in any way. In other words, if you take Sadat's two initiatives together, this version maintains, you have a form of the process that actually took place in the five years after the 1973 War: a combination of a partial agreement and a complete peace agreement with the Israelis. Therefore, February 1971 was the turning point.

The second version maintains that no Egyptian leader could have offered peace before the war. After the humiliation of 1967, no

Egyptian leader would have been ready to make peace from a position of weakness. There was a need to restore the Egyptian self-esteem, and this happened only after the crossing. Therefore, in Sadat's speech on 16 October, when he felt that the crossing was an established fact and was unaware of the extent of the Israeli counter-crossing, he made a peace offer. According to this second version, this was the turning point. It couldn't have happened before.

Now there is clearly a contradiction between these two versions but it is a controversy that does not take place between doves and hawks – as is usual with these controversies in Israel – because both positions are based on an acceptance of the sincerity and the seriousness of Sadat's departure from the road of war to the road of peace. If we examine these two versions more closely, we find that both have strong arguments and evidence. In fact, they are based on some conceptual premises that put stress on different aspects of this process.

The first version puts stress on Sadat as a person – the role of personality. It says that the actual difference between February 1970 (when peace with Israel was impossible) and February 1971 (when suddenly it was offered by Egypt) was that in February 1970 President Nasser was in power and in 1971 was President Sadat. The personality of President Sadat can be studied, and his record (it is better-known today than it was in the past) shows some consistency. We know that when he appeared, perhaps for the first time, before Egypt's National Security Council in late 1970, the issue at hand was the question of the cease-fire. It was limited in time and the Egyptian leadership command, the political command, had to decide what to do when this cease-fire expired.

Sadat listened most of the time and at the end he said: there is a lot of talk here about resuming hostilities, about wars, about military operations. I didn't hear anybody speaking about the houses that we shall have to build when our soldiers come back from the front when all this is over. I didn't hear much talk about the schools that we shall have to build for their children, and so on.

This was not an isolated expression. We followed his interviews at the time, and now perhaps we understand better their significance, but consistently he was speaking in a language, and using a peace vocabulary, that had never been used before.

We can also support the first version by what we know about his basic previous position and outlook. We know that he was a highly pragmatic, not an ideological person; that he initiated a process of de-radicalization and de-Nasserization of Egypt; that he was ready to depart from almost all other principles of the Nasser era. So why wouldn't he be ready to depart also from the policy of belligerency toward Israel? We learned later that he was a person capable of taking great decisions. In other words, according to this version, personality is the key and all the analysis of the objective situation at that time, and of the fundamental factors, is relatively less significant.

There is, on the whole, a growing skepticism about the interpretative value of this analysis of fundamental causes and factors. When Sadat came to Jerusalem in November 1977, every commentator was capable of explaining how the situation left him no other choice because of the economic hardships in Egypt, its need to go with the United States, Sadat's high priority on regaining the Sinai, and so on. But had it happened the other way around and, as a result of the stalemate in November 1977, he had returned to the track of war and hostilities, it would have been as easy to explain why the fundamental factors made that necessary and gave Sadat no choice but to take such a course.

Take the case of a traffic accident. There are fundamental causes of that particular traffic accident: one of them would be the invention of the internal combustion engine; another would be this tendency of human beings to move from one place to another. But when you examine the immediate causes, you may discover that the driver was drunk, and the interpretative value of the fundamental causes in this case would be very very limited.

Supporters of the first version would say: watch the driver. The driver was Sadat. We know what we know about his personality and his preferences. Therefore it is very plausible that in February 1971 he indeed made a serious peace offer to Israel. As some political scientists would say, we should watch his operational code – a concept that was very popular in academia for many years to explain decision-making. Some reservations about this concept that have developed. But I think the basic truth should be accepted: Sadat did have an operational code and it explains the possibility of his suggesting peace at that time.

The other version also has a lot to rely on: the depth of Egypt's sense of humiliation required a military achievement to make it possible for an Egyptian leader to offer peace. Here you can go back to all the Orientalist literature about honor in Arab society, and shame societies, and explain how important these factors would be in a society like the Egyptian society, therefore making an earlier peace simply impossible.

Even if you ignore the psychological aspect, there is here a question of balance of power. Advocates of this version would say that whatever people's feelings, or intentions, or hopes or expectations, these are relatively secondary. What is important in any process that tries to establish a regional or global order is a balance of power. This balance was achieved by the outcome of the October War; therefore, for the first time, there were conditions for peace.

Others would speak about ripeness, about the fact that somehow war often becomes an integral part of the process leading to peace. People need this catharsis in order to bring themselves to be ready for peace. They would argue that in this case the humiliation of 1967 was not enough; the pain of the War of Attrition was not enough. What was needed was another war that would make it clear in Egypt that this course was leading nowhere – only to more suffering – and create the mood that would make peace possible. To sum up this line of thought, it is a combination of a new self-esteem and a certain fatigue, a certain weariness.

We may draw here a comparison to what is happening among our Palestinian partners, where we can watch a very similar process evolving. I think it would be correct to say that the readiness of the PLO to make with Israel the kind of agreement that would have been unthinkable in the past is a result of the new self-esteem gained by the Palestinians through the *intifada*, plus the weariness, declining position, and weakness of the PLO, at this particular time. So this school of thought would be, I think, justified in saying that you need a combination of these two things in order to make a leadership or a society ready for peace, and this happened only after 1973.

Before giving my own perspective on this question, I would like to deal briefly with a third version occasionally found in the literature, because I think it's very unconvincing. This school of thought maintains that in reality the change started not in 1973, and not in 1971, but in fact with Nasser, as a result of the exigencies of the situation. It was simply carried on by Sadat. Nasser's 1 May speech in which he addressed Nixon, indicated that he wanted to open a new page in relations with the United States, and that he accepted the Rogers Plan, and so on. I have had the opportunity to watch in Egypt how this school of thought sometimes rises, sometimes falls among the Egyptians. When peace was very popular in Egypt, after Sadat's trip, then those who were Nasser's sympathizers of course made this suggestion. They said: Sadat is simply continuing what Nasser would have done any way, so Nasser should get the credit for this.

Later, when peace got a bad image and became a cold peace – during the war in Lebanon and so on – the same people said: Nasser would never have made such a peace. What Sadat did was treason. It would have been impossible under Nasser.

And then once again, in recent years, when Egypt returned to the Arab world or the Arab world returned to Egypt, and peace became more convincingly an inevitability and a necessity for Egypt, once again the same people started writing articles on how Nasser had started thinking about peace not after '67 but in 1954 and 1955, and had secret contacts with the Israelis, and so on. So this was an intrinsic and inherent Egyptian policy which Sadat simply implemented.

I do not think that this is a serious argument. Certainly 1967 started a number of important changes in Egypt, but if we think about the transformation to peace I would say there is simply no evidence. Nasser never put on paper the words – "peace agreement with Israel." He remained in all his interviews very vague and ambiguous, and you could not extract from him clear statements like those made by Sadat. The fact is that he accepted the Rogers Plan but, when it came to implementation, his basic commitments somehow took over and expressed themselves in moving the missiles forward, violating the agreement.

Remember, Sadat was not Nasser. Nasser was personally responsible for the defeat not only in Sinai but also in the Golan Heights and in the West Bank and Gaza. For him to get back Sinai would have been an admission of defeat. For Sadat, anything regained from the Israelis was net profit. He was not responsible for the blunder of 1967. Thus he had a much wider scope for maneuvering than Nasser, whose whole ideological system spoke against acceptance of Israel: his historic struggle against imperialism, his Soviet orientation, and so on. I think that we can dismiss this version completely.

What then of the two major versions: 1971 and 1973? I think that the peace offer of 1971 was a sincere offer. It was serious. Sadat meant it. To illustrate this, I would like to direct your attention to some of the conversations that took place in Jerusalem when Sadat arrived in 1977. One of the first questions he asked everybody was: Why didn't you accept the initiative in 1971? We could have saved ourselves this war. And Dayan also on one occasion said something like: if I am ready to admit one mistake, it is the fact that we did not accept Sadat's initiative in 1971. This could have prevented the war.

But the question is: assuming that Sadat was sincere in his peace offer, could he have succeeded with his initiative? This is an entirely different matter. It might have made one step toward reconciliation in the future, but in the situation in which Sadat was still surrounded by all the Nasser elite, who were – and are up to this day – against reconciliation with Israel; when he did not have full control of the country itself, of the state (this happened only in May 1971); when his prestige in Egypt and in the Arab world was at a very low ebb and nobody took him seriously; with the Soviets still present on the soil of Egypt, and with no serious dialogue with the United States, what chances were there for success? Added to all this was the fact that a self-confident Israel was pouring money into military bases in Sinai, building new towns, and believing that "Sharm a-Sheikh without peace was better than peace without Sharm a-Sheikh." There was really no chance for success. Only after 1973, when first the bridges with the United States were prepared, when the Soviets were finally out, when the prestige of Sadat was enhanced, and Israel had learned a lesson and showed greater readiness for a compromise, did this become possible.

So Sadat succeeded on his second chance, and I think the change in the Israeli position was of primary importance. It is regrettable, but looking back at Israeli political behavior, Israel needed the October War in order to make a peace with Egypt based on the principle of territory for peace, and Israel needed the *intifada* for making a compromise with the PLO. Yet we were saying: "*Ha'aravim mevinim rak et s'fat hakoach*" (the Arabs understand only the language of force).

Having said so much about the importance of conditions, the role of personality is still of great importance in this case. We must give Sadat credit for the ability to put questions in a broad context. The best evidence, the best witnesses, to this aspect of Sadat's capabilities are his opponents, and I would like to finish by mentioning two of them and the clash they had with Sadat on this particular question – one from the Foreign Ministry, one from the military.

In the Foreign Ministry, Sadat worked during Camp David with Ibrahim Kamel at a certain point. And Sadat had a certain vision of what peace should be and what the importance of peace was. Ibrahim Kamel represented the Foreign Ministry, a very professional but very narrow perspective. And at one point Sadat said to Ibrahim Kamel, according to Kamel's own testimony: "Listen to what I have to say to you. I heard you, I did not interrupt you. Nobody will say that I am not listening or that I don't read the material. But I would like you to know that what you have just said entered one ear and came out from the other. You people in the Ministry of Foreign Affairs are under the impression that you understand foreign policy. Actually you don't understand anything at all. In the future I do not intend to devote any attention to what you say or to the memoranda that you send me. My actions are directed by a higher strategy which you are not capable of understanding. I don't need your misleading memoranda and your insignificant papers." This was not addressed specifically to Ibrahim Kamel, but to the Foreign Ministry, to the bureaucracy of foreign policy in general.

There was a similar clash with Shazali, who represented narrow military thinking, and, once again, he is the best witness. In his memoirs, he tells about the many clashes that he had with Sadat whenever he came to Sadat with what he understood to be prescribed by military logic, and Sadat dismissed it. When the Israeli crossing of the Canal took place, Shazali came to Sadat and said: military logic demands that we bring back forces from the east bank to the west bank. Sadat said to him: I'm not interested in military logic; I have a higher strategy. He needed the symbolic presence of Egyptian troops on the other side for the political negotiations that would take place afterwards. His book is full of these kinds of clashes that represented the narrow perspective of professionals *vis-à-vis* the broad perspective of a leader who is one of the greatest decision-makers, I think, in the history of the Middle East.

To sum up, I think that Sadat pioneered this peace process. Without Camp David, I think it would have been very difficult, if not impossible, to have Oslo or to have Madrid. He did not really legitimize peace with Israel completely in the Arab world, but he made a great step in that direction. His pioneering role was actually broader than that of preparing the ground for a comprehensive peace, because his peace with Israel was part of a package. Let us not forget that. His peace with Israel was part of a package that included economic liberalization; reorientation toward the United States; completely ignoring the Soviet Union as a marginal factor in the area; the beginnings of democratization, at least in the sense of political pluralism; and peace with Israel. All these things together form part of what he called the higher strategy.

These elements of his policy are actually the elements of what is now called the new world order: the stress on economics, the United States, the West, a peaceful solution to problems, and so on. It is regrettable that Jordanians, Syrians, Palestinians did not follow him after Camp David. They did so 15 years after his peace initiative. In fact we can show some forgiveness for all the opportunities that were missed at that time if we bear in mind what Abba Eban said on this subject. He said history teaches us that men and nations behave wisely once they have exhausted all other alternatives. I think this applies to all the actors in the Middle East.

6

Policy and Back Channels: 1970–1973

Amnon Sella

Most of the factual data about the October Yom Kippur War is common knowledge, although time may reap some new revelations. As rational people who believe that history is human made it is speculative to argue: "what would have happened?" But it is also banal to argue that we must bow to our fate and that history as it is unveiled is inevitable. The question that I want to address is why nation-states need to go through an excruciating process of learning to achieve goals that on the face of it look so obvious; and why, when these are achieved, only historians remember that once upon a time people were ready to kill each other in order to prevent their achievement.

Between 1970 and 1973 the Middle East seemed to have returned to its precarious normalcy after the cease-fire that terminated the War of Attrition. Sadat's declaration that 1971 was the "year of decision" would have created a crisis after October 1973, when Sadat became a prominent international figure, but not when it was uttered. Israel's impervious smugness prior to the October War could not have been an incentive for an ally like the United States to bring pressure to bear on either side, or to risk a confrontation, be it even a diplomatic one, with the U.S.S.R. When we take into consideration that the U.S. and the U.S.S.R. at the time were engaged in an effort to reach a global agreement, we can understand how Israel's over-confidence joined Egypt's need "to regain by force what had been taken away by force" to produce a war in order to make peace.

Time runs differently for small powers and for superpowers. As an illustration we may imagine the movement of a pendulum. At the head of the rod the oscillation is hardly perceptible, while near the weight, down below, the oscillation is considerable. The superpower at the top of the rod need make only a slight move for a dependent country at the bottom end of the rod to feel a tremor.

For instance, Israel must be able to mobilize all its forces in a couple of days because it lacks strategic depth, while the Soviet Union took a whole month to deploy one army against the Japanese in May 1939. The difference between a superpower and a small country is perhaps less obvious at a time of peace, when a superpower has a timetable which may affect a small country directly, but it is by no means less significant. It does not make a great deal of difference whether the two countries, the big and the small, aim at the same goal and have many common interests. This may only signify that goals and interests should be elaborated upon and worked out to the finest details to make sure that they are really the same and that the interests are truly common.

Obviously, the goals and interests of the superpowers were not congruous with those of Egypt and Israel before and during the October 1973 War. Egypt wanted to get back the Sinai Peninsula but not through direct negotiations with Israel and not by means of a separate deal; Israel was prepared to give back most of Sinai, by no means all of it, but only in return for a full peace agreement with Egypt that would not bear on other territories occupied during the Six Day War, and only if a settlement was stretched over a long period of time.

A main concern of the political-military leadership of Israel prior to the October War was that any sign of a looming war or of weakness might encourage the United States to move the wheels of negotiations again. The United States wanted to see a settlement in the Middle East because President Nixon and Kissinger believed that U.S. interests, such as the free flow of oil at reasonable prices, are better served at a time of peace, and that American diplomacy was superior to the Soviets', in particular when there is no crisis.

The U.S.S.R. did not want to see a strong American influence in the Middle East but was not prepared to involve its own forces in fighting to achieve this aim, nor did it want to see its allies involved in a hopeless war. Evidently, neither party, small or big, wanted to see the Middle East go up in flames. Furthermore, Israel's defense doctrine was based on the assumption of deterrence, meaning that the Arab countries would not risk a war against Israel's superiority in the air and against the odds that it could use the weapon of "last resort."

On the face of it then, after the end of the War of Attrition and up to the May 1972 summit meeting in Moscow there was a tacit agreement between the main parties – the United States, the U.S.S.R., Egypt and Israel – that no-war is better than war and that diplomacy is better than violence. The Egyptian restlessness with the status quo was noted, but the grievances were never considered seriously by Israeli-American teams, nor did the American administration ever reveal to Israel its strategy and tactics with regard to the U.S.-Soviet rivalry in the Middle East.

During the years preceding the October War, and during the war itself, the division of power and interests in the Middle East seemed to be clear cut. The United States was an ally of Israel, the U.S.S.R. sided with Egypt and Syria and with the Arab side in general. It was therefore assumed that any Arab move, even if not engineered in Moscow, would certainly receive the blessing of Moscow automatically after the event.

It was also assumed in Israel that any American move aimed against the U.S.S.R. was of necessity beneficial to Israel. During the years 1970–72 Nixon and Kissinger worked out the strategy and tactics that were aimed at reducing Soviet influence in the Middle East. The diplomatic maneuvre needed a long period of time in which nothing would happen so that Sadat would be able to see for himself that Soviet economic and military aid as well as diplomatic support was getting him nowhere. Kissinger, who became the chief formulator of American foreign policy in the early 1970s, said:

> My aim was to produce a stalemate until Moscow urged compromise or until, even better, some moderate Arab regime decided that the route to progress was through Washington.[1]

At that time, the first half of 1971 – which for Sadat was his year of decision – Kissinger wrote to Nixon, on 31 May 1971:

> The Egyptian Army is dependent on Soviet support. In turn, Sadat is at the moment dependent on his military for his base of power, having purged the party and the bureaucracy. Rather than strengthening Sadat's flexibility with respect to negotiating the Canal settlement, the treaty could give the Soviet Union a veto over the future

negotiations. Thus, whatever the outcome of the negotiations – and after all, *the Soviets are the chief beneficiaries of a Suez settlement* (emphasis added) – recent events may have enhanced Soviet long-term influence. Certainly the Soviets are committed to engage themselves as never before in case of resumption of hostilities.[2]

Apparently, there were too many assumptions on all sides. The United States assumed that Egypt was a staunch ally of the Soviet Union; Israel assumed that the U.S. interest in a blocked Suez Canal would last; Egypt assumed that the United States condoned the status quo in the occupied territories; the U.S.S.R. assumed that its position in Egypt was secured. Only perceptive eyes detected the weaknesses of the Soviet system in the early 1970s. Most strategic and military analysts believed that the U.S.S.R. was prepared to challenge the predominance of the West even in a region of crucial interest, like the Persian Gulf. This supposed challenge was called "penetration," whereas the West's position was called "presence". No wonder that the signing of the Treaty of Friendship and Cooperation with Egypt (27 May 1971) was considered another proof of the assumption that Egypt was a Soviet "client".

The Soviet aim at the time was to strengthen its position in the Third World and in the Arab world through diplomatic means. After the treaty with Egypt in May 1971 there followed a treaty with India in August and a treaty with Iraq in April 1972. These treaties were signed when it became more and more difficult for the U.S.S.R. to supply generous credits for the purchase of arms. Thus, after several trips to Moscow where Sadat was promised that he would get deliveries of modern arms which he needed urgently because the "year of decision" was nearing its end with no tangible achievements, Marshal Grechko and Air Marshal Kutakhov came to Cairo on a visit, five days before the summit meeting between Nixon and Brezhnev was convened in Moscow. The two marshals brought with them the new Sukhoi-7 but Egypt was forced to sign a joint communiqué to the effect that it had received long-range bombers.[3]

During the years 1970–74 American foreign policy accomplished a great deal. It managed to break the ice in relations with China, which had been frozen since the establishment of the Communist regime in 1949; to sign the SALT agreement, which professed diplomatic "parity" but maintained the American technological and strategic edge; to end the futile war in Vietnam and to undermine the Soviet position in the Middle East.

In domestic politics, however, the Watergate scandal was brewing and Kissinger replaced Secretary of State William Rogers as the chief engineer of foreign policy. In his words, "What finally got me involved in the execution of Middle East diplomacy was that Nixon did not believe he could risk recurrent crises in the Middle East in an election year. He therefore asked me to step in, if only to keep things quiet. My first move was to explore whether the Soviets were in fact willing to moderate their proposals; if not, I intended to draw them into protracted and inconclusive negotiations until either they or some Arab country changed their position."[4]

By the end of 1971 the division within the American administration, the State Department's pursuit of a comprehensive peace and the U.S.S.R.'s unwillingness to complicate its relations with Egypt, Syria and Iraq had, in Kissinger's words: "produced the stalemate for which I had striven by design."[5] In the words of another observer, who was later to become involved in the Camp David Accord: "U.S. diplomacy continued to aim at what Kissinger was later to term the 'complete frustration' of the Arabs, a policy that he later admitted was shortsighted and may have contributed to the October 1973 War."[6]

The aims of Nixon and Kissinger at the time, then, were to reduce the risk of a global crisis. They were prepared to negotiate with the U.S.S.R. and to link global agreements to regional understanding. On the regional level they were prepared to negotiate with the U.S.S.R. some settlement in the Middle East when that country was prepared to compromise, or better still when Egypt was prepared to deal directly with Washington. The technique was to manipulate incalculable frustration in order to achieve manageable negotiations.

In March 1971 Nixon gave Kissinger a mandate to explore the possibilities of an interim agreement with the Soviet Union. However, the U.S.S.R., sensing the limits of its influence in the Arab world, did not dare to wander off the main course of Arab policy, which at the time was not ready to go for anything less than a complete withdrawal of Israel from all the occupied territories. In March, then, Dobrynin, the Soviet Ambassador in Washington, was not ready to discuss an interim agreement. However, on 20 September 1971, Dobrynin told Kissinger that when Gromyko met Nixon on 29 September he might propose putting the Middle East into a "special channel." When Nixon and Gromyko met, Nixon accepted Gromyko's suggestion that Kissinger and Dobrynin "undertake a serious exploration of Middle East issues – though not without linking it again to Soviet help on Vietnam."[7]

Superficially it was a complete victory for the strategy worked out by Nixon and Kissinger. Negotiations were conducted between the superpowers; a linkage was established between global and regional affairs. Gromyko even agreed that if there was a linkage between the interim agreement and a final settlement, the U.S.S.R. would be prepared "to withdraw its forces from the Middle East, join in an arms embargo in the area, and participate in guarantees of a diplomatic settlement."[8] Israel did not agree to any linkage between an interim agreement and a final settlement.

To crown the success of Kissinger's strategy at the beginning of April 1972, Egypt had opened a secret channel to the White House. However, "preoccupied with the Vietnam offensive and then my forthcoming trip to Moscow, we did not respond immediately" and "after SALT was settled, any remaining tension disappeared from the summit. No serious effort was made afterward to resolve any outstanding international problem."

All seemed quiet on the global level. That very tranquility started off a train of events which led eventually to the October War. Sadat was so exasperated with the endless delays in arms deliveries from the Soviet Union that in July he decided to expel the Soviet advisers from Egypt. In other words, Kissinger's strategy succeeded beyond all expectations. The secret channel with the Soviet Union did not push forward the negotiations because Nixon and Kissinger did not believe that the U.S.S.R. was ready to compromise on the Middle East. Sadat decided to change orientation from Moscow to Washington, but Washington was so preoccupied elsewhere that it could not respond. What might have become a secret channel to make peace turned out to be part of a great deceit, which climaxed in the Egyptian-Syrian surprise attack on 6 October 1973.

The first part of this chapter established that the superpowers' interpretations of stability and "peace" were neither congruous nor identical with those of the parties involved in the region. Indeed, the global idea of stability and peace at the time immediately preceding the October War was detrimental to the advancement of regional stability and peace. It was not for lack of empathy for the warring parties, nor was the American administration deaf to the lengthening toll of Israeli casualties. It was a cruel scale of priorities which dictated the pace of response. *Detente* was at stake and the U.S. measured its response to the intensity of the war by the margin it was prepared to allow for Soviet success in influencing the fate of the Middle East. Says Kissinger: "The Soviet Union never launched a diplomatic offensive to embarrass or isolate us at the United Nations. The war was contained, and the United States maneuvered successfully to reduce the Soviet role in the Middle East."[9] In his first news conference on 12 October, Kissinger said: "We also do not consider that Soviet actions as of now constitute the irresponsibility that on Monday evening I pointed out would threaten détente."[10]

It is arguable that had Israel been better prepared for the surprise attack by Egypt and Syria, another Israeli victory could have frozen the Middle East for a long time. Furthermore, due respect must be given to the fact that the military stalemate that was imposed on Israel by the end of the war facilitated the ensuing agreements and that a crushing Israeli victory might have postponed the peace process indefinitely. My main argument is that a readiness to go on a defensive alert, shuttle diplomacy, and a reassessment could have achieved much the same results in 1971. The fact that all these happened only after a bloody war and that the United States made the most of the opportunity, once the circumstances allowed it, shows the painful process of learning by nation-states.

Notes

1. Henry Kissinger, *White House Years*, p. 1279.
2. Ibid., p. 1284.
3. Anwar el-Sadat, *The Story of My Life*, pp. 174–175.
4. Kissinger, *White House Years*, p. 1285.
5. Ibid., p. 1289.
6. William B. Quandt, *Peace Process*, pp. 116–117.
7. Kissinger, *White House Years*, p. 1287.
8. Ibid., p. 1288.
9. Ibid., p. 507.
10. Ibid.

Decision-Making and Bargaining in the Arab-Israeli Conflict

Zeev Maoz

Political scientists are interested in analytical insights into long-term negotiation processes. An important distinction is between bargaining and negotiations. All negotiations entail bargaining, but not all bargaining processes entail negotiation. Strictly speaking, a bargaining situation is a situation in which two or more parties are interlocked in a situation of mutual interdependence, wherein the decisions of one party are affected by the decisions of the other party. So the best choice depends on what you think your opponent is going to do, and your opponent's best choice is based on what he attributes to you as your choice. Bargaining can take place in war, even when parties don't talk to one another: fighting and shooting and escalating is bargaining, because by making decisions in which you try to foil your opponent's plan, and by your opponent trying to do likewise, you are bargaining with this opponent. You don't have to talk to the opponent either directly or indirectly. It may involve tacit communication, but it doesn't require explicit communication.

Negotiation, on the other hand, is a process whereby two or more parties are engaged in a joint decision-making process, designed to bring about an agreement. This situation can come about only if all parties involved are convinced that some joint resolution of the conflict of interests is preferable to a unilateral attempt to resolve the conflict. If one party believes that it can resolve the conflict merely by its own action, then there is no place for bargaining. If both parties, or more parties in the case of multilateral negotiations, are convinced that they cannot do so, or that some agreements are achievable and preferable to a lack of agreement, then they have to start to talk. They don't need to talk directly. They can talk through intermediaries. They can talk through all kinds of indirect messages. They can talk through secret channels. They can talk publicly. But some communication is required, and some joint decision-making process is required. Obviously, in a negotiation process, as in bargaining situations, we have mutual dependence, and each party's decision is based on the decision of the other parties.

Let us illustrate this by taking two cases. The first case is the situation immediately preceding the outbreak of fighting in the Yom Kippur War, that is, roughly between 3 October and 5 October 1973. We can describe the Egyptian choices broadly defined, as to attack, or not to attack. Israel's choices were to mobilize reserves, or not to mobilize reserves. Israel had the option of pre-empting, but we are not considering it here in order not to complicate the presentation.

What each party gets depends not only on what it decides to do, but also on what the other party decides to do. Since we have two parties that have two choices, we have four possible situations. If Egypt attacked, and Israel mobilized, Egypt and Israel perceived a high probability of Israeli victory, major defeat for Egypt with numerous casualties, and some Israeli casualties. Egypt felt that even in that situation it could get some inter-Arab support, because it would be doing something in order to reverse the consequences of the Six Day War.

The second situation is if Israel mobilized, and Egypt did not attack. If that took place, we would have from Israel's perspective a good situation in terms of strategy because there would be no war. Israel's deterrence could be said to have prevailed, but at a cost. Israel had mobilized in May 1973 and this had cost it a tremendous amount of money. A renewed mobilization would have inflicted a heavy economic burden on the Israeli economy and drawn some international criticism, because the Israeli decision-makers felt that the United States and others would criticize it for potentially setting off a war situation. From Egypt's point of view, this situation had some pluses, but if it didn't attack, it would be criticized by the Arabs for failing to do something about the situation.

The third situation was that which actually took place in '73. Israel decides not to mobilize. Egypt decides to attack, in which case we have heavy Israeli casualties; from the Egyptian perspective, a high probability of perhaps not major victory, but of accomplishing certain objectives that Sadat set for himself in the war; and obviously a boost to Egyptian morale and potentially a domestic political problem in Israel.

Finally, the last situation: Israel does not mobilize and Egypt does not attack – the status quo. The status quo implies for Israel a very good situation. Israel does not spend money on mobilization. It preserves its territory. It doesn't suffer casualties in a war, and obviously that would have been, from its perspective, the best of all possible worlds. It would have been a very bad situation from the Egyptian point of view, because Sadat was bent on reversing or altering the status quo, and failure to do so would have caused domestic problems, economic problems, inter-Arab criticism, and so on, potentially some risk for his regime.

Obviously, in a situation like that, the choice depends on what you think the other party is going to do. You must figure out what the other party is going to do and you have to know something about what makes the other party tick, what motivates its choices. There is a major potential for misperception.

To illustrate this situation, consider the same problem from the Israeli point of view. Obviously, from Israel's perspective, no mobilization/no attack is the best outcome. The worst outcome, from its perspective, is for it to be caught unprepared by an Egyptian attack.

What is important here is that Israel's choice depended on how it evaluated Egypt's best choice. If Israel thought that Egypt would attack, then its best choice would have been to mobilize. However, if Israel's assessment of Egyptian intention was that it would not attack, its best choice would have been not to mobilize. So Israel's perception of the Egyptians was of major importance. Israel thought that Egypt's worst outcome would be for Egypt to attack, and for Israel to be prepared, because then Egypt would suffer a major defeat. And the next worst outcome would be the status quo. Now, by placing the Egyptian preferences in such a manner, Israel figured that Egypt's best choice would be not to attack, hence its own decision not to mobilize. And I am not going to go into the intelligence assessment, but basically this is a theoretical description of what we know about Israel's intelligence failure in that case.

What we know also, because surprisingly we had fairly good primary sources about Egyptian decision-making in that event – including verbatim transcripts of an Egyptian General Staff meetings – is that Sadat really thought the worst possible outcome would be the status quo, and preferred an attack when Israel was mobilized, as offering a pretty good outcome for himself because of the very limited objective he set for the war. Sadat wanted war in order to negotiate. He didn't want war in order to win. He didn't want war in order to capture the Sinai. He wanted war in order to bring in the superpowers, because he felt that the détente between the United States and the Soviet Union presented a major risk for Egypt, some sort of understanding that they would freeze all conflicts in order to avoid situations where local proxies could draw them into escalation.

What we got was our worst outcome. What the Egyptians got was a better outcome than they had expected because, according to this depiction, Egypt was prepared to attack, even if it knew that Israel was mobilized.

This is one description. No communication, but a bargaining situation, a situation where each party's choice depends on the other party. Another situation, which takes us a couple of years ahead, immediately precedes Sadat's 1977 visit to Jerusalem. Again, Egypt has two choices: to recognize Israel or not to recognize Israel. Israel's choice was to withdraw from the Sinai or not to withdraw. Again, the four possible worlds are described in the four cells.

Now, this is a situation where bargaining, or tacit communication, is insufficient. Why? Because Egypt's best choice in this situation, from a theoretical perspective, would be not to recognize Israel. Whatever Israel did, Egypt would be better off not to recognize Israel than to recognize it. Israel did not have a unilateral best choice. Its choice depended on Egypt's choice, but it knew that Egypt's best choice was not to recognize.

This situation suggests that the outcome of this interaction would be no peace. Israel would continue to control the Sinai. Israel could have justified this policy because the Arabs were not willing to recognize us. From the Egyptian perspective, Sinai would not have been returned, there would be a deterioration in Egypt's leading role in the Arab world, and potential domestic costs as well. That would have been Egypt's next worst outcome. Now Egypt and Israel could have done better. They could have done better if Egypt had recognized Israel, because Egypt would have obtained its next best outcome, with Israel withdrawing from the Sinai. From Israel's perspective that would have been the best outcome. However, in order to do that, Sadat had to convince Israel that he would behave in a manner that was seemingly irrational in order to accomplish a rational outcome. And we call this kind of strategy a "self-binding commitment," namely, Sadat's visit to Jerusalem. Although Sadat had already received some sort of promise in Morocco that he would be granted some degree of withdrawal from the Sinai, it is unclear how much. A public move was a move of establishing trust, of telling the Israelis, "I unilaterally recognize you. I cannot reverse it. I cannot reverse this recognition. The moment I come to Jerusalem, the moment I decide to speak to the Knesset, I have recognized Israel. Now it is your turn. It is your turn to reciprocate." Under these circumstances, Israel's rational choice would have been nothing other than to withdraw from the Sinai, and this is indeed what we got in the Camp David agreement.

This is a very crude characterization of two very complex situations. I am trying to derive some general findings about the characteristics of the process as a whole, not merely of one episode or another.

First, we have learned, especially in the first period, how considerable misperception led to numerous missed opportunities. In the period between 1971 and 1973, it was mostly misperception on the part of Israel on the one hand, and the United States on the other hand. What both Israel and the United States failed to perceive was that they were dealing with a leader who followed a very consistent strategy. Despite all the statements that Sadat made throughout this period, he was discredited and was really misunderstood. I think that an exception to this rule was Moshe Dayan, who felt that Sadat was serious and that some serious deals could be struck with him. In the United States the exception was William Rogers. But Dayan, for domestic political reasons, and Rogers, because he was really shut out of any kind of major decision by the President and Kissinger during that time, didn't get their way. The policy that Israel and the United States pursued was based on a fundamental misperception of Egypt. The problems leading up to the surprise in 1973 were not only strategic military problems but also political problems. I think it would be fair to state that the war could have been avoided – not for sure, but there is a reasonable chance that an interim agreement would have avoided the war. And what we did in 1974 and later on in 1975 in Egypt could well have been agreed upon in 1971 or 1972.

Secondly: Sadat followed a consistent strategy throughout his reign in power. Israel did not have a consistent strategy. It usually followed the lead of others. Initially, it was the lead of the United States in 1970 with the Rogers cease-fire initiative; then the Kissinger initiative in 1974 and 1975, the step-by-step diplomacy; and in 1977 it really followed what Sadat determined in his moves, as we have seen.

The United States did have a strategy but this strategy shifted from one administration to another, from one secretary of state to another, from one president to another. Each one developed a strategy. In some cases, leaders did not follow their own strategies. Kissinger really followed his step-by-step diplomacy throughout, until he eventually felt that it had exhausted itself. Carter started out with a general agreement, a kind of Geneva Conference framework, but very quickly he realized that it was a non-starter, and had to follow Sadat's initiative. The Reagan administration started out with the Reagan plan but didn't really follow it through. It is very difficult to characterize any kind of strategy on the part of the Reagan administration, or the Bush administration, up to the Gulf War.

However, Israel really did not have a clear strategy. Only if you would describe the strategy of following what everybody else does as being a strategy, could you say that Israel had a strategy. The only cases where Israel really succeeded, when it accomplished major breakthroughs, were either when it overcame its own self-perceived constraints, or when it launched a major initiative, as happened in the last year or so in Oslo. In most other cases, we can really say that we didn't plan ahead. We followed other actors.

Now the third point I wish to make is that domestic politics had a major impact on the process. Despite the fact that we are engaged in a regional system where major power interaction has a major influence on local actors, domestic politics both in Israel and to some extent in the Arab states played a major role that leaders had to contend with. Now in some cases – in almost all cases – major breakthroughs took place not because of public pressure but despite public pressure, when leaders decided they could risk severe – sometimes very severe – domestic criticism in order to move ahead. That happened in 1977 with Sadat. That happened to a large extent in 1978 when Begin felt that he had to overcome opposition in his own party in order to move ahead. And of course that is happening with the Israel-PLO agreement, with the Labor Party moving on very, very unsafe ground, in terms of public and parliamentary support. When leaders said, "we will take the domestic risk in order to accomplish major breakthroughs outside," that is when progress took place.

To a large extent, in the United States, domestic pressure has very little impact on diplomatic progress, but it has had some constraining effect on presidents. When they attempted to launch major initiatives – for example, the Carter Geneva plan, or the September 1977 Vance–Gromyko statement of principles – they were always blocked by domestic pressure, and mostly Jewish pressure, causing those leaders to retract.

Generally speaking, there are trends that teach us a lesson that these events are not isolated. They affect one another, and what we do now may affect the future of negotiations. Several myths have been broken in the recent period.

First, we had always assumed that we should avoid at all costs simultaneous negotiations with several Arab states or other actors. We felt that such negotiations would create simultaneous pressures on us, not only from our negotiation partners, but also from the United States. Such pressures would be lessened if negotiations were handled one at a time. The Madrid process showed that we could actually use simultaneous negotiation processes with several actors to our advantage. By making progress on one front we could exert psychological pressure on our counterpart in the other front. That actor, fearing that it would be left behind and that we would lose our incentive to make concessions if the agreement with the other party was concluded, would be more inclined to make concessions than if it were to negotiate with us all by itself.

Second, we have always felt that to make painful concessions that may be necessary in order to accomplish peace, the government would need wide-ranging parliamentary support. This, incidentally, has been a major claim of those who pushed the initiative to change the electoral system in Israel. The Oslo accords, and the way they had been approved in Israel show that even a government without majority support in the Knesset can go a long way in its foreign policy.

Third, and most important, we learned that he who dares, wins. Diplomatic initiatives are necessary if progress is to be made. A daring strategy pays off not only in war-making, but in peace-making as well.

8

Drums of War and Bells of Peace: Egypt's Perspective on the 1973 War

Yoram Meital

Almost every concept related to the 1973 War is presented in Israel and Egypt in opposite manners. The Yom Kippur War, as the 1973 War is called in Israel, is linked with labels such as the *"mekhdal"* (omission). This term reflects the political and military leadership's incompetence as well as the over-confidence dominating most of Israeli society in the six years between the military triumph of 1967 and the outbreak of the 1973 War.

The Egyptians, on the other hand, perceive the October War, as it is called in Egypt, in a totally different way, regarding it as a glorious turning point in the course of the Arab-Israeli conflict as well as in Egypt's domestic situation and foreign relations.

In fact, the Egyptians perceive the 1973 War as the basis of most events in the Middle East during the past two decades. From this perspective, Sadat's historic visit to Jerusalem and the negotiation and signing of the peace treaty with Israel, as well as the economic and political "opening" to the West, could not have happened without victory in the October War. Even the dramatic breakthrough of the Israel-PLO Accord and multilateral talks is connected by Egyptians to the 1973 War. Officials, scholars and journalists in Egypt have argued that its roots were in the Egyptian-Israeli reconciliation during the 1970s, which itself had evolved from the October War. In October 1993, in his traditional speech to commemorate the 1973 War, President Hosni Mubarak described Egypt's perspective on the Israeli-PLO agreement in the following words:

> The glorious October War had opened wide the chance for peace to all the peoples of the region. The Palestinian-Israeli agreement could

not have happened without the deep influence the October War had created in the region of the Middle East.[1]

For most Egyptians, the October War was an Egyptian (and an all-Arab) victory, neither to be questioned nor doubted. The surprise offensive was started in the early afternoon of 6 October. By 9 October, the Egyptian army had reached most of the first stage's tactical aims: the achievement of surprise, the crossing of the Suez Canal, the building of several bridges over it, and the advance crossing of infantry and armored forces with their equipment. The Egyptian army's fighting qualities and discipline as well as the technological level of its arms and ability to use them were considerably higher than ever before. The initial attack's success marked the rehabilitation of the army and the restoration of its prestige and morale. Egypt's major achievement was that it had broken the status quo against the desire of Israel and the superpowers, who, from Cairo's perspective, wanted to perpetuate it.

Between the war's outbreak and conclusion, the public mood in Egypt changed radically from frustration and bitterness to a state of elation and joy. The writer Yusuf al-Qa'id, for instance, wrote on the day the war ended: "You people in the land of Egypt are living in times of victory, of happy laughter and boundless joy. You're a happy people, happier than our forefathers ever were, and happier than our grandchildren will be".[2] Even writers formerly as skeptical as Tawfiq al-Hakim, now sounded a different note. On the war's third day, he wrote:

> When we crossed into Sinai, we "crossed" the defeat [of 1967]. Whatever the outcome of the fighting, the important thing is that we have cleansed ourselves. That is the meaning of the slogan: "Egypt always remains Egypt". The world thought [Egypt] had sunk into torpor; but its spirit had not became inert. If it dozed for a while, it woke up quickly, roared, and stood on its feet.[3]

Egyptian historians, as well as much of the general public, came to distinguish between the military events as such – which they regarded as secondary – and the realization of the country's basic strategic aims, which they considered the more important aspect. Najib Mahfuz had this to say on the matter:

> Did we win the battle or were we defeated? Let us ask ourselves what criterion to apply to the question of victory or defeat. Without

claiming expertise in military matters or politics, I say that the objective laid down for it is the criterion for any war; the aim, not the land or the casualties or even the fighting. There is, then, no doubt that the outcome is a victory for the Arab armies. It is certainly not a defeat, even if it is not the final victory which will only be attained by another, crushing victory, or else by just and honorable peace.[4]

If measured in terms of the targets they had set themselves, both Egypt and Israel had indeed cause to claim victory in the 1973 War. Egypt's objective had been to overturn the status quo and to accelerate political efforts, and Cairo had indeed succeeded in doing both. Israel for its part regarded the war primarily as a military challenge and its chief aim was to foil the Egyptian military threat. Therefore Israel also attained its most important war aim.

In the short term, what counted was the Egyptian-Syrian threat to Israel's security. In this regard, the Arab offensive called into question Israel's concept of security and the reliability of its intelligence services. This remains true despite the fact that Israel eventually gained tactical military superiority and ended the war holding Syrian territories beyond the 1967 cease-fire line in the Golan – halting only some 40 kilometers from Damascus – as well as large Egyptian areas west of the Suez Canal, within 100 kilometers of Cairo. In purely military terms, these were the marks of victory. But if we look at the outcome from the perspective of a longer time span and broad political and strategic results, we find that Egypt made undeniably important long-term strategic gains.

According to Egyptian sources (during March and April 1973), Sadat gave the war plan a firmer shape by merging military and political aspects into a single strategy. The war was to begin with a surprise attack on both the Egyptian and Syrian fronts, reach limited objectives on the battle-field, but be sufficient to shatter the Israeli security doctrine. The Suez Canal was to be crossed at several points and bridgeheads were to be established on its eastern bank. The longer the Egyptian forces succeeded in holding a strip of land east of the Canal, the greater the chance for the great powers' intervention. The overall international and regional situation would thus undergo a radical transformation. Under the new circumstances, steps leading to a political solution could be set in motion on much more favorable terms than had been possible before.

Cairo's actual military and political wartime moves show that

Sadat himself and the forces under his command clung closely
to the aims he had laid down. The initial Egyptian assault was
carried out by five divisions who established three bridgeheads
and, exploiting the advantage of surprise, conquered most forti-
fied posts of Israel's Bar-Lev line during the first few days of
fighting. The surprise factor was the result not only of the Israeli
intelligence failure, but also of the use of novel tactics. These
enabled the Egyptians to bring quickly across the Canal much
larger bodies of troops than had been anticipated and, once they had
crossed, to conduct their operations by means of tactics unforeseen
in Israel.

The Egyptian army was able to stand up to the Israeli armor
by sophisticated use of infantry equipped with anti-tank weapons
and trained in the rapid preparation of defensive positions in the
open, sandy ground of Sinai. This was often done at night (a
period of full moonlight having been chosen to open the war).
Consequently, initial Israeli losses of armor were heavy. Moreover,
the Egyptian troops east of the Canal were protected from air
attacks by a dense deployment of ground-to-air missiles on its
western bank. Their range sufficed to neutralize the Israeli air
force in the zone of the initial fighting. The Israeli armor and
the Bar-Lev strongpoints were thereby deprived of effective air
cover.

Egypt's strategic aims in the October War had been to break the
status quo; to cause the United States to change substantially its
policy toward the Arab-Israeli conflict; and to create circumstances
in which a political solution more advantageous to Egypt would
become feasible. In retrospect, it was the change in U.S. policy that
turned out to be Cairo's most significant achievement. Egyptian
and U.S. documents alike show that after the 1973 War both Cairo
and Washington revised their attitudes toward each other. Subsequently, the U.S. administration attributed increasing importance to
Egypt's positions in the regional system.

On the Egyptian side, the *rapprochement* with Washington was
part of an overall reorientation of the country's policies, which,
in turn, resulted from a broad reassessment of national priorities.
The need to manage the conflict with Israel and the economic
and monetary challenges facing Egypt were the factors underlying the turn toward the United States. Egypt's decision-makers
argued that in the prevailing global, regional and domestic circumstances Israel's positions could not be changed by force of

arms alone. Equally it was not feasible to seek a radical solution such as the elimination of Israel. Quick and realistically attainable results could only be the outcome of a more reasonable policy.

Consequently, in the 1973 War's aftermath, establishment spokesmen frequently stressed the interdependence of progress toward a political accommodation with Israel and the rehabilitation of Egypt's social and economic fabric. In other words, socio-economic conditions could only be bettered in times of peace. The same *motif* was used to persuade both the domestic public and other countries of the need for a far-reaching policy change. The present poor state of the economy, it was argued, resulted directly from past huge investments in the struggle against Israel. Looking back at this period, Sadat wrote:

> If we look back through history we see the horrors brought upon Egypt by war – the martyrs, the destruction and the delays in development. Egypt became a backward country because of the slogan "war is supreme". This is why I opted for peace. I thought it was important to create an atmosphere that fostered development, so that Egypt could survive and become a partner in the twenty-first century before it was too late.[5]

From Egypt's perspective, the October War had opened the road toward a peace settlement with Israel. Furthermore, Sadat argued that Israel's and Egypt's commitment to the political process in the aftermath of the 1973 War had created a new tendency in the Arab-Israeli conflict which succeeded because it was based on reality. In this connection, it is worth recalling his words on this point in his November 1977 Knesset speech. His words reflected his broad and correct assessment of the new trends in the Arab-Israeli conflict:

> There are certain facts that have to be faced with courage and clear vision. There are Arab territories which Israel occupied [since 1967]. We insist on complete withdrawal from these territories. As for the Palestinian cause, no one can deny that this is the heart of the whole problem . . . In all faith I tell you that peace cannot be achieved without the Palestinians . . . The only language to deal with it, for a just and lasting peace, is the establishment of their state. With all the international guarantees you request. There should be no fear of a new-born state . . . When the bells of peace ring, there will be no hand to beat the drums of war, and if there is any, it shall be soundless.[6]

Notes

1. *Al-Ahram*, 6 October 1993.
2. Yusuf al-Qa'id, *War in the Land of Egypt* (London, 1986), pp. 93–94.
3. *Al-Ahram*, 9 October 1973.
4. Ibid., 14 December 1973.
5. Anwar al-Sadat, *Those I Have Known* (New York, 1984), p. 106.
6. Arab Republic of Egypt, *White Paper on the peace initiatives undertaken by President Anwar Al-Sadat, 1971–1977* (Cairo, 1978), pp. 175–179.

9

Confidence-Building and the Peace Process

Gabriel Ben-Dor

The peace process in the Middle East has been around for so long that it is difficult even to pinpoint its beginning. Most of us may think of Madrid 1991 as the genesis of the process in its present manifestation, or else we may go back to the Sadat initiative in 1977 and the Camp David conference a year later, when the idea of autonomy for the Palestinians attained the status of an international obligation by the parties. Of course, the matter is more complicated than that. In a sense, for as long as there has been a conflict and there have been wars, there has been a peace process, because both regional and international forces have been at work for facilitating a peaceful resolution of the conflict almost from time immemorial. Certainly each major war in the Arab-Israeli conflict witnessed the birth of initiatives to avert the next war, and at times these initiatives were public and well known, as in the case of 1967 which yielded United Nations Security Council Resolution 242, the Gunnar Jarring mission and several projects called the "Rogers Plan." In other cases, the issues were so obfuscated by external factors that little of consequence, or at least public consequence, came to see the light of day.

However, in a very real sense the ongoing peace process is one that can and should be traced back to the 1973 Yom Kippur War. There are many reasons for this. The first one, which some observers may consider somewhat technical, is that this was the last war between the major protagonists in the conflict. If Egypt is considered historically as the linchpin of the Arab coalition against Israel, clearly this is the watershed in the Egyptian-Israeli

to the eventual peace treaty between these two
ch changed the face of the entire Middle East.
war in which there was a meaningful Arab
he apart in the latter part of the fighting. It was
effort against Israel, producing the high point of
," which then gave way to Arab countries quite
openly p———   heir separate national and state interests.

Of course, it was also an ambiguous enough war in terms of
results, because the Arabs could, and did, claim victory and, in
many ways, justly so. But at the same time, the leadership in
countries such as Egypt clearly recognized that – notwithstanding
the excellent, almost optimal, opening conditions – the war ended
badly for the Arabs, and that moreover, such conditions (surprise,
the oil weapon, intelligence failure) were not likely to be repeated
any time in the foreseeable future. Thus the conclusion was that
this victory, such as it was, had to be translated into political
settlements of lasting value, because the Arab achievements in
the war – contrary to popular perception – did not signify a new
trend for the future that would assure victory with any degree of
certainty or even probability.

The war also involved the external powers to an unprecedented
degree. The oil embargo made it relevant to all the Western industrial democracies, and in fact almost to every single citizen who
drove a car. The brink of U.S.-Soviet nuclear confrontation in the
very late stages of the war demonstrated the great powers' strong
commitment to their local clients, but also the dangers inherent in
such clashing commitments in the nuclear age. Such confrontations
had not been seen as imminent before the 1973 War, so that this was
a watershed in this sense as well. As far as Israel was concerned,
the lack of success in the war's initial stages, its generally difficult
course, and the high casualty rate – to say nothing of the high
economic and social cost – all combined to convince the leadership
that political settlements intended to avert future wars were now a
necessity rather than a luxury that one could choose to adopt or not
to adopt. Hence, the psychological climate of the war made ripe for
the first time a peace process.

Of course, one can argue that the real turning point was the 1967
War, in which the objective conditions for the peace process were
created in the first place. The resounding Israeli victory and the
resulting loss of Arab territory, which was impossible to accept
from the Arab point of view, were the main factors persuading

the Arabs that the status quo was unacceptable for practical as well as psychological reasons. But of course this did not mean it had to be changed via a peace process. That was not the case after the 1973 War, and this difference was of decisive importance.

Needless to say, historians (never mind the interested parties) will probably continue to argue about whether a genuine peace process would have occurred between 1967 and 1973 had the parties reacted differently. For example, much has been made of the Sadat initiative of February 1971, and much ink has been spilt about the relative doses of blame that the parties have to bear for its failure. The same can be said about the Jarring mission and various Rogers plans during the interwar period. But this begs the question. The fact that these initiatives did not succeed in itself indicates that the conditions, objective and/or subjective, did not exist as yet for initiating a massive peace process that would involve a genuine commitment on the part of the major protagonists. This kind of commitment came about only in the wake of the 1973 War, after which the difficulties in proceeding stemmed not so much from the lack of will to make progress as from the lack of knowledge of how to go about making progress under difficult and complicated circumstances.

Some of the difficulty was eventually alleviated by the set of steps and devices that we now refer to under the generic term "confidence-building measures." This term – born during the late stages of the Cold War in Europe and concomitant diplomatic processes in inter-bloc diplomacy – refers to the ability to avert a mutually unfavorable outcome in a relationship as a result of misunderstandings or poor communications. At most, it refers to a systematic effort at improving the political climate between strategic adversaries by pointing to a lack of hostile intentions and a general reassurance that the other side has no built-in animosity incompatible with your own interests, notwithstanding the basic relationship's competitive or conflictual nature.

Scholars point out that confidence-building measures are understood differently in various contexts. In some cases, the term refers merely to a process of verification or monitoring. This means that agreements can be concluded with a reasonable certainty that they will be adhered to because there are means of monitoring and verifying compliance. While this understanding of confidence-building sounds somewhat technical, it has in fact profound connotations in the political process since it facilitates agreements for regulating conflict and reduces armed confrontations arising from a conviction that there is no alternative.

A second meaning of confidence-building is less technical and more psychological. This refers to measures intended to reassure the adversary about the basically peaceful nature of our own intentions. We can make any number of gestures to open our society to the adversary and share various kinds of information so as to minimize the danger of misunderstanding and inadvertent breakdowns due to the lack of knowledge and the resulting uncertainty. At times this may take the form of trying to expose societies and not just governments to each other's scrutiny by exchanging diplomats, students, artists, scientists and tourists, by opening boundaries for trade, and the like. The idea is one of relatively free interaction and movement to stress the willingness to learn about the other side as well as allow the other side to learn about ourselves. In addition, gestures of a humanitarian nature and verbal behavior reflecting a sensitivity to the other side's concerns are also made in order to show sufficient concern with issues dear to the adversary's heart, showing determination to put these issues higher on the agenda. This may be a relatively inexpensive way of handling conflict and transforming it into a less vehement type of competition.

A third meaning of confidence-building usually refers to a gradual strategy of progress in negotiations, to make all the gestures and moves necessary to reassure the adversary that the previous stage in the negotiations has been fairly implemented, and that by observing it scrupulously it is now possible and desirable to proceed to the next stage, where greater risks have to be taken, justified in light of the parties' record and the general good will.

This approach facilitates the complex, lengthy process of conflict regulation when a single agreement will not resolve the range of difficult issues.

A fourth type of confidence-building has to do with mediation, but in the broad sense of the term. It may merely be that a reliance on a mutually acceptable, trustworthy mediator is all that is needed, but at other times we refer to mediating concepts (such as national sovereignty) or structures (such as membership in the United Nations) or even cultures (such as being part of a world-wide elite educated in a major English-speaking university, reading the *New York Times* and watching CNN or Sky cable television).

Of course a strong commitment to a set of values, concepts, and ideological slogans may be seen as contributing to fanaticism rather than to conflict resolution, but when the norms of the commitment are shared, at least there is some common language which allows a dialogue with some meaning. These types of confidence-building reflect the different approaches that stem from different definitions of the concept according to quite different levels of expectations. Yet there is a fundamental difficulty that must be addressed by all those who use the term confidence-building, namely the argument that confidence-building is not very useful, because it refers only to matters of process rather than substance. Proponents of this argument mean by this to say that the best way to build confidence is to make progress on the substantive issues of a given conflict and that once such progress is made it is easy to see that success in one stage of negotiations inevitably breeds confidence, toward the following stages.

Obviously, progress on substantive issues is the best way to proceed, and such progress is indeed a superb confidence-building measure. But there are many conflict situations in which such progress is simply not possible, and the question arises as to how to bring about a breakthrough or at least keep the negotiating process alive when the resolution of basic issues is not yet in sight. Confidence-building measures may help bring about the kind of progress that will then generate a momentum of its own. This can be seen in many other kinds of conflicts, such as industrial disputes, in which confidence-building techniques have proven very useful.

In many ways, process is substance. This is not always true and sometimes the greatest confidence cannot help when the basic divisions are too deep and irritating. As Dante put it, the road to hell is paved with good intentions. Still, good intentions may just prevent the need to go to hell. We know now that conflicts feed on themselves and breed more conflict, by definition forcing adversaries to distrust each other and to assume the worst about each other. In fact, lack of trust and worst-case assumptions about the adversary in and of themselves are central ingredients of a conflict situation, so that lack of confidence is as important as anything more "real" in the empirical sense of the term.

Conflict breeds lack of confidence and lack of confidence breeds conflict. So confidence-building measures can help break this escalatory, self-perpetuating cycle and initially, without touching on the basic issues too much, at a time when dealing with these issues is very difficult precisely because of the harsh psychological conditions surrounding the parties and their grievances. Also, the difficult psychological conditions make it impossible to seize the opportunities to make progress on substance because such progress invariably requires important psychological conditions, such as the willingness to take risks. In order to make these risks more manageable, a measure of trust in the adversary's intentions must be created as well as ability to make sure that whatever has been agreed will be implemented.

Of course, this does not mean that automatically, in *every* situation, we can hope for the enemy to wish for peace if we wish for peace ourselves. To the contrary, as is well known, in cases of appeasement the wishes of one party to make peace have been taken advantage of by the other belligerent. Still, what was so special about the Yom Kippur War, making the parties wish for peace more than they had before the war?

First, there was the devastation of the war. The scale of the destruction, unprecedented in the Middle East, made the leaders think twice about the next war, if there was to be a next war.

Second, there were the special circumstances of the outbreak of the war, such that it could be regarded as a defeat for everyone. Israel considered itself to be on top of the world after the 1967 War, when its enemies were in humiliating disarray. Yet the lines were breached, and the casualties so heavy that Israel could not bear them, and all this even without looking at the economic costs of the war.

On the Arab side, after the initial joy of "winning," a second, more sober thought led to similarly sober conclusions. The Arabs started the war under optimal conditions, in a situation of total surprise, reinforced by a devastatingly effective oil embargo which caught everyone unprepared. All in all, the kind of situation that can be expected to occur perhaps once in a lifetime, but should not be expected to reoccur with any kind of regularity. Yet even these optimal conditions did not lead to Arab victory. In fact, when the war ended, in 18 short days, Israel had managed to recapture everything lost in the north, taking an extra salient that put Damascus within its artillery range. In the south, Egypt managed to hang onto considerable territory on the Suez Canal's east bank, but at what a price! Half of its fighting force, the Third Army, was surrounded by Israeli forces. Across the Canal, a large Israeli force gained a huge foothold, putting them only 60 miles from Cairo.

Third, there was the question of dependence on outside powers. This is not only a matter of psychology, although it is that, too.

There is more to it; there is the problem that the dependence factor takes away whatever fruits you may have gained in victory, and it subjects you to the kind of political constraint that you were fighting to avoid in the first place. Moreover, while local problems, no matter how serious, may be temporary, subjection to the whims of foreign powers is much more difficult to reverse or overcome.

All small powers, as a rule, like to play games involving greater powers, and many of them get away with these games for a long time. When there is a confrontation between outside powers, this certainly presents a great opportunity to exploit the differences between them and thereby enhance the opportunity to add to the national resources in times of conflict with local powers. In the case of the Middle East, the Egyptians, to take just the most conspicuous example, had been very adroit at this game indeed. But all good things come to an end, and this did too.

The ability to maneuver among the great powers is little consolation when in either case – meaning in case of "alliance" with either of the two – the situation is that of extreme dependence, which makes the concept of alliance a mockery to begin with. The cost of pursuing a local conflict is so high that whatever benefits one may gain from it are cancelled out by the gigantic consequences of the dependent relationship with the external patron. In addition, there is the fear of the next war. Even if this war is somehow pursued to the very end, after all, in the realities of the Middle East, this war will not be the last one. There will always be another one after that. And the outside powers themselves may not wish to be involved in that one, because the costs for them are becoming so prohibitive that supporting their clients, any clients, may not be worthwhile any more.

One never knows, of course. But the uncertainty makes the local powers think twice about continuing a conflict in which it may no longer be possible to acquire outside support, and in which there is no chance of winning without such support, because of the developments in technology. No amount of national pride and willingness to make sacrifices can make up for the inability to produce or even maintain the advanced weapons systems in the electronic age.

Fourth, there was the fear of the nuclear factor. This is one of the great enigmas of Middle East politics. But the assumption has long existed that the Israelis have the nuclear capacity to inflict huge damage on their enemies in the case of a conventional defeat. When such conventional defeat started to loom large, in early October 1973, there were rumours (which have not ever been substantiated) that Israel was getting ready to arm some of its missiles with nuclear warheads in order to deter the Arabs from penetrating deeply into Israel proper. In the final stages of the war, there was the mysterious matter of the Soviet "nuclear ship" appearing in the waters off Egypt, and finally there was the American alert, bringing the superpowers to the brink of a possible nuclear confrontation. At the time, this appeared rather frightening, perhaps more so to the superpowers themselves than to the local ones, but it started people in the Middle East thinking seriously about the nuclear dangers inherent in the explosive situation.

Whereas in the 1967 War there was no nuclear question whatsoever, in any manner, shape or form, in the 1973 War the nuclear question came up and came up big. From the Israeli point of view, the very possibility of needing to use the nuclear option was very frightening, and of course the fact that the superpowers reached the brink of a nuclear confrontation led the Israeli leaders to think somberly about the future of American commitments to Israel. All this, of course, merely added to the hesitations of the U.S. administration in resupplying Israel at a time when the Soviets were already doing wonders for their Arab clients.

From the Arab point of view, things did not look good either. True, in this war, unlike in the previous one, the Soviets finally delivered – at least as far as technology and doctrine were concerned. But the brink of the nuclear confrontation made the Soviets so obviously unhappy that one could have very real doubts as to what they would do next time around. In this war victory in the end eluded the Arabs, notwithstanding their huge early momentum, so there was no need for Israel to use the nuclear option. But to many thinking Arabs it was obvious that the near disaster of the war's opening stage would push the Israelis to accelerate their nuclear program. Every day brought Israel closer to a nuclear capability that would make it much more intransigent and reluctant to agree to changes in the territorial status quo. This fear appeared in many of Sadat's interviews, in which he argued that the Arabs had to make a settlement with Israel before the situation would freeze for an indefinite period due to progress in the Israeli nuclear capability.

It is tempting to argue from analysis of the case of the Yom Kippur War that it is always sensible to assume better things about the enemy, but it would not be always true. Yet there are ways to test the intentions of the enemy without taking unacceptable risks: by engineering interim agreements, involving security arrangements and the like. So to some extent the lesson does stand.

A second general lesson is a more pessimistic one. While one may argue that a more creative statesmanship might have prevented the war and would have established an earlier peace process, this is not necessarily true. Let us keep in mind the Kissingerian argument that the time must be ripe for a political move, and that at times there is no choice but to let the parties fight another round or two in order to create the necessary will for a political settlement.

The fighting itself may not prove anything that dispassionate analysis cannot prove at a much lower cost from every point of view. Yet nations at times feel that they must fight and are reluctant to make peace without having had this dubious "benefit." Much has already been made of the Arab insistence on restoring the "honor" lost in the 1967 War. This insistence had a clear psychological component. Even the most generous Israeli offer for the restoration of the territories (and this admittedly was not forthcoming) would not have made the impression that a round of fighting did. A peace treaty based on the results of the 1967 War, no matter how sensible, would have somehow perpetuated the results of that war, whereas another war created a different starting point which made a huge difference. This makes one think somberly about the limitations of diplomatic creativity in the face of the primeval urges that nations have.

A third general conclusion is that the 1967 War, after all, became the basis for all later political activity in the Middle East, notwithstanding the psychological point just made (there is no contradiction, for the two elements coexisted side by side). Until the 1967 War the conflict was difficult to grasp, because it involved heavily ideological themes taken from the lore of radical nationalism, involving, of course, the right of Israel to exist. In any case, the conflict changed drastically in 1967 and from then on involved concrete territories in terms that nation-states traditionally understand and are well-equipped to deal with. Even so, in the period between 1967 and 1973 the concrete territorial issues were hopelessly tangled and confused with lingering ideological themes. This is one of the reasons for the difficulties in peace-making in the interwar period, although, as we have already seen, there were others as well.

The 1973 War, however, was one in which the immediate interests of the territorial nation-state were dominant, and moreover, they were the only real issue at stake. The war could not be understood in terms other than *raison d'état* of the two Arab states concerned, who started the war when and because it suited their own interests. Moreover, the Egyptians also stopped the war when this suited their interests, as the Syrians then bitterly remarked. So all in all, this was a war of normalization in the inter-Arab system, which in turn increasingly allowed a protracted peace process which could not have been successful in a more ideological age. Kissinger is reported to have complained to Muhammad Hassanein Haikal that he could only negotiate with states, and not with states of mind. The more the countries in the region behaved and thought like states and less as states of mind, the better the chances of the peace process. And never had the countries in the region acted more as states than in the 1973 War.

This was more true, it seems, with Egypt than with Syria, but the Syrians still behaved in a surprisingly state-like fashion, concluding an agreement with Israel under very tough bargaining conditions and then meticulously sticking to their word. In Lebanon, they were part of a complex set of unwritten understandings that allowed these two countries to stay out of all-out war when the dangers of conflagration were immense. The rhetoric continued to be much more ideological than in Egypt, but the practical conduct of business was very state-like indeed. One might say that the voice continued to be that of the revolutionary *Bath* party, but the actual business to be that of the increasingly pragmatic Syrian state.

Then there is the question of the oil boycott. This was, in many ways, the unexpected high point of Arab solidarity, precisely at a time when the high expectations of unity, merger, or solidarity were already a thing of the past. This was the Sadat-like concept of the unity of action in practice. But there were many different issues involved. First of all, there was a huge economic factor which in fact later dominated the considerations of OPEC members, eventually glutting the market and bringing the once mighty cartel to the brink of collapse. Then there were huge differences between large and small countries, which made the long-term restriction of production virtually impossible. And there was the cooperation of large oil companies from the West, which had their own domestic and economic agendas. In light of all this, it would not be correct to consider the oil boycott as a purely ideological act in the old sense of the term. Although it did have ideological elements, it was a move of greater complexity, combining elements of protest against the dominance of the Western industrialized countries with diverse economic interests. The Arab component of the oil boycott does seem to signify the end of an era, just as the military cooperation in the war signified the end of the same era on the strategic level.

What has transpired since seems to reiterate these changes. Since then, in the early 1980s we witnessed the Israeli invasion of Lebanon, which sorely tested the Egyptian adherence to the peace treaty, but no Arab country came to the rescue, and the Syrians managed the confrontation with Israel with great caution and prudence, averting an open overall war. Even more conspicuous is the outstanding event of the early 1990s: the Gulf War and the Iraqi action that preceded it. The old politics of unification by changing boundaries and sovereignties was completely discredited, and the Arabs who felt threatened resorted to military action dominated by an outside superpower. The mainstream of the Arab world cooperated willingly enough, but even Syria played a role in the coalition and then was well paid for it, a sure sign of the new, pragmatic conception emanating out of Damascus.

While few Arab leaders would admit this publicly, the fear of the Iraqi nuclear shadow became much more frightening than that of the Israeli nuclear option, and the interests that Israel, Syria and Saudi Arabia had in common in opposing this danger are very strong and obvious, whether or not publicly articulated and acted upon. It would have been too much to expect that the Arabs would simply abandon the old agenda, and simply articulate the explicit expression of the new perception, according to which Iraq threatens Saudi Arabia far more than does Israel, notwithstanding the ideological mumbo-jumbo that had dominated for so long in the region. Eventually, though, the new realities began to sink in. The region is increasingly a region of states. None of these states is likely to disappear, and the territorial status quo is not likely to be changed by force.

The realities created by the Yom Kippur War led to an almost classic demonstration of a confidence-building process. The objective conditions surrounding the war's end left a residue of uncertainty and high risk which simply had to be reduced. And the deployment of the forces and their proximity made it imperative to undertake some confidence-building that would then allow the parties to withdraw and disengage, thereby reducing the risk of outbreaks of war undesirable for all concerned. To do that requires

trusting the adversary to have the same interest in averting mutually destructive outcomes, which is the very basis of the original
minimalist approach to confidence-building. Then there is the recognition that the resemblance between oneself and the adversary
is much more striking than previously assumed, brought home in
practical negotiations about the implementing of arrangements for
mutual benefit.

Immediately after the Yom Kippur War, and even before it came
to a complete halt, the need for such measures began to sink in. The
Egyptian attack, so successful in the beginning owing to the element
of surprise, gave the Egyptians not only confidence that they were
able to stand up to Israel as equals, but also some understanding
of Israel's fears and traumas about being surprised in the future.
One can argue that it is easier to understand the fears of the enemy
when one does not lose the war, and this may well be true.
A successful campaign is also an important confidence-building
measure for oneself, and only a confident self is able to understand
the traumas of the other. In any case, once this gap was overcome
and some insight into Israel's problems could be seen in Egypt, a
much higher level of understanding in communications could be –
and was – accomplished.

The travails of a war intended to liberate territory lost to the
enemy in a recent war, decisively contributed to the reemergence
of the concept of the sovereign state among Egypt's political and
intellectual leadership. The 1973 War had very little to do with the
country's inter-Arab involvement, and everything to do with its
self-interest in regaining land and reestablishing the prestige of the
national leadership. Hence the war's favorable results enhanced the
self-image of the Egyptians as living in a state with a distinct existence and a sharply differentiated identity of its own, an image more
and more dominant ever since. Enhancing one's sense of stateness,
by definition, leads to a perception of the stateness of others. In
other words, a country caught in a nationalist fervor regards others
more or less in the lens of how they affect the fortunes of one's
own nation, and hence tends to divide the world into friends and
foes. But a country looking upon itself as a state, with boundaries,
sovereignty and security concerns, is likely to regard other political
entities as having very much the same kinds of characteristics.

The very concept of the sovereign state as a major organizational
category in the focus of international realities is a most important
self-confidence-building measure which allows a state to relate to

others in much the same way as to the self, hence creating some common values and standards. Once Egypt started cultivating its state identity more strongly, it quickly discovered how greatly this helped in understanding the anxieties of Israel also stemming from legitimate concerns that all states have in common. This is not to deny the many unique characteristics of Israeli security concerns, but they also have many general ingredients which are universally comprehensible. It was through this universal mediating concept of the sovereign state that Egypt and Israel managed to establish a businesslike relationship. This is a complex and gradual mental and cultural process, but it seems that the biggest push and greatest momentum it gained had to do with the 1973 War more than with any other event in the history of the Arab-Israeli conflict.

On the other fronts, even in retrospect, things do not appear quite so clear. As far as Syria was concerned, the war ended dismally from the inter-Arab point of view. Syria felt betrayed by Egyptian willingness to terminate the war when it suited Egyptian rather than all-Arab interests. But this could hardly have been a surprise since it was well understood that all the rhetoric in the world will not override the considerations of a state pursuing its own interests and security.

Hence, the Syrian regime started doing the same in its version. The best example of this policy is the disengagement agreement of 1974, which stands as an outstanding example of the Syrian strategy in this respect: a difficult, almost obnoxious, conduct of negotiations; driving a hard bargain; sticking to every single point on style as well as substance to make the regime look good to its own people as well as to a possible Arab constituency across the border; and a scrupulous sticking to the letter of the agreement, with very few exceptions. Of course, this had very little to do with the general Syrian position on the Israeli question, because the general hostility continued, and the Syrians still confronted Israel in Lebanon, built up their forces beyond the Golan Heights, and aided various acts of terrorism.

The main point, however, is that precisely in the midst of this hostility the Syrians continued to adhere to the disengagement agreement conscientiously, even though in the beginning they used to inject a measure of uncertainty about the semi-annual renewal of the United Nations Disengagement Observers Force in the Security Council, utilizing each occasion for public relations and diplomatic purposes, often in a form approximating blackmail. Yet the agreement survived and continued to be observed under harsh circumstances. Obviously, the Syrians felt that it was in their interest to observe it, while confronting Israel elsewhere.

In any case, the agreement's very survival and the consistent Syrian compliance served as important confidence-building measures. It became obvious to Israel that it was indeed possible to do serious business with Syria and that the word of Syria was meaningful and credible. All the while, the Syrians could continue to argue that adhering to inter-state agreements was good form, which, however, did nothing to undermine their willingness and ability to continue pursuing the national interest as defined by them in ways other than breaking their word.

Jordan participated in the war on a very limited basis. It sent an expeditionary force to Syria in order to demonstrate its adherence to the common Arab war effort, but scrupulously refrained from confronting Israel head on. In fact what Jordan did could be regarded as absolutely compatible with the long series of understandings with Israel, including secret meetings with Israel on the highest level. There have been reports that Jordan explicitly warned Israel against the surprise attack in September 1973, a warning which was not heeded. In any case, the Jordanian-Israeli relationship was reasonably well institutionalized by October 1973 and the way that the parties conducted themselves in the war was clearly compatible with their history and helped continue building a relationship of confidence and partial cooperation.

On the other hand, the Palestinians were almost marginalized in the period of the war and its immediate aftermath. The war was one between states, by and large pursuing their well-defined state interests, and using large-scale military forces. This strategic configuration made the Palestinians unimportant and unnecessary for the Arab cause at that particular moment. It appeared that the Palestinians were useful for keeping the Arab struggle alive between wars, and their forces used in irregular formations could inflict damage and show that the fight continued even in the midst of cease-fires among the institutionalized states. But once the guns started firing, none of these considerations seemed to apply: the usefulness of the Palestinians seemed to come to an end.

Moreover, the political process in the war's immediate aftermath also concerned itself with the results and the need to prevent future wars along the same lines. In this respect, too, the Palestinians were unable to carve out a useful role for themselves. It was only when the interim agreements between Israel, Egypt and Syria were fashioned that the Palestinian issue became more salient again. The ultimate result of the processes launched by the war was the Sadat initiative, considered by the Palestinians the classic act of betrayal. They had to consider the Yom Kippur War not as a great victory for the cause, but as a reminder that the lack of a Palestinian state made the Palestinians unimportant in the games which states play. The result was a lack of confidence in the normal processes of regional politics which froze the Palestinians out, and an energetic attempt to liberate the Palestinian cause from the shackles of inter-Arab politics. For a long time many Israelis failed to understand that slogans such as the PLO being the sole legitimate representative of the Palestinian people were directed against the leading Arab states as much as they were directed against Israel.

The war ultimately gave way to a political process which built simultaneously on the territorial and strategic realities created in 1967 as well as on the political and psychological ingredients of the regional game of nations as forged in the crucible of the 1973 War. Interestingly enough, while the Six Day War yielded much talk about winning the next war, the Yom Kippur War brought a lot of talk about the forthcoming peace settlements. It was no longer assumed that this war was something that could be rectified in the next one. The devastation and the difficulties made everyone understand that there would not be many more like this, so that one had to build on the results of this one and make the best of it. Of course, not everyone understood this right away, but in retrospect it appears remarkable that the talk about peace and politics started as early as it did, in the midst of such a large-scale destructive war.

One may argue that all this is easy to see in retrospect, but that at the time things looked very different. That is certainly true, and there is absolutely no assurance that positive opportunities inherent in a strategic situation would not be missed through the perceptions of the leadership. After all, the peace process that started was not inevitable and it would have been quite possible to adopt a *revanchist* attitude, throwing the Middle East yet again into a cycle of violence; and there certainly were enough people in the region who would have done just that had they been given the opportunity. But there was also a leadership in Israel, Jordan and Egypt which understood correctly that the hour was opportune for statesmanship, and this statesmanship did in fact materialize. It first institutionalized the cease-fire between Israel and Egypt, then expanded it into a series of political agreements until peace was also attained. Confidence-building measures made a decisive contribution to the process, all the while cultivating the existing de facto peace between Israel and Jordan and the success of the Syria-Israel disengagement agreement, which allowed these two countries to regulate their relationship with the minimum danger of a violent outbreak, even in the midst of a heated strategic race between them. Only the Palestinian issue gained no confidence-building from the 1973 War.

It is noteworthy that the great achievement of peace between Israel and Egypt was accomplished while the Soviet-American rivalry in the Middle East was still very vehement. There was no Soviet contribution to that part of the peace process, and many have argued that it was the strong support of the Soviets to the cause of Syria that kept the Syrians out of the process at the time. But the Soviet Union's collapse in the beginning of the 1990s completely changed the balance of power, and coupled with this has been the drastic decline in the potential and actual importance of the Arab oil weapon. These two factors account for a completely different political map of the Middle East twenty years after the Yom Kippur War. Yet real progress in the peace process has been accomplished mainly through indigenous regional developments and, among these, the relative success of confidence-building measures among some of the major protagonists.

The Yom Kippur War was the logical outcome of the neither-peace-nor-war situation prevailing after the Six Day War. This abnormal, unstable situation could have been changed by war or peace, and peace apparently was premature as an option, because war looked an attractive way to change the status quo and its intolerably high cost was not yet witnessed or foreseen.

It was only the Yom Kippur War that started to close the historical cycle created by the Six Day War. The latter changed the equation dramatically by generating the question of Arab territories in Israeli possession, which transformed the ideological question of Israel's destruction into a pragmatic question of liberating territories, obviously at a cost that was seen initially as military but later increasingly as political. But it was only the 1973 War which made it inescapably clear that the military option was much too costly for the regional as well as the outside powers, and hence that the political option had to be pursued with great vigor and a sincerity not witnessed before. Since then, the political momentum has had its ups and downs, according to the concrete historical circumstances in the various countries and regional as well as global constellations. It was in 1973, however, that the agenda changed drastically.

References

On the relationship between state, peace and war in the region see Gabriel Ben-Dor, *State and Conflict in the Middle East* (New York: Praeger, 1983) and Gabriel Ben-Dor and David B. Dewitt (eds), *Confidence Building in the Middle East* (Westport, Conn.: Greenwood Press, 1993) and *Conflict Management in the Middle East* (Lexington: Heath, 1987).

10

The PLO: From Armed Struggle to Political Solution

Moshe Shemesh

All the wars waged between Israel and the Arabs, including the Lebanon war and the *intifada*, brought about the exacerbation of the Palestinian problem, an increased Arab awareness of the Palestinian issue, and the crystallizing and strengthening of the Palestinian national movement and national identity. The Arab-Israeli conflict became the sole focus of Arab nationalism and the Palestinian issue became the focal point of the Arab-Israeli conflict.

For the Palestinian national movement, 1974 was a significant year in terms of political achievements. These achievements began with the resolutions of the November 1973 Algiers Arab summit, continued with the decisions of the 12th session of the Palestinian National Congress (PNC) convened in June 1974, and ended with the resolutions of the Rabat summit in October 1974. One cannot conceive of all these achievements without the relentless efforts of Egypt and above all those of Sadat himself.[1]

The aim of this chapter is to outline the Arab background to the 12th PNC resolutions, Sadat's efforts to bring about a change in Fatah-PLO strategy, and finally the components of the turn in Fatah-PLO strategy embodying the decisions of the 12th PNC, and its repercussions. In other words, it traces the origins of that change of strategy.

Sadat, as "the hero of the crossing" of the Suez canal, dictated to the Algiers summit his strategic concept of a solution to the conflict and to the Palestinian problem. Already, in a speech of 16 October 1973, he had defined the principles of his "peace plan." Central to it was "an international peace conference" which would include the

Arab confrontation states and the PLO. The "top secret" resolutions of the Algiers summit marked a change in the Arab strategy toward the conflict. The summit defined for the first time an "interim aim" (*hadaf marhabi*) and gave the go-ahead to negotiations with Israel for a permanent peace in the region. The summit decided on a number of "present aims of the Arab new strategy":

First: In the territorial sphere: "Full liberation of all the Arab territories which were occupied in the aggression of 1967, (and) the liberation of Arab Jerusalem." The summit called for "the restoration . . . of the inalienable national rights of the Palestinian people."

Second: In the Palestinian sphere: "Adherence to restoring the national rights of the Palestinian people in accordance with resolutions of the PLO, the *sole* representative of the Palestinian people." Jordan had objected to this article.[2]

During 1974, Sadat tried persistently to convene the Geneva conference to discuss the final solution and lasting peace. The components of such peace as he envisaged were the return to 1967 borders and the establishment of a Palestinian state. In order to secure a successful outcome to the conference Sadat stipulated that Egypt, Syria, Jordan and the PLO should go to Geneva united as "one bloc."

To achieve such solidarity, Sadat saw the need to overcome the opposing positions of Jordan and the PLO regarding the Palestinian representation at Geneva. This he did in two stages. The first stage lasted from October 1973 until June 1974. During this period Sadat urged Fatah to adopt an interim aim which would correspond with the interim aim of the Algiers summit; in the second stage, which lasted from July 1974 until September 1974, he needed to find a formula acceptable to both Jordan and the PLO for representation of the Palestinians, or their case, at Geneva.

Sadat defined the interim goal to which the Palestinians should aspire:

First: "The establishment of a Palestinian homeland is inevitable."

Second: "Palestinian national rule must be established on every centimeter of the liberated land of Filastin."

Third: "The goal is, the establishment of a Palestinian state on the West Bank and the Gaza Strip with a linking corridor." This state should decide on the nature of its relationship with Jordan, on the assumption that there must be some kind of link between the two states.[3]

Sadat believed that "there is no escape from Palestinian representation at Geneva." He therefore strove for a definition of a Palestinian interim aim by the PLO that would enable it to participate in the peace talks. To attain this goal, Sadat used all his weight and prestige in pressuring the Fatah leadership, rightly believing that the Fatah position was synonymous with that of the PLO. Indeed, Sadat's efforts were a decisive factor in convincing the Fatah leaders to change their policy and in persuading the rank and file of the organization and most of the Palestinians to accept this change.

What were Sadat's tactics?

First: With astute understanding of the character of the Fatah leaders, Sadat did not attempt to impose his policy on them. He did his best to persuade them. Sadat was supported by the Egyptian media and the Arab leaders, who encouraged Fatah to accept an interim aim. Already on 26 October 1973, Sadat summoned a number of Fatah leaders, and suggested that they participate in a peace conference. On 12 November 1973, Arafat informed Sadat of their resolution: "Not to decide either positively or negatively before receiving an official invitation to the Geneva conference."[4]

Second: Sadat argued that participation in a peace conference was unlikely as long as the PLO's strategic aim was "the set up of a democratic state in the entire land of Filastin," which meant the liquidation of Israel. He reiterated that the Palestinians have the right to reject UN resolutions 242 and 338. Egypt opposed any change in resolution 242, as the PLO had demanded. In his talk with Fatah leaders, Sadat claimed that the mere invitation of the PLO to Geneva, and its participation there, would automatically mean a change in 242 and recognition of the PLO.

Third: Sadat stressed that "a Palestinian entity should be established even on a single square centimeter of the liberated Arab land."

Fourth: As the 12th PNC approached, Egypt stepped up efforts to help Fatah leaders in persuading the PNC members to adopt the turn in Fatah's strategy. Egypt's commitment to the PLO and the Palestinian cause was conveyed extensively through the Egyptian media. Sadat's letter to the PNC (1 June 1974) was a final attempt in the Egyptian marathon. Sadat did not deliver a speech at the opening session of the PNC, so as not to be seen to apply pressure. His letter stated, among other things: "A historic responsibility is placed on you"; "The decision should be purely Palestinian"; "We have committed ourselves, together with our Arab brethren in the Algiers Summit, to recognize the PLO as the sole legitimate representative of the Palestinian people." Moreover, the Egyptian media called on the PNC "to reach a brave and wise decision which would take into account realities, such as the three million Jews who live on the land of Filastin, and the existence of the State of Israel, which is recognized by almost the entire world."[5]

Against this background of Egyptian and Arab political campaign, and as a result of their assessment of the situation, the Fatah leaders came to the conclusion that they had reached a stage which required a radical change and reappraisal of previous aims. The Palestinian National Covenant set out only one strategic aim, "The liberation of all Filastin and the liquidation of the Zionist imperialist presence." It further declared that "the armed struggle is the only way to liberate Filastin, and is therefore a strategy and not a tactic."[6] Abu Iyyad even admitted that the situation was one of "to be or not to be," adding that "we face a new reality which requires realistic solutions. We should know our precise size and the extent of our influence over events, without exaggerating, which misleads both us and the masses." Furthermore, not joining the Arab "phased concept" would mean, according to him, "a confrontation with the two Arab central states [which] conducted the October War and with the U.S.S.R."[7]

The change in the Fatah position occured in December 1973 when the organization's leadership made a decision in principal to adopt a "phased concept." The interim aim was defined as "the establishment of a national rule over the Palestinian territories from which Israel would withdraw."

Fatah embarked upon a campaign to promote the "phased concept" among the Palestinians, presumably to prepare the ground for the debate in the PNC, which would have to endorse this concept. The campaign was led by Abu Iyyad, who contributed much to the approval of the new strategy by Fatah leadership and later by the PLO institutions.

But, whereas the Popular Democratic Front for the Liberation of Palestine (PDFLP) and Sa'iqa, sponsored by Syria, supported Fatah, the Popular Front for the Liberation of Palestine (PFLP), headed by Habash, was bitterly opposed, insisting that "national rule" should only be achieved by "armed struggle." Fatah ultimately prevailed, but not without considerable difficulties, including opposition from the grass roots and from its leadership.

What were the arguments and considerations which Fatah leaders raised in support of the phased strategy?

1.   *The failure of the armed struggle to achieve its goals*: "The Palestinian resistance reached in early seventies its maximum ability to wage its armed struggle and to achieve tangible accomplishments. The events in Jordan in 1970–71 proved this conclusion," wrote Dr. Yazid Sayigh, a Palestinian scholar from Oxford.[8]

The Palestinian leadership had begun to realize this truth and to absorb its meanings and consequences. They concluded that the armed struggle would lead to the implementation of far less than their slogans and their long-range goal. The Yom Kippur War and its repercussions vindicated their assessment. The phased programme was the lesson.

2.   *The need for Palestinian land*: Following the liquidation of their bases in Jordan in 1971, the organization suffered a deep crisis.[9] The organization's leaders became more aware that the Palestinian resistance could not exist without a Palestinian land under its control; a land which might serve as a substitute for Jordan as a "safe base." Abu Iyyad claimed that "until we achieve the strategic aim we need a safe base, whose fate should not be similar to that of Jordan." In his view, "Gaining a small part which constitutes 23 percent of Filastin is an interim achievement."[10] Thus, in early 1972, the organizations asked themselves: "Whither the Palestinian resistance?"

The year 1972 was characterized by what Fatah leaders called "lack of action." The organizations continued to be more an Arab problem than an Israeli problem. Abu Mazin, a Fatah leader, admitted in August 1972 in a closed Fatah forum that "the Palestinian revolution is in a state of fundamental contradiction to the Arab regimes. We cannot declare that . . . all the Arab states are strategically against the revolution."[11]

Indeed, the search for "Palestinian land" led the organization, at the same time, to change its concept of how to realize the strategic goal. The PDFLP was the pioneer in this direction. The fourth PDFLP central committee endorsed, in August 1973, the "interim plan" calling for "the struggle to liberate the Palestinian area occupied in 1967, the West Bank and the Gaza Strip, and guaranteeing freedom of self-determination of the Palestinian people in these areas."[12]

3.   *The historical lesson*: The Fatah leadership was imbued with the reflex of rejecting any suggestion "which characterized the

Palestinian traditional leadership for fifty years." "They said 'no' without proposing an alternative for the continuation of the struggle in different ways." Fatah attacked what it called "negative rejection" by the PFLP. Abu Iyyad argued that "the rejection path would lead the revolution to a dead end."[13]

4. *The struggle with King Hussein*: Fatah claimed that to argue against the return of the West Bank to Palestinian rule would appear to mean its return to Jordanian rule. This was a strong and persuasive argument. Abu Iyyad stressed that: "leaving the future of the West Bank to a settlement between Jordan and Israel would mean an admission of PLO denial of responsibility for the West Bank and for its representation of the Palestinian people." Hence "absence from the discussion would mean leaving the political arena to Hussein."[14]

5. *The U.S.S.R.'s position*: Fatah attached great importance to the Soviets' attitude. On its visit to the U.S.S.R. in November 1973 a PLO delegation found that the Soviets encouraged Palestinian representation at Geneva and rapid PLO integration in the political process. They also encouraged the PLO to adopt an "interim aim." As a possible solution to the problem of Palestinian representation in Geneva, the Soviets proposed that a delegation from the West Bank and Gaza participate on behalf of the PLO.

And finally *the Israeli factor*: Fatah presented the establishment of a "Palestinian national rule" as an answer to Golda Meir's and Rabin's declaration which "rules out the establishment of an additional Arab state between Israel and Jordan, and seeing the Jordanian state as the expression of the political identity of the Palestinians and Jordanians."

So, the debate in the 12th session of the PNC (1–8 June 1974) revolved around two major topics: The Geneva conference and resolution 242; between "absolute refusal," and "positive refusal"; between a clear position on the Geneva conference and a vague one which would leave the PLO leadership considerable freedom of political and diplomatic maneuvering.

"The phased political programme"[15] (*al-Barnamij al-Siyasi al-Marhali*), or the "ten points," was endorsed by a large majority of the PNC, as suggested by the PLO Executive Committee. Only four delegates voted against. That was indeed a victory for the Fatah leaders.

The political programme was a strategic breakthrough in three major areas:

1.   It was a conceptual turn. The strategy of stages was substituted for an "all or nothing" strategy. The interim aim was defined by the PNC as: "The establishment of the people's independent fighting national authority over any part of the Palestinian territory which would be liberated." The notion of "national authority" was later replaced by that of "a Palestinian state." By this strategy the PLO brought itself into line with the Arab interim aim.

2.   The readiness of the PLO to integrate into the political process to resolve the conflict or the Palestinian problem without conceding the armed struggle. The second point of the interim plan stressed that: "The PLO would struggle with all possible means at its disposal, the foremost of which is armed struggle, to liberate Palestinian territory . . . and establish the national authority." Thus the PLO did not rule out political negotiation.

3.   Accordingly, the PNC decided on a qualified negation of the "242" resolution. The PNC objected to the resolution on the ground that "it obliterated the national (*watani*) and pan-Arab rights (*qawmi*) of our people, and regards our people's cause as a refugee problem; therefore the PNC rejects cooperation with this resolution on this basis, at any Arab or international forum, including the Geneva conference." The impression is that Fatah was willing to accept "242" on the basis of recognition of the "legitimate rights of the Palestinian people" and to participate in the Geneva conference provided that the invitation recognize the right of self-determination of the Palestinians, and the PLO as the sole legitimate representative of the Palestinian people.

The Rabat Arab summit (October 1974) adopted the PNC resolutions. It reaffirmed "the right of the Palestinian people to set up an independent national rule led by the PLO, the sole legitimate representative of the Palestinian people."[16] King Hussein reluctantly joined the Arab consensus, thus giving the resolutions a historic dimension.

As regards the leadership of Fatah / PLO, it is pertinent to compare the composition of the leadership of Fatah / PLO today with that of 1974. The picture today seems less promising for Arafat. Today Arafat is mostly surrounded by so-called leaders who emerged from the second echelon of Fatah leadership, except for Abu Mazin and Farouq Qaddumi, who are both grey figures.

In 1974 the Fatah / PLO leadership comprised, besides Arafat, two charismatic leaders, namely Abu Iyyad (Salah Khalaf) and Abu Jihad (Khalil al-Wazir). Indeed, Abu Iyyad successfully led the campaign to convince the Palestinians of the need to change the PLO strategy. The lack of strong and charismatic Fatah leadership might explain the difficulties confronting Arafat in trying to achieve endorsement of the accord with Israel by the PLO's institutions, and gain acceptance from Palestinian public opinion. Yet, though it would be no understatement to describe the status of the Fatah leadership as weaker today than in 1974, Arafat still has power and authority as the veteran leader of Fatah / PLO.

The endorsement of the phased strategy by the PNC exemplified the dominant status which Fatah had been enjoying within the PLO's institutions since 1969 when the *fidai* organization took over the PLO establishment. This dominance had been proved again in the 17th PNC, held in 1983, when the radical organizations boycotted the congress; and in the 19th PNC, convened in 1988, when the PNC approved the "two states concept" and accepted the "242" resolution; and again when the PLO central committee endorsed the agreement of principles with Israel. In March 1975 Abu Iyyad astutely described the status of Fatah: "The decision of Fatah is the Palestinian decision. Any decision unacceptable to Fatah will not see the light."[17] As a result the Fatah leaders vaunted themselves as leaders of the PLO in both theory and practice.

The decisions at both the 12th PNC and the Rabat summit defined the tenets of the Palestinian national rights, that is, the territorial and national elements of the future Palestinian state. They strengthened the linkage between the territorial and national components of the West Bank problem. A formal Arab commitment emerged to make the PLO a party to political process in solution of the Palestinian problem.

On the other hand, the resolutions exempted Jordan from any formal responsibility to negotiate directly the future of the West Bank after Israeli withdrawal. In fact, in 1974, from the Arab and Palestinian point of view, little was left of Jordan's stance in determining the future of the West Bank. With that, in my opinion, the Jordanian option came to its end. The only card which remained for Hussein to play was the Israeli card, namely, Israel's refusal to recognize the PLO or to negotiate with it.

The PNC's and Rabat resolutions intensified the political allegiance to the PLO of the traditional leadership in the territories, including those considered pro-Jordanian. They created a consensus, among the entire range of the political leaders in the territories, that the PLO had the decisive position concerning the solution of the Palestinian issue. The first tangible proof of this conclusion was the results of the municipal election held in the West Bank in 1976.

To conclude, both the phased strategy and the agreement of principles with Israel were a return to Fatah's political ideology, in its early days when, in November 1960, its organ *Filastinuna* had called for "the establishment of a revolutionary Palestinian national rule in the Arab parts of Filastin,"[18] namely the West Bank and the Gaza Strip. In that statement, *Filastinuna* suggested, in fact, that the Gaza Strip might be the territory in which the national rule would be set up. Fatah indeed returned also to Farouq Qaddumi's suggestion of July 1967 to the central committee of Fatah calling for "the establishment of a mini-state in the West Bank and Gaza, after Israeli withdraw from them."[19] After the war Abu Iyyad claimed that this idea "met (then) with fierce opposition, in spite of its realistic nature."[20]

The agreement of principles between Israel and the PLO had endowed the 12th PNC resolutions with better historical perspective and dimension than before, albeit the basic significance given to these resolutions during the previous two decades had remained valid. Arafat reiterated these resolutions in order to legitimize the agreement. He argued, and rightly so, that the agreement was in fact the implementation of the 12th PNC decisions. Thus, the resolutions of the 12th PNC may be seen, retrospectively, as the start of a process which led to the 19th PNC decisions of November 1988, culminating with the signing of the agreement between the PLO and Israel.

Notes

1. On these achievements and Sadat's efforts, see Moshe Shemesh, *The Palestinian Entity 1959–74, Arab Politics and The PLO*, London, 1988.
2. For the text of the Algiers summit top secret resolutions, see *al-Nahar*, Beirut, 4 December 1973.
3. See Sadat, *Cairo Radio*, 30 October 1974; *Middle East News Agency*

(MENA), 30 March 1974, 24 October 1974, 19 January 1975; *al-Anwar*, Beirut, 22 June 1975; *al-Hawadith*, 21 March 1975; *Observer*, 24 October 1974; *NBC Television*, 5 November 1975.

4. On the talks between Fatah's and Egypt's leaders, see Abu Iyyad, *Filatini Bila Hawiyya* (Palestinian Without Identity), Kuwait, n.d. pp. 205–210; *al-Ahram*, 26 March 1974, 7 April 1974, 2 and 18 May 1974.

5. On Sadat's tactics, see for example: Sadat, *Cairo Radio*, 31 October 1973; *MENA*, 23 January 1974, 29 March 1974; *al-Ahram*, 2 June 1974; Abu Iyyad, *Filastini*, pp. 205–210; *al-Nahar*, 21 February 1974; Arafat, *al-Ahram*, 17 May 1974.

6. For the text of the Palestinian National Covenant, see *PLO, al-Majlis al-Watani fi al-Qahira* (The Fourth PNC convened in Cairo), 10–17 July 1968.

7. Abu Iyyad, *al-Balagh*, Beirut, 24 November 1973, in Shafiq al-Hut, *al-Filastini Bayna al-Tih wa al-Dawla*, Beirut, May 1977, pp. 135–140; *Iraqi News Agency* (INA), 9 December 1973; *al-Yawm*, Beirut, 24 December 1973.

8. Yazid Sayigh, "Mawqi' al-Kifah al-Musallah wa al-Intifada fi Atar al-Nidal al-Watani al-Filastini," *Shuun Arabiyya*, Summer 1991, No. 67, pp. 65–79.

9. On the organizations' crisis during 1971–2, see Shemesh, op. cit., pp. 233–249.

10. Abu Iyyad, *Filastini*, pp. 200–225, "Afkar Jadida Amam Marhala Ghamida," *Shuun Filastiniyya*, No. 29, January 1974, pp. 5–10; *al-Nahar*, 12 December 1973.

11. Abu Mazin, *Lecture*, on 15 August 1972, in Fatah's course for its cadres, "Fatah, al-Maktab al-Amm, Dawarat al-Kawadir al-Ulya," 14–24 August 1972 (unpublished).

12. PDFLP, resolutions of the 4th session of the PDFLP Central Committee, August 1973, in *al Wad' fi ul-Munatiq al-Muhtalla wa Muhimmat al-Thawra*, Beirut, August 1975, pp. 7–9, 120–124.

13. See note 10 above and "Farouq al-Qaddumi, al-Nidal al-Siyasi al-Filastini," *Shuun Filastiniyya*, No. 39, November 1974, pp. 6–10; Isam Sakhnini, "Mukawwanat al-Qarar fi al-Majlis al-Watani al-Filastini, al-Dawra al-Thaniya Ashara," *Shuun Filastiniyya*, No. 35, July 1974, pp. 4–12.

14. See Abu Iyyad, note 10 above.

15. For the text of the "phased programme," see *PLO, al-Barnamij al-Siyasi al-Marhali, al-Bayan al-Siyasi*, the 12th PNC session.

16. For the text of the Rabat summit top secret resolutions, see *al-Safir*, Beirut, 30 November 1977. On the debates in the Rabat summit and its resolutions, see Shemesh, op. cit., pp. 306–311.

17. Abu Iyyad, *al-Nahar*, 27 March 1975.

18. *Filastinuna*, No. 11, November 1960, p. 3.

19. See Abu Iyyad, *Filastini*, pp. 219–222.

20. Ibid.

11

Changes in Egyptian Society since 1973

Joseph Ginat

Egyptian society is not a single, homogeneous entity but rather a conglomerate of several communities. Within the demographic-geographic structure of Egypt, one can distinguish several entities. Starting from the south, the first is the Nubian group, a direct continuation of the Nubians of northern Sudan, inhabiting mainly the region between Aswan and Luxor. The group inhabiting the region further north – halfway between Miniyah and Cairo – is known as the Sa'ids. (The demarcation line between the two groups is discernible in particular in the Sunday market, held in a valley south of Luxor, where one can see both Nubians and Sa'ids trading, buying and selling side by side.)

The third group, called the Fellahin, dwells in the Delta region, itself divided into two sub-regions, the eastern and western Delta. Outwardly, Sa'idis differ from Fellahin in their headdresses – the Fellahin wear a rather tall brown hat, resembling a large fez, while the Sa'idis wrap a length of fabric around their heads.

The next ethnic group is the Sinai desert Bedouin, some of whom retain their semi-nomadic way of life, while others are already sedentarized. They are organized in tribes and tribal federations and try to perpetuate their traditional social structures, manners and customs, including their traditional courts (see Hobbs, 1989).

The two largest Egyptian cities are Alexandria and Cairo. In the former, one encounters the offspring of intermarriages – various groups of immigrants from the Mediterranean basin and Turkey marrying into other immigrant groups, as well as immigrants marrying into the local population. Most of the Egyptians who have immigrated into the Alexandria region are Fellahin from the Delta villages.

Cairo, the capital, attracts villagers from all over the country who come to the city in an attempt to find a livelihood, and is therefore a mosaic of different ethnic groups. When a resident of Cairo asks a fellow resident as to his origins, and is told, "I'm from Cairo," he usually responds, "But where were you from *before* Cairo?" since most of Cairo's inhabitants are descendants of immigrants into the city.

The famous Egyptian dialect of the Arabic language, which can be heard on the radio and television, in films and the theatre, is actually limited to Cairo, Alexandria and their outskirts. It is spoken by approximately one-third of Egypt's population, some 20 million people.

One doesn't have to be a Marxist to realize that social change is a direct result of economic developments. The late President Sadat wanted to change the system, as well as the entire atmosphere that had prevailed in Egypt since 1952. In order to understand the changes which took place after 1973, one has to refer to an earlier, specific date – 15 May 1971. It was then that Sadat realized that drastic measures would be required to overcome the Nasserist opposition. This opposition emerged right after the death of Nasser (28 September 1970), and regarded itself as "the backbone of Arabism." Interestingly enough, it was this self-styled "backbone of Arabism" that opposed most bitterly the proposed plans for a confederation between Egypt, Syria and Libya, claiming that such a confederation would be premature. Most of the previous regime's leaders were arrested, tried and sentenced to imprisonment. The arrested politicians included Vice-President 'Ali Sabri; Minister of the Interior Sharawi Gum'a; Minister of Defense General Fauzi, one of the most powerful political figures of the day; Minister of Information Muhammad Faiq; Minister of Housing Sa'ad Zayed, and many others, such as Sammy Sharaf. In the judicial system, Sadat established a special court for political activity, as well as a prosecutor appointed specifically to deal with political issues. Only one party – al-Ittihad al-Ishtiraq al-'Arabi – was granted official recognition, and this state of affairs lasted until 1975, when Sadat abolished the one-party system.

These dramatic and drastic measures enabled Sadat to remove the Soviets and establish relations with the West, mainly with the United States. In 1975, about a year and a half after the October War,

Sadat announced an economic open-door policy. The parliament passed a bill to encourage foreign investments in Egypt by granting foreign investors tax-exemptions. Initially, the investments were very cautious – the first factories founded in Egypt by foreign companies were branches of Coca-Cola and Seven-Up. Sadat's opponents stressed the fact that these factories produced consumer goods, rather than products that might add impetus to Egypt's economy.

Due to the economic development, a limited group of people within Egyptian society managed to get rich very quickly, mainly as a result of partnerships with foreigners, and the establishment of licensed agencies marketing foreign goods, such as cars, electric appliances and electronic equipment. The following anecdote illustrates the situation at the time: When told by Minister of Interior Mamduh Salem that the town of Port Sa'id already boasted 90 millionaires, Sadat remarked, "Why not 900, as long as they pay their taxes?"

The open-door policy enabled Egypt to export Egyptian labour, both skilled and unskilled. Within a relatively short period, over a million Egyptians found employment in the Gulf states, Saudi Arabia, Iraq and other countries. This was an unprecedented phenomenon. Most of these workers left their families behind – many only came home once a year, or even once every two years or more. This greatly affected the social structure, and most of all women's status and roles: in the absence of the head of the family, the woman accumulated more responsibilities within the family, including decision-making in various areas of life. The changes in the family structure throughout the period will be discussed below.

The economic upheaval brought about changes in the structure of Egypt's socio-economic pyramid. Up to the late 1970s and early 1980s, the pyramid consisted of a proportionally larger lower class, divided into lower, middle and upper sub-strata. Above it was a narrow middle-class stratum, and the even narrower stratum of the upper class. Since the 1980s this stratification within the pyramid has undergone two principal changes. The upper class has expanded. Within the lower and middle class, however, one can detect a two-way mobility.

On the one hand, certain classes of people got rich and ascended from the bottom of the middle class to an upper layer, still within the middle class – people such as lawyers and physicians, who increased the rates they charged for their services and consequently made more money. The ascent from the lower to the middle class, on the other hand, is much less pronounced.

The import, assembling and acquisition of cars and electric appliances brought about a significant increase in demand for the services of various mechanics and technicians. Fellahin owning relatively large plots of farmland raised the price of their crops and also accumulated more wealth. The salaries of civil servants and hired employees, in comparison, remained about the same, while their expenses grew considerably larger. The mechanic or the technician, unlike the civil servant, needs no suit for work and has no additional expenses. Thus, a group originally belonging to the lower middle class drifted downwards, into the upper lower class.

The change, however concrete in its manifestations, is conceptual in nature. The recently established materialistic competition leads to an increase in individual status and concurrently decreases the cohesiveness of the descent group as well as the extended family. The individual is less dependent on his family for support and thus the extended family loses some of its past roles. In other words, in this process of a fast shift from the *Gemeinschaft* to the *Geselschaft*, the achieved status becomes far more significant than the ascribed status.

Until the period covered by this study, marriage was always a family undertaking, from the mate selection stage up to the purchase of an apartment and furniture and the wedding ceremony itself. These days, however, in many cases, the financial burden of buying an apartment and furnishings falls upon the prospective groom, who can expect no help from his relatives. The apartment is usually bought and furnished in the period between the engagement and the wedding.

Therefore, engagements may sometimes last several years – five to seven, and in some cases even longer – until the groom manages to acquire the necessary funds. Quite often, this leads to friction between the bride's father and the groom – the former pressing to shorten the engagement period, and the latter struggling in vain to meet the demands of his future father-in-law. Sometimes these pressures even cause engagements to be called off.

A rather interesting system has emerged, in an attempt to solve this problem. Some ten youths establish an association – *Gam'iyya* – each chipping in and paying a minimum of 100 or 200 Egyptian pounds a month into a communal fund. The sum thus accumulated serves as a loan, intended to finance the basic needs of the grooms-to-be. Members of the association determine the order of priority, that is who will be first, second and so on to enjoy the loan. This mutual aid system is independent of the family structure.

Since newly-weds find housing relatively expensive, quite a few couples resort to renting apartments in villages located several dozen miles outside of Cairo, where they can also save on food and daily expenditures, which are much lower in the village. Those urban residents who have moved to the villages are not cut off from the city – they commute daily between the city and their village residence, which only serves as a dormitory. The universal tendency for a shift from the village to the city does exist in Egypt, since people come alone to find employment in the city, and later send for their families. The above-mentioned pattern, of a shift from city to village, is characteristic of third- or second-generation urban residents. This pattern also distances the individual from his family of origin.

One should note a different pattern, of a shift from village to city, by people who emigrated into the city several decades ago and have lived there ever since (Fakhouri, 1972; Harik, 1974). Although city-dwellers, they preserve their connections to the village. They travel to their village of origin during weekends; a considerable number retain their inherited plot of farmland, which they lease to tenants or relatives who till it for them (for a poor neighborhood in Cairo, which was formerly a rural area, see Wikan, 1980). On weekdays, when they return to the city, they bring back agricultural produce such as fruit and vegetables, and thus save money on food. The family ties are reciprocal – when relatives, usually women, come to sell their crops in town, they stay overnight at the homes of their city relations.

A further pattern of transfer from city to village is still at the planning stage. The Egyptian ministry of agriculture has initiated the establishment of several villages in the Fayyum oasis, on both sides of an irrigation canal connecting the Fayyum and the Nile. Currently, unemployed university graduates are interviewed as candidates for future settlement in these villages. At university these candidates did not necessarily specialize in agriculture, but rather studied various unrelated subjects, such as Humanities and Social Sciences. The future settlers are mostly urban residents, lacking any knowledge or experience in agriculture. Furthermore, the various candidates are not previously acquainted with each other, and share no communal background – they did not go to the same schools, grow up in the same neighborhood, etc. These couples, most of whom are in their mid-twenties and have only just begun their married life, will have to adjust to an entirely new life style in close proximity to total strangers, far from the city where they were born, raised and underwent socialization for nearly a quarter of a century. The idea is innovative and interesting, and might present the solution to housing and unemployment problems.

On the other hand, it is radically different from the project of the five cities, some of which were built in the vicinity of Cairo, and others on the roads from Cairo to Isma'ilia and from Cairo to Alexandria. This project, begun in the early 1970s, involves a shift from one city to another, not very far away. Some of the relocated residents have found employment in their new towns in trade and municipal work, while others commute daily to Cairo. Unlike Fayyum, these cities are close enough to enable former neighbors, relatives and friends to visit and be visited, and old ties retained. The Fayyum project is a first Egyptian attempt at a planned shift from city to village.

Within the family, there exists a special relationship between sons and their mothers. The mother is held in great respect. Mother's Day has become a major event. At the first stage of this process, Mother's Day gained importance mainly in families where the father worked abroad. As mentioned above, the woman in such families gained status, being the only one responsible for the education and upbringing of the children, and making decisions that would normally have been made by the husband. In that, she takes upon herself the role of father, as well as fulfilling her traditional role as a mother. Sons in such families express their appreciation through gifts given to the mother, and the custom has spread to families whose head never left to work abroad. Thus, this emphasis on Mother's Day has eventually become a general behavioral norm in Egypt.

In particular, the woman's status has increased in families where the woman is employed outside the household. The number of working women has grown in recent years, so much so that women's work outside the home has become the prevailing norm. In recent years, one can also detect quite a few women drivers in the heavy traffic of Cairo and Alexandria. Another noteworthy, albeit limited, phenomenon involves the promotion of working women. The women are then transferred to a different branch of their firm, located in another city. In several such cases, the entire family has followed the wife and moved to the new location.

The high rate of population growth is one of the most important issues in Egypt. There have been some attempts at family planning but so far they have gained only limited success. As more females are allowed to gain higher education, in both high schools and universities, they stand a better chance of reducing the number of children per family. The common view holds that illiteracy is higher in the villages.

Apparently, in recent years the number of female students in the universities of Miniyah and Asiut has risen considerably. The university of Asiut has 29,000 students. Miniyah university has a total of 14,000 students, 40 per cent of which are female. Only 3,000 of the Miniyah students come from the city itself, the others hailing from small towns or villages. The principal departments at Miniyah university are agriculture, medicine, education and literature. In Asiut, on the other hand, the principal departments are pharmacology, veterinary medicine and Semitic languages, including Hebrew. The 1992 graduates of the departments of agriculture and education had no trouble finding jobs immediately after graduation.

Many female students found employment as teachers. The female graduates, including village girls, tend to put off marriage and marry on the average at a later age. In the villages of the Sa'id, women only slightly older than the female students and recent graduates are illiterate or have spent very few years in school and also married young. The status of female university graduates both in villages and towns is doubtlessly higher, and their influence on the family and community larger than that of illiterate or semi-literate women. Not only can these women influence decision-making processes within the nuclear family, they will probably strive for family planning and birth control.

Concerning the social aspect of fundamentalism, Esposito maintains that "Egypt's militant groups remain fragmented and small. They do not enjoy broad popular support." Esposito emphasizes also that "During the 1970s the number of private mosques doubled from approximately twenty to forty thousand. Out of forty-six thousand mosques in Egypt, only six thousand were controlled by the ministry of religious Endowments" (Esposito, 1992).[1]

One should stress that, as illustrated above, in recent years we see a large number of newly erected mosques, and an increasing number of women and girls who adopt the custom of covering their heads with a scarf or a shawl. Both phenomena are explicit signs of a revival of religion. One should beware of equating this religious revival with fundamentalist Islam. In the last decade, the revival of religion has become a universal phenomenon common to Christianity, Judaism and Islam alike. In Egypt, the revival of religion is also characterized by people joining Sufi mystic orders (see Gilsenan, 1973; Reeves, 1990). These orders, which until quite recently suffered a decline, now experience a revival and growth, and are quite unrelated to the extremist Islamic movements.

The extremist movements are commonly called fundamentalist movements. However, the president of the supreme court for state security, Dr. Sa'id el-Ashmawy, scholar and the author of several books on Islam and fundamentalist Islam, repudiates the application of the term "fundamentalist" to these movements but prefers to use the term "fundamentalist" to describe himself, since he studies the fundamentals of Islam. According to him, any use of violence contradicts fundamental Islam. Therefore, the only suitable name for organizations representing extremist Islam would be Political Islam (el-Ashmawy, 1992).

The most prominent structural change in the extremist organizations of the 1980s and 1990s is the addition of unemployed university graduates who have joined their ranks. Whereas in the past, extreme movements mostly operated locally and sporadically, these days the new members from among the intelligentsia manage to join the separate links into a continuous chain. The Egyptian government takes drastic measures against acts of violence aimed at foreign tourists, as well as at Egyptian officials and police officers. Apparently, the government has scored several successes in its effort to put a stop to those waves of violence. On the other hand, the problem has also required a thorough in-depth treatment, that could solve both the social and economic problems of the unemployed youths in provincial towns and villages. Beyond supplying them with jobs, it is vital to give them a sense of belonging, an involvement in the social and political development of the state. It is frustration that pushes these youths to extremes, and drives them to join Islamic movements in an attempt at protest.

As to whether these movements threaten the regime, I can answer categorically "No." Obviously, the militant activity has heavily damaged Egypt's economy, affecting mainly tourism, which is a principal source of national income. Further, no political personage is immune to bullets. Nevertheless, all these phenomena are a far cry from an actual threat to the government.

In conclusion, changes in the economy, in the open-door policy toward the West, have resulted in social changes. The individual competition greatly reduces cohesiveness within the extended family. Materialism has become so widespread that street slang has developed special code names for certain sums of money – one hundred Egyptian pounds are called *"astic,"* one thousand pounds are called *"bakko,"* and a million is called *"Arnab"* (a rabbit). These terms have penetrated into Egyptian culture. And what is culture if not beliefs, values, signs and signals?

Many claim that the materialistic influence detracts from the tolerance and patience characteristic of Egyptians. The change in the structure of the social pyramid is unique, since it includes both an ascent and a descent of various social groups. In the past, salaries of four-star generals were among the highest in the country. This social group does own villas by the seaside, but the computer programmer, daughter of such a general, may earn a higher salary than her father. In sum, the changes occurring during the last two decades have altered irrevocably the equilibrium of economy, society and family alike.

Note

1. See also Esposito, John L., *Islam and Politics*, 3rd edn, Syracuse, N.Y.: Syracuse University Press, 1991.

References

el-Ashmawy, Sa'id. *el-Islam el-Siasi* (Political Islam), 3rd edn, el-taba'a el-thalitha. Cairo: Sina lil-Nasher, 1992.

Esposito, John L. *The Islamic Threat: Myth or Reality*. Oxford: Oxford University Press, 1992.

——. *Islam and Politics*. Syracuse, N.Y.: Syracuse University Press, 1991, 3rd edn.

Fakhouri, Hani. *Kafar el-Elou: An Egyptian Village in Transition*. New York: Holt Reinhart and Winston, 1972.

Gilsenan, Michael. *Saint and Sufi in Modern Egypt*. Oxford: Clarendon, 1973.

Harik, Iliya. *The Political Mobilization of Peasants: A Study of an Egyptian Community*. Bloomington: Indiana University Press, 1974.

Hobbs, Joseph J. *Bedouin Life in the Egyptian Wilderness*. Cairo: The American University Press, 1989.

Reeves, Edward B. *The Hidden Government: Ritual Clientelism and Legitimation in Northern Egypt*. Salt Lake City: University of Utah Press, 1990.

Wikan, Unni. *Life Among the Poor in Cairo*. London: Tavistock, 1980.

Part III

Israel and the PLO as Negotiating Partners

This section analyzes Israeli and PLO policy and interests in the era of their September 1993 mutual recognition agreement. Given the PLO's original objective of destroying Israel, and its frequent use of terrorist tactics, the organization long found compromise with the Jewish state impossible to contemplate, while Israel wanted to avoid the PLO's involvement in diplomacy, or the creation of a Palestinian state. The gap to be bridged before an agreement was possible between them was one of the widest in the history of international affairs.

Yair Hirschfeld was the main Israeli negotiator during most of the secret talks held with the PLO. Using archival sources, he explains in "Dynamics of Israeli-Palestinian Negotiations" how Israeli-Palestinian talks in the 1970s made no progress because of the PLO's high level of demands. He shows how the victories and defeats of both parties in the ensuing years gradually moved them to a point where compromise was possible and gives a first-hand account of the turning point at the 1991 Madrid conference. Especially useful is the concept of the periodization of the two sides' relationship and the importance of the interplay between Palestinian interests and the interests of the various Arab states.

Abraham Tamir, former director of Israel's National Security Council, in "Israel's Security Policy and the Peace Process," shows how Israel returned to its original post-1967 policy a quarter-century later, redefining its goals and interests to make peace on the basis of the pre-1967 borders. This was an abandonment of the more

ambitious goals – which coincided with more pessimistic assess-
ments of the prospects for peace – during the 1980s and early
1990s.

Matti Steinberg's article, "You Can't Clap with Only One
Hand," shows the complex relationship between West Bank/Gaza
Palestinian leaders and the PLO leadership. The former group's
power increased during the *intifada*, but it still required the
legitimacy offered by Yasir Arafat's endorsement and role to
make possible a negotiated solution. Manuel Hassassian's article,
"Policy Dynamics of the Palestinian Leadership," also discusses the
interrelationship between the leadership and Palestinian groups and
constituencies.

Shmuel Eisenstadt considers "Changes in Israel's Society since the
Yom Kippur War" which moved the country to a greater acceptance
of a drastic break with its long-held policy of refusing to negotiate
with the PLO, though stressing the pivotal role of leadership in
changing public opinion.

12

Dynamics of Israeli-Palestinian Negotiations

Yair Hirschfeld

In January 1977 Issam Sartawi, a leading PLO diplomat and moderate, sent a letter to Austrian Chancellor Bruno Kreisky. Sartawi was then the leader on the Palestinian side of secret negotiations in Paris between Israelis and Palestinians, while Lova Eliav, Uri Avineri and Matti Peled led on the Israeli side. The letter not only encapsulates the dilemma of the first stage of negotiations; it reveals the dynamics and difficulties of Israeli-Palestinian negotiations in general.

> There is nowadays a unanimous agreement that the Middle East crisis should be brought to a speedy solution. Unfortunately, there has been a great deal of confusion over what constitutes the basic ingredients of a just and lasting solution. So far two formulas have been under consideration. The one assumes that the crux of the problem is the dispute between the Arab confrontation states and the state of Israel, while the other insists that the essence of the crisis is the contradictory claim of both Palestinians and Israelis to the same country. The first formula assumes that a settlement is possible between the Arab states and the state of Israel, with the Palestinians relegated to a vassal status under Jordan, whereas the other insists that peace can only be achieved when the Palestinians and Israelis reconcile their contradictory claims amicably and satisfactorily.[1]

What formula would enable progress? Should there be peace between Israel and the Arab states – and was this possible – or should there first be a peace between Israel and the Palestinians? In the first stage, between 1973 and 1977, the Palestinian position was clear. It maintained that the PLO must have a complete monopoly over the peace process. Whether it decided to move towards negotiations or to postpone negotiations, all members of the PLO – even the most moderate, including Sartawi – would do everything to prevent direct negotiations between Israel and the Arab world. The PLO insisted that the only partner which had a legitimate right to negotiate was the Palestinians.

The Israeli position at that time, between 1973 and 1977, was more open. A discussion was taking place in Israeli society with different formulas under discussion. The official policy taken by the first Rabin government was to try to advance towards peace with Egypt, the largest Arab state. At the same time, with the knowledge of Rabin, a back channel was opened in Paris where negotiations were held with the Palestinians.

The outcome of these negotiations in Paris, and of those between Israel and the Egyptians, was to reinforce the Israeli understanding that, while it was not possible to come to an agreement with the Palestinians at that time, it was possible to come to an agreement with Egypt. Sartawi's letter shows that the Palestinian demands in January 1977 harked back to 1947, attempting to turn back the clock to a stage of history which had long since passed. Thus, the back-channel activities strengthened the Labour Party leadership's belief that progress on the Palestinian track was not possible since the Palestinians were not prepared to advance towards any understanding that was feasible for the Israeli government at that time.

January 1977 begins the second stage, characterized by clear confrontation. The Israeli position was that it would make peace with Egypt. This, incidentally, ran contrary to the position of President Carter, who had just been elected. Israel nonetheless wanted to go ahead with Egypt. And the Palestinian aim was to prevent this.

This second stage, between 1977 and 1982, represented a knockout victory on the Israeli side. The Egyptians had said "yes" to recognition, to negotiations and to peace with Israel. Sadat came to Israel and signed a peace agreement with the government of Egypt. The PLO and Arab states tried to undermine the agreement because it not only ran contrary to the basic concept of the radicals, those in the PLO who wanted to confront Israel, but also ran contrary to the basic concept of the moderates. These insisted that if there was to be an understanding with Israel, Palestinians must lead the way.

Israel established peaceful relations with Egypt and maintained them beyond the 1982 Lebanese war and assassination of Sadat. An understanding of peace grew between Israel and Egypt that could be built upon. If this concept was right, it meant that the next

Israeli step would not be towards negotiations with the Palestinians but towards negotiations with Jordan and Syria.

The third stage lasted from 1982 to 1989. In this stage, the Palestinians were those who scored a victory – but not a knock-out victory, only a victory on points. The Israeli policy was to circumvent the Palestinian issue and to find other ways to solve the problem. One way was thought to be coming to an understanding with the Jordanians, who could then become a vehicle for bringing in the Palestinians. There were also attempts to make peace with Lebanon. A peace treaty was signed on 17 May 1983, though it didn't last for very long. There were attempts to come to a public understanding with Syria. All those attempts failed.

This failure was not predetermined by history. During this period of negotiations, Israeli talks with Jordan brought about the agreement with King Hussein in April 1987 – which has become known as the London Agreement. This agreement, focusing on procedure over substance, did represent a serious option for moving ahead in negotiations. It failed, not because of historical necessity, but due to the fact that Shimon Peres and Yitzhak Rabin did not succeed in obtaining a majority in the Israeli government to support this approach.

At the end of 1987, the *intifada* broke out, bringing about the end of the Jordanian option. It strengthened the Palestinian cause and made the Palestinians the main interlocutor with Israel. At the end of July 1988 King Hussein of Jordan announced that he was no longer a potential negotiating partner for the future of the West Bank and the Gaza Strip. Worse, from his point of view, the Jordanian camp within the West Bank and Gaza had lost its influence and ceased to play a meaningful role.

At that moment, Israel might have taken political advantage of the *intifada*. The civil backbone of the uprising, the various local citizen committees, had turned into genuine and effective political grass-roots organizations and had gained, in cooperation with the united national internal leadership, sufficient power to start negotiations of their own. However, for security reasons, the Government of Israel decided to break the political power of these grass-roots organizations and thereby eliminated the option of reconciling with the internal Palestinian leadership. This was the end of stage three.

By 1989 the fourth stage had started, when the Israeli leadership, even the government led by Prime Minister Yitzhak Shamir, understood that if they wanted to go ahead, there was no serious possibility of doing so without confronting the Palestinian problem. By May 1989, Shamir and Rabin came out with what became known as the Shamir-Rabin plan. It emphasized the need to come to terms with the Palestinians and suggested a method for bringing the Palestinians into the negotiating process. Moreover, on the Palestinian side the *intifada* created the need to achieve practical political results on the ground that were attainable only by means of negotiations with Israel and thus induced the Palestinian leadership to adopt a more flexible attitude and seek – like the Government of Israel – an acceptable formula that would enable the beginning of the peace negotiations. Hence, since May 1989, there has been an understanding, on both the Israeli and Palestinian sides, that the Palestinian problem will be tackled through a formula to be worked out in pre-negotiations, in a manner acceptable to both leaderships. While this has led to serious ups and downs, it led to the convening of the Madrid Conference. There, both parties agreed that the issue of the Israelis and Palestinians must be tackled through direct negotiations, and both parties accepted that the negotiations must also include other parties.

The developments in Madrid cast us into a new situation. The negotiating framework created under the umbrella of the Madrid Conference permitted Israel to negotiate simultaneously and directly in bilateral negotiations with Syria, Lebanon, Jordan and the Palestinians. In practical terms this meant that Israel's policy makers had obtained the option to choose.

Israeli negotiation tactics could be directed at obtaining a break-through on either the Palestinian or the Syrian front. This, of course, would only be true if the Palestinian leadership was determined to make progress with Israel, independent of the Arab states. As a matter of fact, at Madrid the Palestinians demonstrated their determination to act independently of other Arab delegations. Whereas the Syrians had threatened on the third day of the Madrid Conference to leave, the Palestinians singlehandedly moved ahead, creating enough pressure on the Syrians to stay. The following story illustrates how this came about.

The first day in Madrid, a Wednesday, saw talks by Bush and Gorbachev. All went well. On Thursday, Israel's leadership spoke, followed by the Syrian and Palestinian delegations. A strong verbal dispute ensued between the Syrian Minister of Foreign Affairs and our Prime Minister Rabin – each accused the other of being a terrorist. Everybody was upset on Thursday, and on Friday the

Syrians said: We have had enough with those Israelis, we have had enough with Madrid. We will pack our suitcases and go home.

On Friday the newspapers declared that Madrid was a major failure. And then, from Friday noon to Saturday night, the U.S. mission, led by James Baker IIIrd, sat and worked in the city's Palace Hotel. Everyone, including the Jews, worked on that Saturday. By Saturday night they reached a dramatic moment – the Palestinians put the Syrians in a very awkward position, saying that, whatever happened, they would come to the bilateral negotiations on the next day, 3 November.

The Syrians had two options and they chose a third. The first option was to say, "To hell with the Palestinians; they won't dare go alone. We will close the door on them and go back to Damascus." The second option was to say, "This is a serious opportunity. We want to take part in it. Despite the difficulties on Thursday and Friday, we will be constructive and we will come, like the Palestinians, at 10:00 on Sunday, 3 November to bilateral negotiations." They did neither. The Syrian delegation chose instead to threaten not to attend and then waited to see whether the Palestinians actually would show up. When they saw that the Palestinians did in fact come at 10:00, the Syrians changed their minds, arriving at the negotiations at 6:00 in the evening.

Thus in Madrid a new pattern was created which demonstrated that when the decision was taken on the political level in Israel to move ahead with the Palestinians, the Palestinians were willing and able to move ahead, even if the Syrians would not go with them. In the fourth stage, then, the deadlock had seemingly been broken. However, this was only half of the truth. The Madrid Conference provided the Palestinians with a platform on which to negotiate, but it did not create the necessary conditions for decision making. In a way, for Chairman Yasser Arafat, the Madrid and ensuing Washington negotiations (which were held within the framework of the Madrid Conference) created a formidable dilemma: If no headway was made in negotiations, Hamas (the Islamic Resistance Movement) would become the main player and put an end to the historic role of the PLO. But if progress was made in Washington, the Palestinian delegation there – representing the "inside" Palestinian leadership of the West Bank and the Gaza Strip – would become the main players; the PLO leadership in Tunis would lose its control and its political leverage. The solution to this dilemma was to exploit the Washington negotiations in such a way as to encourage an intense Israeli-Palestinian dialogue outside the Washington talks.

Thus, the fifth and decisive stage in the history of Israeli-Palestinian peace negotiations began. In Norway a secret back-channel was created and the way for secret negotiations between the Government of Israel and the PLO was being prepared, leading finally to the signing of the Israeli-Palestinian Declaration of Principles in Washington, on the White House lawn, on 13 September 1993.

In summary, the dynamics of Israeli-Palestinian negotiations followed a circular path, and quite an interesting one. Throughout the entire time, the Israeli-Arab and the Palestinian-Arab relationships were the main factor determining the negotiating strategy and tactics of either side. Whereas in the beginning, the outside Arab factor was a serious obstacle to promoting negotiations, from the 1991 Madrid conference until 13 September 1993, the Palestinian competition with Syria, the competition within the Arab world, and the willingness of the Arab world to look favorably on an Israeli-Palestinian agreement, became major factors in making the negotiations a success.

13

Israel's Security Policy and the Peace Process

Abraham Tamir

Several major factors linked Israel's national security policy with its peace policy. Since the establishment of the State of Israel, its national security policy has been designed to defend its existence, integrity and security, and not for expansionist territorial aspirations. Hence, if the Arab confrontation states did not initiate wars against Israel or pose threats to its existence, then Israel would not start a war, neither to extend its territories, achieve control over water resources, unite Jerusalem, nor prevent Jordan and Egypt from establishing a Palestinian state in their former controlled territories of the West Bank and the Gaza Strip.

Our national security policy created from its very beginning the linkage between Israel's political willingness for peace and Israel's military capability to repel aggression of any kind and scale. Up to the Six Day War, Israel's willingness for peace was on the basis of the pre-1967 boundaries, and after the Six Day War, on the basis of Security Council Resolution 242, which also determined the principle of returning occupied territories for peace.

After the 1973 War, we began to realize the scope of territorial concessions required for peace, in an internal political structure in which the two big parties, the Likud and the Labour Party, fed public opinion with territorial expectations that became a main obstacle for peace. The main reasons for this realization were the beginning of negotiations with an Arab party instead of talking only to ourselves; the U.S. role in providing peace initiatives along with aid, allowing for a trade-off between Israeli security based on territories and security based on military means; and U.S. guarantees, including involvement in security arrangements. Another reason for this realization was the psychological effect of the '73 War, to which I will refer later.

For these reasons, all of Sinai was returned to Egypt for peace, and we may assess that it will not take long before the Golan Heights will be returned to Syria for peace. As for the West Bank and the Gaza Strip, it will be necessary to make amendments to the 1967 boundaries that will include the united Jerusalem under Israeli sovereignty, with extraterritorial arrangements for the Islamic holy places. The change in the fate of the West Bank and the Gaza Strip results mainly from the dominant influence of the Palestinian national movement, the PLO, on the future of the Palestinian people within a framework of a Palestinian state, through the Israeli-Palestinian mutual recognition agreement and the Oslo agreement of principles.

It also seems likely that – for reasons of demographic, economic and security considerations – the future Palestinian state will be eventually integrated within a confederation with Jordan or with both Jordan and Israel. A national security policy with provisions for Israel to defend itself on the basis of the 1967 boundaries can also provide the security solutions for all possible resolutions of the Palestinian problem in the West Bank and the Gaza Strip.

The inability of the Arab confrontation states to force terms upon Israel by military force, terror or economic blockade, and, on the other hand, the ability of the United States to deter the Soviet Union during the Cold War from intervening in the region, gradually motivated the Arab regimes to prefer political means for solving the conflict with Israel.

This motivation was mainly fed by the Israeli military victories in all wars, especially the 1973 War, by the U.S.-Israel strategic cooperation, and by the Arab states' assumption that Israel possesses nuclear weapons. This change had already paved the road for peace after the Six Day War. Hence it may be argued that, with wise strategy, it would have been possible to start the peace process before the 1973 War, including solving the Palestinian problem. On the other hand, the 1973 War created in Israel – regardless of its battlefield military victories – an awareness of its inability to maintain the territorial status quo gained in the Six Day War until the Arab side was ready to accept Israel's territorial aspirations, which were a boundary with Egypt stretching from el-Arish to Ras Muhammad; all of the Golan Heights, according to the Likud movement's concept, or a part of it, according to the Labour movement's concept; and all of the West Bank and Gaza Strip, according to the Likud movement's concept, or a part of these areas, according to the Labour movement's concept.

Today, in a period in which extreme expansionist ideologies are collapsing one after the other, we are returning to the principles that we set before the Six Day War for a military strategy that would link war and peace. These principles were:

1.   Israel can achieve its national goals on the basis of the 1967 boundaries with Egypt and Syria, and amendments to the '67 boundaries with the West Bank and the Gaza Strip.

2.   Israel should develop an infrastructure and capability to deter its potential enemies from using force, conventional or non-conventional, that might endanger its existence.

3.   If a war is forced on Israel, the Israel Defence Forces should transfer the battles as soon as possible to the enemy states, including the possibility of launching a preventive offense in order to remove a stranglehold on Israel, as happened in the Six Day War. This is why we give first priority to being able to maintain air superiority on all fronts, to mobile warfare, and a to long-range strategic arm.

4.   The Israeli goals for war will be to destroy the enemy's infrastructure for war and to force on it a cease-fire that will pave the road for peace negotiations.

5.   Occupied territories will be returned only for peace, and not as happened after the Sinai Campaign of 1956, when we returned territories captured from Egypt for security arrangements only, whose violation by President Abdel Nasser caused the deterioration into the Six Day War.

6.   In peace negotiations, Israel will require security arrangements on the bilateral and regional levels, and these should include not only military arrangements but also normalization of relations.

7.   Israel will require amendments to the boundaries in the West Bank and the Gaza Strip that will include a united Jerusalem under Israeli sovereignty.

On the basis of this approach, we started to plan, after the 1973 War, for a comprehensive peace process between Israel and its neighbors that would be based on three strategic stages. The first stage was confidence-building measures, including direct communication and contacts that would bring an end to hostile activities and establish mutual security arrangements. This stage potentially included interim territorial agreements. We achieved this with Egypt and with Syria.

The second stage was to be for the achievement of bilateral peace agreements between Israel and its neighbors on the basis of permanent boundaries and resolution of the Palestinian national rights (after a transitional period of autonomy) within a confederation framework with Jordan or with Jordan and Israel. These peace agreements were to be based on normalization of relations and security arrangements at the bilateral and regional levels.

In the third stage, we sought to develop a comprehensive peace in the form of a Middle Eastern community, based on a common market; on international projects such as water systems, research and development centers, transportation systems; and regional security arrangements such as arms control, and demilitarization of the region in terms of mass-destruction weapons. This would require a world order that could prevent the proliferation of nuclear weapons and which would also control arms supplies to radical regimes. In the period of the Cold War, it has already been demonstrated that the existence of nuclear weapons outside the region might endanger states in the region. It is also clear that disarmament of conventional weapons in the region depends on the frustration of the arms race, which has its sources in states outside the region producing sophisticated weapons and technology. We have already experienced how fast military power can be created when resources and capital for buying it are available.

We may propose several scenarios for a world order capable of achieving the goal of comprehensive security in the region. The question remains, however, of who will lead the world toward this goal. Will it be the United States? This seems impossible, not only because of the objection of other states but also because the United States itself is unqualified, because of its internal structure, to assume such a role. Or perhaps it will be the UN Security Council, on the model of the Gulf War, when the U.S. led a coalition operating under the auspices of its resolutions. This method, too, is questionable because of the appearance of cracks in that coalition. Or perhaps the UN secretary-general has aspirations that the Security Council will have permanent international forces for military involvement to prevent threats to world peace. This is also for the time being unimaginable.

The other possibility, which is achievable, is the development of regional communities, based on economic and strategic cooperation, in a world moving toward a new century in which economic strategy will hopefully replace military strategy as the dominant factor in international relations. But the movement toward a comprehensive peace in the region is still on the starting line and there remain forces of fundamentalism and extreme nationalism. We should continue to rely on the United States in order to be strong enough to march toward peace, and for strategic cooperation designed to prevent threats by extreme regimes that might endanger regional peace and stability, including by developing weapons of mass destruction – to put it simply, to prevent the rise of a new Saddam Hussein.

14

"You Can't Clap with Only One Hand": The Dialectic between the PLO "Inside" and "Outside"

Matti Steinberg

The PLO originated outside of Palestine.[1] The liberation of Palestine was envisioned by its leaders to be a dynamic process which would devolve "from the outside inward," with the Palestinian armed struggle serving as the main catalyst. Indeed, when the PLO demanded that the Palestinians take fate into their own hands and act, this call was directed primarily at Palestinians "outside" – those in the Arab confrontation states – and it refrained from assigning an active role to the Palestinians on the "inside." In those early days, before the PLO had struck roots among Palestinians in the territories, there was a marked contrast between the PLO's admonition to Palestinians to view Palestine (the inside) as an ultimate aim and its practical demand that the process of liberation must take place primarily on the outside. This approach was reinforced after the Six Day War following the abortive attempt to penetrate the territories and foster a popular uprising against Israel.

Until enhancement of the PLO's status in the Arab world and internationally following the Yom Kippur War (October 1973), support for it from Palestinians in the territories was far from assured.[2] A fierce struggle for their loyalty developed between the PLO and loyalists to Jordan, coming to a head with publication (in April 1972) of the Federation Plan of King Hussein, which proposed turning the West Bank into a Palestinian district of the Kingdom of Jordan.

From External to Internal Consensus

The Federation Plan was defeated more by the opposition of Arab leaders than by the opposition of the Palestinians in the territories. In the days before the Yom Kippur War, as noted, the territories were still divided between supporters of the PLO and Jordan loyalists. The consensus that formed around the PLO after this war derived from external Arab factors. Indeed, consolidation of an Arab consensus viewing the PLO as the "sole legitimate representative of the Palestinian people," following the Yom Kippur War, had an impact on its status not only within the Arab world, but internationally as well. It was not long before the external consensus – Arab and international – was clearly manifested in the territories as well, with the formation of an internal Palestinian consensus. The direction of influence was thus from the outer environment inward. Almost the entire world gave its blessing to the PLO (including Jordan, which at least officially accepted the verdict of the resolutions taken at the Arab summit in Rabat in October 1974), hence the residents of the territories under Israeli rule were unable to defy Arab national and international consensus.

The external consensus was understood by the Palestinians in the territories as the imperative of "international legitimacy" which supported Palestinian "national legitimacy." The more they internalized this recognition, the less their support of the PLO depended upon the external environment, and it took on a life of its own, standing on its own feet. The PLO also had to accommodate itself to the new circumstances, and it adopted the striving for a Palestinian state in the territories as its present interim goal. Prior to the Yom Kippur War, the PLO had asserted that all the territories of Palestine should be regarded as one entity, with no differences or preference among them. This new development was thus interpreted by residents of the territories as placing their vital interest as the paramount concern of the PLO, and this strengthened their connection to it.

The PLO did not rest content with a declaration, but sought to translate it into concrete budgetary and organizational terms. In the 1970s, financial aid to the territories in various forms began to take priority in the PLO budget, and feverish efforts to establish various front organizations in the territories were given equal weight with – and even preferred to – military action. This was clearly expressed in the decisions of the 13th Palestinian National Council (PNC) in

March 1977, which for the first time presented a detailed plan of actions to be taken by the PLO and Palestinians in the territories in the context of *sumud* (steadfastness), foremost among them the development of national institutions such as universities, labor unions, youth organizations (*shabiba*), etc.[3]

The landslide victory of PLO candidates in the municipal elections of 1976 in the West Bank proved to the PLO that its efforts had been rewarded. In these elections, Jordan's candidates were routed by PLO candidates, even though the Palestinian voters certainly understood that their vote for PLO rather than Jordan's loyalists carried the danger of extending Israeli rule. In those years, the PLO assigned to the residents of the territories an obstructing role in the context of *sumud* in an effort to block Israel's attempt to swallow up the territories and to establish an "alternative leadership" (*qiyada badila*) to the PLO. Indeed, the decision of the PLO to instruct its supporters to vote in the 1976 municipal elections derived from the fear of losing control to the Palestinians loyal to Jordan, who would have constituted an alternative to the PLO.

The preventive role of PLO supporters in the territories was clearly demonstrated in their opposition to carrying out the "Palestinian part" of the Camp David accords. Because of the PLO's intense opposition, local Palestinians could not be found to conduct the negotiations. The lesson drawn from this, repeated frequently by Faisal Husseini, is that the Palestinians in the territories have the power to thwart any political process that they do not want, but they do not have the power to initiate a political process that they do want. Hence their power is to respond negatively, rather than to initiate positively.

There was a good reason that the PLO leadership assigned only a preventive role to the Palestinians inside. The more prominent the centrality of the territories, the greater was the concern among the PLO leadership that the *golem* would turn on its creator and demand a role worthy of its importance. The PLO leadership on the outside thus had a vital interest that the inside should not deviate from its role as obstructor, and that the inside should serve the outside as a tool against those conspiring against it. The initiative taken by the mayors elected in 1976 could have threatened the PLO monopoly, this time by an alternative leadership that was clearly nationalist.[4]

The PLO could have easily retaliated against an "alternative leadership" which leaned on Jordan or Israel, but not against those elected from inside, the most prominent of whom followed organizations which rejected the approach of the PLO mainstream. The principal differences among the Fatah and the organizations of the Popular Front and the Democratic Front derived from the shape of their relations with the inside. Fatah, which felt its supremacy threatened, advocated centralism of the highest order, which did not leave freedom for the inside to maneuver beyond what the Fatah was willing to allow, while the Fronts sought to cultivate the inside as a counterweight to the dominance of the Fatah outside. Indeed, in the early 1980s, the Fatah leadership was so concerned that it made a concerted effort to clip the wings of the Committee of National Guidance, which was led by the recalcitrant mayors suspected of threatening Fatah's exclusivity, such as Bassam Shak'a, then mayor of Nablus.[5]

The Reversal: From Internal to External Consensus

The next milestone in the process of strengthening the Palestinians in the territories came in late 1982, following the ouster of the PLO leadership from Beirut and the dispersion of its organization throughout the Arab world. It was clear that pushing the PLO forces away from the Israeli border in Lebanon drove the armed struggle into a dead end as a strategy for liberating Palestine from the outside. The weakening of the PLO outside forced it to lean for support on the Palestinians inside. Because it held out against Israel during the months-long siege of Beirut, its international status was not impaired but, without the support that it received from the Palestinians inside, its international credit would have quickly dissipated.

In contrast with the early 1970s, when the external consensus in favor of the PLO spilled over into the territories and solidified the internal consensus, the situation was now reversed, and it was the internal consensus which maintained international legitimacy for the PLO. The weakening of the PLO outside forced its leadership to focus its main attention on the inside. This had practical implications for its entire approach: with the increased importance of the West Bank and Gaza, the PLO was in urgent need of using Jordan and Egypt as transit links to them. Indeed, Arafat began to invest great effort in strengthening these ties. For Egypt in particular, this at least implied the beginning of rehabilitation of the agreement format that it had created, i.e., the Camp David model. The growing rapprochement between the Fatah leadership and Jordan led directly to a relaxation of the tension between their supporters in the territories. The United States was eager to exploit these new circumstances, and President Reagan presented his plan (September 1982) based on the principles of Camp David.

With the territories rising to the top of the PLO's order of priorities, leaders in the territories also rose in prominence as of late 1982, and this meant having to take their views into consideration. Indeed, these individuals now began trying to influence PLO policies. Thus, in November 1982, supporters of the PLO and Jordan (the mayors of Bethlehem and Gaza, Elias Freij and Rashad al-Shawwa, the former mayor of Hebron, Mustafa Natsha, and Sa'ib Ariqat, and others) initiated the Palestinian Peace Document, which included a fervent request that the PLO and Jordan cooperate in the political process. They called upon the PLO to recognize UN Security Council resolutions 242 and 338, and they declared their support for "mutual and simultaneous recognition of the PLO, our legitimate representative, and Israel." The emphasis was on there being no alternative to a peace agreement.

Most daring of all was Rashad al-Shawwa, who did not rest content with a general declaration, but formulated a plan based on the principles of Camp David, i.e., a 3-to-5 year interim arrangement followed by a permanent agreement. Al-Shawwa brought his plan to the attention of the leadership of Fatah-outside.[6] To this new circumstance of the leaders in the territories speaking out in the wake of the Lebanon War, a factor of incomparable importance was added: the fear of inhabitants of the territories, whose spokespersons these were, that the ground was being pulled from under their feet as settlements in the West Bank and Gaza were stepped up by the Likud government. The Palestinian Peace Document emphatically sounded the alarm about this: "It is crucial that the process of Israeli settlement in the occupied territories be halted. The establishment of settlements is an obstacle to peace, and will transform the historic, demographic, social and economic situation in the occupied territories."[7] It was only natural that the "insiders" were more sensitive to this than the leadership outside. For the former, this was not an abstract political claim, but a basic existential need.

The assumption that the residents of the territories supported him was critical to Arafat's willingness to make common cause with Jordan (the Amman Accord in February 1985), despite opposition from all the other large organizations led by the Popular and Democratic

Fronts. He believed that the legitimacy drawn from the Palestinians in the territories was sufficient to justify the internal split of the PLO. In his view, unity of the leaders with the people in the territories was more important than unity of the organizations on the outside. This common cause floundered when Arafat concluded that the United States, Israel, and even Jordan had collaborated to prevent the PLO from having any role in the political process.

The growth of the uprising in the territories was the outcome of a cumulative process of increasing salience of the Palestinians inside, although it also embodied a major turning point. Through the uprising, residents of the territories signalled that they were tired of waiting endlessly for initiatives from the outside and fed up with the limited reactive role which PLO had assigned them. The uprising was generated by the force of the spontaneous climate of opinion, rather than a formal decision that the time had come for the inside to take action for itself. The act of uprising thus carried a message of complaint over the inefficacy of both the Arab world and the leadership of the PLO outside, whose efforts to regain the territories until then had all failed.

The inside was not, however, seeking to separate from the PLO, but rather to strengthen the tie. Indeed, the uprising had not gone on for long before it began to lean on the organizational structures set up by the PLO in the 1970s. Even though the PLO had not initiated the uprising, once it broke out the organization began to fill a key role in sustaining it and setting its direction. A clear manifestation of this was the establishment in the territories of the Unified National Command as the execution arm of the PLO outside, a body which reflected the same configuration of forces and which was responsible for daily command of the uprising.

With the Palestinians inside willing to bear the daily burden of the uprising, senior Fatah leaders in the territories attempted, even unilaterally, to translate the uprising into political achievements. Though these initiatives were coordinated with the PLO outside, they were generated inside the territories. The most prominent of these was formulation of a plan for a Document of Independence, found in the office of Faisal Husseini on 1 August 1988.[8]

The Document of Independence expressed the feelings of the Fatah leadership in the territories that the time was ripe for realizing political gains from the uprising. Arafat based himself on this general desire when he led the PLO to adopt the "Declaration of Independence of the State of Palestine" in the 19th PNC (November 1988). Even though this declaration did not match the Document of Independence of Faisal Husseini in every detail, the similarities were too striking to be purely coincidental. The Document of Independence called for the declaration of an independent Palestinian state within the borders of the partition plan (of 1947), to be headed by a provisional government composed of equal numbers of leaders from inside and outside the territories. The provisional government was to declare in the name of the PLO its willingness to establish a "functional delegation," its members drawn from both inside and out, which would seek a permanent settlement with Israel.

Thus the seeds of the idea to declare a State of Palestine in the 19th PNC were sown in the Document of Independence of Faisal Husseini, which set as its goal "passage from the stage of uprising by stone-throwing on the battlefield to the stage of political initiative, with the Palestinians adopting a technique of creativity and initiative, which will spur the commendable uprising to new action in order to arrive at an international conference."

Awareness of the importance of the uprising radiated from every line in the Document of Independence, and justified its demand to award a central role to those inside in the institutions of the state-in-the-making and the state itself. The demand by the inside to share in the responsibility, which would have been perceived in the past as presumptuous, appeared quite natural given the reality defined by the uprising.

Prominence on the part of the inside as prime bearer of the burden of the uprising was given concrete expression in the key role it was given in representing the Palestinian side, according to the Baker Plan of 1989. Were it not for the uprising, this development would have been hard to imagine. To this was added the weight of Israel's unflinching stance against any contact with the PLO leadership. This strengthened the role of the inside since it could potentially circumvent the political dead end. Because the uprising raised the question of why the inside was not qualified to take a significant role in representing itself after having become the focus of the Palestinian struggle, the leadership of the PLO outside was forced to take note of the desires and the constraints of the inside. The character of the relationship between the outside

and the inside became less lopsided in favor of the outside, and
mutual accommodation and adaptation became necessary between
the main camps and organizations on the outside and those inside.
Thus, despite direct dialogue between the United States and the
PLO leadership in Tunis (1988–90), the latter had to agree that
the inside would be the main representation in the early stages
of the political process according to the Baker Plan. The outside
would not have agreed to give this up, had it not been concerned about the inside distancing itself from it. This detachment
was obviated, however, by virtue of their mutual need for each
other.

Hence, because of the uprising, the character of the "inside–outside" relationship was transformed from absolute hierarchical sub-
servience of the inside – as a subordinate obeys his commander –
to one of mutuality and mutual dependence, albeit not always that
of equality. The rise in importance of the inside forced the outside
to take it into consideration and to refrain from dictating to it from
above. The inside was no longer in the pocket of the outside, a
group whose response could be taken for granted. Although the
inside continued to look toward the PLO in Tunis as the leadership,
it began to demand to be consulted.

Thus, the uprising blunted the dimension of coercion and veto
power in the relationship between the outside and the inside. In
addition, the central command of the outside had eased in the
absence of the guiding and organizing hand of Abu Jihad. The
vacuum created by his absence could not be filled by the many
who competed for his place, especially since the ranks of leadership
in the "PLO outside" dwindled with the murder of Abu Iyyad and
Abu-Hawl in 1991.

Unlike the situation following the 1982 Lebanon War, the basis
of legitimacy of the PLO leadership outside was indeed impaired
following the Kuwait crisis and Gulf War (1990–91). Its recovery
was largely contingent upon support from the Palestinians inside.
The more the outside depended upon the inside, the more weight
accrued to the inside. With the waning of the PLO in the wake of
the Gulf War, the inside – which had already functioned as the
area of the uprising – now became the primary diplomatic arena.
If, during the political moves around the Baker Plan, the United
States had searched for a way to circumvent Israel's opposition
to participation by the PLO through communicating with representatives from the inside, this became even more pronounced

now that the PLO leadership had contaminated itself by contacts with Saddam Hussein. The stock of the inside shot up by virtue of the sharp distinction the United States made between barring the PLO leadership from negotiations at the present stage and the legitimizing of prominent individuals on the inside for the task.

The failure inherent in relying on an external power such as Saddam Hussein corroborated the view inside that originally drove the uprising, i.e., that the Palestinians in the territories must take matters into their own hands, and that neither profit nor salvation will come from elsewhere. Hence, the importance of the inside was reconfirmed as it became clear that the connection with Saddam had been a strategic blunder. The economic bankruptcy of the PLO lessened dependence on the PLO outside. Despite the severe economic crisis in the territories, the PLO leadership could not come to the assistance of Palestinians there since payments from the Gulf states, led by Saudi Arabia, had ceased.

The growing prominence of Hamas in the territories as the main opposition to the PLO had an effect in opposing directions. On the one hand, this development underscored the conversion of the inside as the main arena of struggle not just between Israel and the Palestinians but also among the Palestinians themselves. On the other hand, by virtue of this, the inside required the legitimation of the PLO leadership on the outside to meet the challenge from Hamas.

Although the six years of *intifada* accentuated the centrality of the internal arena, this came at the expensive price of consider-able havoc and disarray. For example, the education of a whole generation of children has been in shambles. In its self-reckoning today, the mainstream of Fatah asserts that the *intifada* succeeded in confronting Israel and compelling it to recognize the PLO and the Palestinian collective identity, but admits that it has failed completely in its second aim – laying the foundations of a viable Palestinian society and institutions. The mainstream of the PLO has realized that it was presumptuous to expect results in this matter. In the wake of the Declaration of Principles (September 1993), they intend to concentrate on this aim of development and reconstruction (*tanmiyya-wa-i'mar*) during the coming interim period. They know that advancing the peace process toward a permanent settlement depends, first and foremost, on the ability of the self-governing authority to function well. This will be the primary criterion on which the capabilities of the Palestinians to govern themselves will be tested.

Leadership on the Inside: Beliefs, Attitudes and Images

Until now, we have focussed on the major milestones in the growing significance of the Palestinian inside. The question that arises is how the "objective" historical trends affected the subjective outlooks and images of the leadership on the inside. It should first be noted that routine use of the term "leadership" creates the impression of a monolithic group, which is far from true. The leaders of the inside are not cut of one fabric, but represent splits into regions and camps, and various personal and ideological tensions threaten unity even within the same camp.

If there is one common denominator that forges unity despite the diversity, it is the connection to one of the main organizations: Fatah, the Popular Front, the Democratic Front with its two factions, and the Palestinian People's Party (formerly the Palestinian Communist Party). This attachment means sharing a certain political perspective, from which conclusions are drawn concerning possible programs and action. Like the outside, the inside is also very diverse, but this does not prevent unity within a broad common framework.

In the absence of elections, which could clarify the degree of popular support for the leaders on the inside, the obvious question is whether they really deserve the title "leaders," or whether they only serve as spokespeople for the real leaders, who are concealed because of their activity in the field (we are referring to those called by the Palestinians *midaniyun* – activists on the ground). One must not conclude from their diplomatic skill as public speakers what their real status is in the population, and in this sense they are not spokespeople but "mailpeople" – both of the PLO outside and of other true leaders inside.

Indeed, so long as elections are not held, we are unable to answer this with certainty, although so far there have been no serious challenges to their status under the banner, "Who made you leader?" In the eyes of the PLO-supporting public (as opposed to those supporting the Hamas), it seems that a leader is not tested only in terms of his or her skills and characteristics, but also requires the approval of the PLO outside as a "nationalist figure."

The division of leaders inside the territories on the issue of the political process following the Gulf War sharpened the differences between two main streams within the PLO. On the one side were those who approved the dialogue as long as there was a possibility of realizing some political gains. These included the Fatah (prominent among them Faisal Husseini, Sari Nusseibeh, and Ziad Abu Zayyad), independents aligned with the Fatah and who joined them, such as Hanan Ashrawi (even though they were not always in complete agreement), the organization headed by Yassir 'Abd Rabbo – FIDA (most prominently 'Azmi Shu'ybi and Zahira Kamal), and the Palestinian People's Party (the former Communists) headed by Bashir Barghuthi. And on the other side were those opposed to the meetings, which included the Popular Front (most prominently 'Abd al-Latif Ghith) and the Democratic Front – the Na'if Hawatma faction (headed by 'Ali Abu Hilal).

This division into two streams illustrated the basic feature that the main dividing line was not *horizontal-geographic*, i.e., those from outside versus those from inside, but *vertical-ideological-political*, i.e., reflective of different perspectives and approaches, each of which has representatives from outside and inside. Although within the vertical division of political and ideological camps there was a geographical division of outside and inside, this was secondary to the primary division. Within each camp, efforts were made toward accommodating inside and outside components, and narrowing the differences between them. Just as the unifying factor on the outside was the institutions of the PLO, unifying the inside was the common desire of the leadership to sustain the uprising, despite differences of opinion and approach.

Although the primary division was by factions and organizations, this did not overshadow the division into inside and outside which cut through each and every faction. From this point of view, the inside was not a perfect duplicate of the outside, and was far from a pure automatic extension. These two divisions combined to create the patterns of thought and action characteristic of the inside as opposed to the outside, despite their belonging to the same faction. There is no doubt in this regard that the daily contact and friction of the inside with Israel distinguishes, for example, the leadership of the Fatah inside from the leadership of the Fatah outside.

This has important implications for the image of Israel in the eyes of the inside and the general approach to it. The different point of view shaped a different approach which created disparities between those on the outside and the inside. To bridge this gap, the leadership of Fatah outside took advantage of the familiarity with the territories of those who had been expelled and had come to Tunis. Throughout the uprising, these individuals served as liaisons to the inside. The Fatah applied to them the Arabic saying, "There are none better than Meccans for knowing its byways." Thus, 'Akram Haniyya and Jibril Rajub were put in charge of links with the West Bank, and Muhmmad Dahalan, of links with Gaza. What is true for the Fatah is true for other organizations, which also reflect divisions between the components from inside and outside the territories.

Even prior to the uprising, which they did not need to reinforce their view, prominent figures of the Fatah such as Husseini and Nusseibeh supported direct negotiations with the government of Israel, then headed by the Likud. Even then they had concluded that contacts with the Israeli left alone would not be useful, and that a path must be found to penetrate the center of the Israeli political spectrum.

The clearest expression of this was the memorandum issued jointly with then-Likud member Moshe Amirav in August 1987.[9] What was innovative about Husseini and Nusseibeh's position in this memorandum was not just the practical willingness of a PLO-identified figure to enter into direct negotiations, but also that, for the first time since Palestinian rejection of the Camp David format, they were authorized by Arafat to agree to an interim arrangement of 3–5 years to precede a permanent settlement. Thus they adopted the component of stages from the Camp David format. We saw, above, that harbingers of this approach had appeared at the initiation of people on the inside (such as the mayors of Bethlehem, Gaza, and others) in the wake of the Lebanon War in 1982. Even though the initiative was approved by Arafat, it was a kind of trial balloon which did not take off. But as time passed, the strains which had fostered this initiative in the first place did not ease but became even more pressing. In addition, during 1985–86, the attempt to devise a permanent settlement based on a joint Jordan-PLO effort failed.

Thus the uprising, which increased the weight of the inside, enabled the leadership of the pragmatic stream in the territories, headed by Faisal Husseini, to exert subtle influence on the PLO to adopt the format of a peace process in stages. Now the inside could demand a more prominent role for its representatives, and its influence became tangible. The role of the PLO outside was relegated more and more to behind the scenes. It was the Fatah leadership in the territories which urged the PLO leadership in late 1989 and early 1990 to take part in the Baker Plan, with the inside representing the PLO by proxy. For example, Sari Nusseibeh proposed in November 1989 the need of the inside to participate in the elections in the territories with a view toward self-rule. Before the Gulf War, Baker's Five-Point Plan had focussed on elections and an interim settlement, without going into detail about what the permanent settlement would entail. Likewise after the Gulf War, a similar plan for resolving the Palestinian issue was on the agenda, and representatives from the inside and Baker were discussing it with the PLO's agreement and authorization. The format of a settlement in stages, rejected by the PLO outside for so many years, has thus become acceptable through pressure from the inside. Its ability to exert influence along these lines has grown with its increased status in the wake of the uprising and the Gulf War.

Three main ingredients are salient in the political culture of the followers of the PLO in the territories:

- First, their experience is stamped with the Palestinian nationalism headed by the PLO. The present generation of leadership inside could be called "the generation of 1967," because most began to assert themselves politically following the 1967 war. This is also true for the Palestinian residents of the territories, 70 percent of whom are under 30 years of age. Thus, for example, eight of the eleven representatives of the inside who met with Baker in various rounds of talks were born in the years between 1940 and 1950. Trailing behind them is the younger generation, for whom the uprising served as a formative period in which it stood up for its political views; this group is already knocking on the door, demanding its share of leadership based on its contribution and sacrifice.

    Though Palestinians on the inside – population and leaders from both the "1967 generation" and the "*intifada* generation" – have not always agreed with the actions of the PLO leadership, and have voiced their criticism, nevertheless, for them the PLO as an institution was equivalent to Palestinian identity. This means that most of them were born into some sort of Palestinian identity; this phenomenon is self-evident for them. Hamas itself can testify that this feeling is firmly rooted, and thus it had to accommodate itself to the spirit of the uprising and to take care not to be perceived as standing apart from the community. This led it to adopt a positive attitude toward Palestinian nationalism, albeit still subordinate to Islam.[10] This feeling of Palestinian uniqueness is further sharpened by virtue of the ongoing contact and friction with the Israeli civil and military regime and population.

- Second, proximity with Israel is a fundamental ingredient in the world view of those on the inside. This influences, and is influenced by, the political character of the various camps. For the pragmatic mainstream, proximity has fostered adoption of a sober and realistic approach, which sets aside psychological barriers and ideological obstacles with which the Fatah leadership outside may still be preoccupied. Thus, the willingness for direct deliberations with the government of Israel, and a process of stages, grew from inside rather than outside the territories. The opposite occurs within the Hamas: proximity and friction with Israel, combined with their basic religious world view, drive them to the other extreme.

- The third ingredient is the obvious fact that the inside is more attentive to – and therefore more constrained by – public opinion in the West Bank and Gaza. The leaders inside cannot ignore their immediate constituency, which has greater influence where there is no state or regime to control it. Similarly, the outside cannot ignore the climate of opinion inside but, by definition, is more detached and less constrained by it. The outside is more sensitive to the vicissitudes in its own arena – the Arab world. From time to time, this different environment pushed the inside to take more intransigent attitudes than the outside, especially when the peace process was seen by the population to be an exercise in futility (for instance following Israel's December 1992 expulsion to Lebanon of Hamas activists). At the same time, the PLO in Tunis had a vital interest in proving itself indispensable by adopting pragmatic positions.

Although the pragmatic camp in the territories was careful not to state this in so many words, it seemed to have an obvious self-interest in starting with an interim arrangement. During the transitional self-rule period, it would rule and could consolidate its power locally and nail down its status – not just in relation to Israel but also in relation to the PLO outside. It would strike roots among the Palestinians through elections.

Since the establishment of self-rule would reflect the disengagement of Israel in the territories in comparison with the previous situation, it would be credited with achievements such as halting the settlements, control over land and water resources, establishment of central governing institutions, etc. This would have consolidated its own power inside and strengthened its influence over PLO decisions.

The plunge by the PLO outside into the interim arrangement known as "Gaza and Jericho First," based on the Oslo Agreement between Israel and the PLO (September 1993), altered the resolve of the Fatah inside to use the interim arrangements to achieve dominance. Indeed, their enthusiasm for interim arrangements has steadily diminished since then. The massacre of Muslim worshippers in Hebron (February 1994) added more objective weight to their skepticism: Since delaying the decisions on difficult issues (such as settlements) obviously did not ease the friction between Palestinians and Israelis, but seemed to aggravate it, the question arose of whether interim arrangements only exacerbate rather than relieve the situation. As a result, Fatah leaders on the inside began a vigorous campaign to deviate from the language of the Oslo Agreement – to skip directly from implementation of "Gaza and Jericho First" to discussions about a permanent arrangement.

Contention and Correction

Although the inside has clearly and consistently gained in importance, the connection of the nationalist public (in contrast to the fundamentalists) with the PLO has not been severed and identification continues on principle. A collision between the inside and the outside is averted through a process of adjustment and mutual accommodation, even though relations are far from harmonious and there are periodic struggles for power and control.

What are the reasons and causes for the strong leverage of the PLO outside over the inside? Heading the list of factors which push from within to preserve the connection is the reality that the vast majority of Palestinians in the territories belong to the generation that grew up equating the institution of the PLO with Palestinian identity and nationalism. For them, the PLO is the "people's representative" and even Hamas' supporters cannot dismiss this fact. Again, this identification is symbolic, and does not mean that the Palestinians have no complaints or grievances against the PLO leadership. But the symbolic identification enables the PLO to preserve its exalted position even during periods of material slump, when the supply of basic needs is difficult.

Preserving the connection with the PLO is, then, a vital need of leaders on the inside. From their connection with the PLO, they draw their authority and legitimacy in the eyes of the Palestinian public. We saw, above, that even when they held a position of unprecedented strength, during the talks with Baker, the leaders of the pragmatic camp claimed repeatedly that their flexibility was dependent upon their credibility among the Palestinian public, and that this credibility derived from their public identification with the PLO. Another factor fostering the connection stems from the search of leaders on the inside for an overall settlement. Although, as noted, they support a settlement in stages, they categorically reject any arrangement that would meet the needs of the inside only. They demand that the permanent settlement be comprehensive and deal with the issue of the Palestinian diaspora, which cannot be addressed outside the PLO.

Another important endogenous factor concerns the divisiveness and heterogeneity of the Palestinian inside. The territories are chock-full of geographical, ideological, social, and economic polarities, and the connection with the PLO constitutes the primary unifying and integrating force. Leaders on the inside frequently appeal to the PLO outside to serve as arbitrator for matters in contention which they cannot settle by themselves. Under Arafat, the PLO leadership exploits this to maintain the dependence of the inside, based on the system of "divide and rule." Thus this factor, which "pushes" from within, is transformed into one which "pulls" to preserve the link of the territories to the PLO. The leadership of the PLO deliberately refrains from locking into one partner in the territories and maintains a multiplicity of partners or centers of gravity, each of which owes its authority to the PLO. Thus, several organizations in the territories – the Fatah leadership, the Unified National Command, the *Tanzim* (the Fatah activists on the ground), etc., operate in parallel.

By maintaining a multiplicity of centers in the territories, the PLO ensures their neutralization and the concentration of power in its own hands, which leads the inside, in general, to do its bidding. Additional means used by the PLO leadership to preserve the connection are threats and awarding or withholding monies to those close to it. Thus, despite the apparent absence of the PLO outside from the peace process in Washington, it maintained, through link-preserving elements, a prominent, behind-the-scenes presence.

Had a peace process developed according to the letter and the spirit of the Madrid format, the relative importance of the PLO inside would have risen and possibly even become dominant over time: a PLO in which the outside has a starring role and the inside serves as its satellite is not the same as a PLO in which the inside occupies the center and the outside revolves around it. If such a transformation had transpired, reflecting a change in personnel and style of leadership, the significance would have been that the inside had taken control of the PLO and represented the Palestinians en masse, including those in the diaspora. Had this happened, the inside would still have insisted on a comprehensive settlement, meaning one which addressed all the open issues, including the right of self-determination and the right of return. With all the significance of such a change of guard, it would have remained within the domain of the PLO.

For this reason, Yassir Arafat was very apprehensive of being marginalized by the political process according to the Madrid format. As a result of the Gulf War, he was forced to approve a political process whose progress could, paradoxically, work against him. His solution to the dilemma took the form of demonstrating his indispensability both negatively – as a force which could obstruct – and positively – as an activating and driving force. In the public channel in Washington, he functioned as an obstruction and undermined the strengthening of the inside; while in the hidden channel of Oslo, he served as a driving force, proving that things could be accomplished only through him.

We know what happened, but we do not know what might have been. Thus it remains an open question what would have happened if events had been reversed – had Israel been willing to give the same concessions to the inside (in a back channel, not in the Washington open channel, which was doomed to failure) that it gave to the PLO outside in Oslo. Could the inside have overcome the disruptive role of Arafat in Washington by showing the Palestinians that only the inside can deliver the goods?

The insiders could have acquired authority only through a dynamic peace process which would have been crowned with an elected self-governing entity, while Arafat was able to obstruct their progress. The only way out could have been for Israel to have made them an offer (such as that made in Oslo) that would have gained the backing of the population and compelled a weakening Arafat to comply with it. To my mind, this option was not exhausted.

Thus, while negotiations were being pursued with Israel, the PLO on the outside and the inside were vying for dominance in a struggle that took place beneath the surface. I have no doubt that this will continue to cast its imprint in the wake of the Declaration of Principles, albeit in another form. While waging common cause against the Hamas, the Palestinian self-government will have to forge a delicate balance between those from the outside and those from the inside. The disparate experiences will become tangibly felt: those from the inside will undoubtedly claim that had it not been for the *intifada*, whose burden they bore, the outside would never have gotten in, and that this should be reflected in the division of jobs and authority. On the other hand, those from the outside will demand their lion's share, reminding them of the sacrifices they made in the more distant past in Jordan and Lebanon. Hence it is not surprising that the insiders are apprehensive that Arafat will try to delay general elections in the West Bank, in order to limit the significance of the inside. Here, too, Palestinian self-government will be put to the test.

Vox Populi: The Formation of Public Opinion in the Territories

Since the outbreak of the uprising in the West Bank and the Gaza Strip at the end of 1987, the Palestinian leadership both inside and out has become keenly aware of the special role played by public opinion in the territories. Before the uprising, the failure of all efforts to replace the PLO with a widely supported alternative fostered a sense of complacency – a sense that the obedient public in the territories was in its pocket.

The uprising – not decreed from above by orders and decisions but as an outburst of popular feeling – proved that public opinion in the territories could move beyond passivity to a role of initiating and activism. The uprising was also the anvil on which the Hamas was forged and organized as the main opposition within the territories, vying with the national camp for public attention and support, which it wishes to woo from the Fatah.

Thus, two necessary conditions evolved in the territories which have enabled formation of the concept of "public opinion" (*al-Ra'y al-'Aamm* in Arabic), as distinct from individual moods.[11] The first is that opinions about public issues are not limited to a small group, but are held by a large majority, both because the constricted geographical dimensions narrow the gaps between city and town, and because the centrality of the national problem – coping with Israeli rule – involves everyone. The second condition for the evolution of active public opinion is a sense of efficacy – the expectation that what people think and express about various issues can bring about change if it consolidates as "popular will." There need not be the expectation that their desires will always prevail, but they must believe that their opinions will always be heard and sometimes will prevail.

Public opinion comprises various convictions, and the Palestinian public is neither unified nor homogeneous. Even when it wins the attention of the leadership, public opinion is but one important component among the many constraints and motives which affect the direction of a decision and its content. Public opinion generally puts its stamp on the order of priorities, but cannot delve into the details and nuances. At most, it can determine an overall attitude, in contrast with a well-formulated position.

Inhabitants of the West Bank and Gaza have relatively high political awareness, but lack a state or a regime and government. This special combination magnifies the importance of local public opinion. In dictatorships and authoritarian regimes such as those in the Arab world, the government controls the tools and media used to direct, oppress and – upon occasion – even placate and appease public opinion.

While public opinion is taken into consideration by individual Arab rulers, it is even more critical in the situation of "un-rule" that exists in the territories. Here a daily battle is waged for the loyalty of the public, a kind of continuous referendum, though latent and unofficial. The uprising made perceptible to all the ability of public opinion in the territories to serve as a motivating force and not just an obstructive force which obeys outside dictates, the role assigned to it in the past by the PLO. A change subsequently ensued in the self-image of the inhabitants of the territories, and also in their image to the outside. It is not surprising that ever since the uprising, the number of public opinion polls conducted in the territories has testified to increased attention to public opinion there. These polls in the territories are unique in the Arab world. In no other Arab country does the ruling power allow independent public opinion polls.

One manifest indication of the formation of political awareness and its diffusion throughout the strata of Palestinian society is the relatively broad willingness to be mobilized for public activities. A clear expression of the breadth of political awareness is the intense rivalry in sectoral elections (trade unions, chambers of commerce, student unions, etc.). Participation in these elections is high and their politicization is immediate, since they tend to deviate from the narrow professional field into the broad political sphere.

Another factor should not be underestimated – the extended experience of the inside living side by side with democracy in Israel. It is superfluous to note that this close proximity to Israel distinguishes the Palestinian public from residents of other Arab countries. Thus Israel has contributed to the formation of Palestinian public opinion in two ways: Israeli military rule in the territories posed a communal challenge that heightened Palestinian political awareness and consolidated its aspiration to eliminate it; while the democratic government in Israel serves as a model for many Palestinians and is con-sidered worthy of learning and even espousing. From their observation of Israel, they have learned to appreciate the role of public opinion in a democratic country and to recognize ways to affect it through the media. The practical experience in democracy has been adopted by some public leaders in the territories, such as Faisal Husseini, in appealing to Israeli public opinion.

The broad political awareness in the territories should not be confused with unanimity and consensus. On the contrary, the more heightened the political awareness, for the reasons noted above, the sharper the differences of opinion and position. Hence developed political awareness has not narrowed the differences, but broadened and exacerbated them.

Testimony to the growing impact of public opinion on the lead-ership of the PLO outside and the public figures inside is the frequency with which they address the issue of their credibility among the population in the territories. This key word "credibility" (*misdaqiyya*) is often used in the context of their image among the Palestinian public, i.e., their reputation or popularity. Thus the

Palestinian leadership evaluates itself and is evaluated by others on this criterion.

In the 1970s and 1980s, the PLO leadership still enjoyed undisputed status as the source of supreme legitimacy. This legitimacy (*shar'iyya*) was enough to advance the popularity (*sh'abiyya*) of whomever it favored. Thus the PLO leadership could grant legitimacy to itself and to those under its aegis. These individuals gained immunity – a kind of seal of approval or imprimatur – against rivals and opponents. Accordingly, fate did not smile on those denied this immunity. Their public credibility was thus derived from the aegis bestowed by the PLO.

However, as the challenge to the PLO increased – from Hamas, for example – the situation reversed and the legitimacy of the PLO became primarily a function of its credibility: the willingness of the public in the territories to support it. It could be said that the factor of credibility thrust aside the factor of legitimacy, and the latter became conditional upon and secondary to the former. As long as the legitimacy of the PLO had been assured, its credibility was not at issue; the moment there were cracks in the consensus and it was no longer immune from mistakes and criticism, the issue of its credibility became paramount.

This should by no means be taken to imply that the PLO no longer has clout; even now, Fatah leaders in the territories require the endorsement of the PLO. But independently of that, their own status in the population carries at least as much weight. This is true for Haidar 'Abd al-Shafi, for example, whose criticism of the PLO leadership not only did no harm to his popularity, but even enhanced it. What is more, while most Fatah leaders are still dependent on the good graces of the PLO leadership, certainly for acceptance among their supporters in the territories, the times are gone when the PLO leadership could bestow legitimacy and impose its will; these too require the consent of public opinion in the territories.

The great Russian historian Kaluchevski summed up his thinking by claiming that for the buds of a trend to bloom into a major historical force, they must evolve into one of the following patterns or their combination: public opinion, institutions, or law.[12] These constitute a kind of "carrier wave" on which events are swept along and gather into a great historical trend. The leaders of various Palestinian camps seem to be locked into a fierce internal battle for

Palestinian public opinion, which will only become more fierce, and whose results will affect development into other patterns: institutionalization and law.

Dominant Trends in Palestinian Public Opinion

In the absence of clear-cut measures of public opinion, such as national elections or reliable surveys, there is no alternative but to use as indicators the results of various sectoral elections (trade unions, chambers of commerce, student unions). If election results during the last three years are examined with regard to how many voted for each camp (and not with regard to who won, since these elections are based on "winner takes all"), there is clearly an equilibrium between the two main camps (Fatah and Hamas), with a slight advantage to the Fatah, i.e., the *number of voters* for Fatah candidates is 5–10 percent more than those who vote for Hamas (40–45 percent for Hamas; 50–55 percent for Fatah).[13] The balance of voters is divided among the factions of the Palestinian left, who were badly hurt by both the collapse of Marxism and the Soviet Union, and the concomitant rise of Islamic fundamentalism at home. This equilibrium between the two major camps has enhanced the bargaining power of the factions on the Palestinian left, enabling them to tip the scales in sectoral elections.

The main drawback of sectoral elections as a gauge of Palestinian public opinion is that they reflect only those who identify with the organized factions (Fatah, Hamas, and the left), but not the large segment of the public which is independent – who do not identify with them and who are not powerful or committed, nor stand to gain by such association. This segment is reflected not in sectoral election results, but in the public opinion polls periodically conducted in the West Bank and Gaza.[14]

Although precise data do not exist about this independent segment, both large rival camps agree as to its size and political tendencies. Both camps claim that this segment constitutes about one-third of the population in the territories, and that it basically holds a pragmatic view closer to that of the nationalist camp of Fatah. Both also agree that as hopes dwindled for concrete achievements from the Madrid Conference, this segment's support for the pragmatic approach diminished, and it moved to the middle ground between the two polarized major camps. Its disappointment in the lack of concrete results has not pushed it into the arms of Hamas, but invested it with skepticism and pessimism concerning the entire process. This is not apathy but rather confusion, as its discouragement with the barren Washington negotiations did not undermine its belief that the Hamas is still not a better alternative to a productive peace process.

Although the fence-sitters are mostly conservative-religious, for whom Islam constitutes an important value in their self-image, they are far from religious fanatics and they do not believe that fundamentalism is the key to a practical solution. For this reason, the expulsion of the Hamas and the economic distress resulting from extended closures did not engender a mass move to the Hamas; also for this reason, the independent segment expressed sweeping support for the Declaration of Principles (September 1993), which appeared to be an escape from the morass. Indeed, Hamas notes with disappointment that economic distress did not push residents of the territories into its camp, but actually reinforced their view that positive economic change is contingent upon progress toward a peace agreement.

The fundamental quarrel between the Fatah and the Hamas about what ought to be done should not overshadow the agreement between them about what ought not to be done. Both share a deep concern about the destructive effects of a civil war (*fitna*) among the Palestinians. This approach reflects the repugnance of the entire public over an internal war that would devastate Palestinian society. Thus the strict opposition to a civil war that has prevailed within both camps until now, is derived from their awareness of the extreme severity with which the Palestinian public regards such a development.

Both sides claim that the main battle between them is over the hearts of this public. Both also subscribe to the prediction that if the hopes raised by the Declaration of Principles are dashed and if the peace process does not produce the promised economic changes, the Hamas will benefit over the course of time. Hamas is not sitting idly by, but seeks to expedite this latter trend. The conclusion is clear: the period of Palestinian self-rule will intensify the rivalry between the Fatah and the Hamas for the heart of the floating voter. And this voter's support for one of these camps will depend on the success or failure of Palestinian self-rule.

Notes

1. The differences between the "outside" and the "inside" in the PLO
   are considered by Palestinians – both intellectuals and PLO activists –
   to be a sensitive issue that should be raised as little as possible. Their
   concern stems, no doubt, from the assumption that the very placement
   of the issue on the agenda can exacerbate it, hence it is better to let
   sleeping dogs lie. Nonetheless, Palestinian political literature does
   include some studies which raise this issue, although even they
   tend to stress the symbiosis between the outside and the inside
   rather than the tension between them. See: Issa al-Shuaibi, *Palestinian
   Statism Entity: Consciousness and Institutional Development 1947–1977*
   (Arabic) (Beirut: Research Center, Palestine Liberation Organization,
   1979); 'Ali al-Jarbawi, *The Political Uprising and Leadership in the West
   Bank and the Gaza Strip: A Study of the Political Elite* (Arabic) (Beirut:
   Dar al-Tali'a, April 1989); Ziyad Abu-'Amr, *The Islamic Movement in
   the West Bank and the Gaza Strip* (Arabic) (Jerusalem: Dar al-'Aswar,
   1989).
2. For the historical background of the West Bank and the Gaza Strip
   until the *intifada*, see Moshe Ma'oz, *Palestinian Leadership in the West
   Bank: The Changing Role of the Arab Mayors Under Jordan and Israel* (London: Frank Cass, 1984); Emile Sahliyeh, *In Search of Leadership: West
   BankPoliticsSince1967*(Washington,D.C.:TheBrookingsInstitution,1988);
   Helena Cobban, *The Palestinian Liberation Organization: People, Power
   and Politics* (Cambridge: Cambridge University Press, 1984), ch. 8.
3. Palestine Liberation Organization, *The Palestinian National Council,
   13th Conference (The Conference of the Shahid* [martyr] *Kamal Junbalat)*
   (Arabic), 12–22 March 1977, pp. 105–107.
4. See the analysis of the Popular Front concerning this Fatah approach:
   Popular Front for the Liberation of Palestine, Office of Occupied Land,
   Regarding the National Guidance Committee on the Inside (Arabic), 30 July
   1980, pp. 6–7.
5. Ibid.
6. Emile Sahliyeh, *In Search of Leadership*, pp. 167–171; "Palestinian Peace
   Document" (Arabic), November 1982 (in my possession); see also, the
   criticism of the Democratic Front on these initiatives of leaders inside:
   Al-Hurriyya, 29 May 1983, p. 13.
7. "Palestinian Peace Document," paragraph 4.
8. Zeev Schiff and Ehud Yaari, *Intifada* (Hebrew) (Tel Aviv: Schocken,
   1990) pp. 370–374 (English edition, New York: Simon & Schuster,
   1990); Emile Sahliyeh, *In Search of Leadership*, p. 172.
9. Schiff and Yaari, pp. 369–370.
10. Hamas, *The Hamas Covenant* (Arabic), place of publication uncited, 18
    August 1988, paragraphs 6–7, pp. 9–11.
11. Daniel Lerner, *The Passing of Traditional Society* (New York: Free Press,
    1958), p. 99.

12. David Pollock, "The 'Arab Street'? Public Opinion in the Arab World," *Policy Papers*, No. 32 (Washington, D.C.: Washington Institute for Near East Policy, 1992) p. 2. See also, Shibley Telhami, "Arab Public Opinion and the Gulf War," *Political Science Quarterly*, Vol. 108, No. 3, 1993, pp. 437–451.

13. Michael Confino, *From St. Petersburg to Leningrad: Essays in Russian History* (Hebrew) (Tel Aviv: Ofakim Library, Am Oved, 1993), pp. 102–103.

14. See, for example, the detailed analysis of Dr. Mahmud al-Zahar, one of the Hamas leaders in the Gaza Strip, *Al-Quds* (East Jerusalem), 1 November 1992.

15. See, for example, Jerusalem Center for Strategic Studies, Maqdes, *Strategic Review* (Arabic), No. 16, Vol. 2, July 1992; Center for Palestine Research and Studies, Nablus, *Analytical Reading of the Palestinian-Israeli Agreement "Gaza and Jericho First"* (Arabic), No. 1, September 1993, Appendix 3, pp. 48–53; see also, the survey conducted by the above center, *Al-Quds*, 23 March 1994, 28 March 1994. Since the Declaration of Principles (September 1993), the Center for Palestine Research and Studies in Nablus conducts a monthly public opinion survey among approximately 2,000 respondents from the West Bank and the Gaza Strip.

15

Policy Dynamics of the Palestinian Leadership

Manuel Hassassian

From the inception of World War I until the signing of the declaration of principles between the Palestinians and the Israelis on 13 September 1993, several options were considered by the Palestinians that were decisive in leading to dramatic shifts in their positions and attitudes at critical junctures of their history. By the 19th Palestinian National Council of 1988, Palestinians endorsed the principles of political accommodation based on Security Council resolutions 242 and 338 with the objective of arriving at a two-state solution.

History demonstrates that territorial conflicts pose a great threat to peace, harmony and interdependence. In spite of dramatic global transformations in technology, economics and politics, regional conflicts based on territoriality continue to command attention in the international arena. Of course, other avenues have been opened to settle territorial disputes beyond war, i.e., the use of bargaining and negotiation as tools of diplomacy. In such a process, perceptions, and beliefs and cognitions enter into the calculus of pragmatism, of "making choices within constraints."

The essential stakes in the Israeli-Palestinian conflict, however, are the core-value systems by which nation-states and peoples define their existence, sovereignty, territory and, above all, security. For Israel, a basic dilemma is the relationship of territory to security and survival, and the question of "secure boundaries" has run through its history as a modern state.[1] Israel's acquisition of territory after the 1967 War has put it into greater opposition to Palestinian claims and those concerning the territorial integrity of neighboring Arab states.

The Palestinians have been deprived of territory and denied status as a sovereign state, two important factors that mold their political identity. The Palestinian concept of how much territory is required for a viable sovereign state has changed over time.[2] From an early policy laying claim to all mandatory Palestine, the Palestinians today are settling for the West Bank and Gaza Strip, comprising 22 percent of historic Palestine. Even with the change, it is clear that Palestinian-Israeli positions collide over the same contested territory.

Since 1945, the dominant issue for the Arab world has been the Palestinian question and the refusal of the Arab nations to recognize the Zionist state in the Middle East. This conflict has exacerbated instability in the Arab world and undermined all hope for unity and cooperation.[3] Palestinian nationalism has developed and matured, however, under the leadership of the PLO.

By a decision of the Arab League, the PLO was officially created in 1964. President Nasser of Egypt, at that stage the champion of the Arab cause, backed the idea in order to coopt the new organization into the League,[4] and to provide a means of preventing any Palestinian action against Israel that might draw Egypt into confrontation with it.[5] The PLO was headed by Ahmad al-Shuqayri, known for his close relationship with Nasser, and the Palestinian Liberation Army (PLA) was directly under the Arab Unified Command, headed by an Egyptian. The inaugural conference of the PLO was held in May 1964 and its chairman spared no effort in raising material and public support from the various Arab capitals, especially the Gulf states.

Since its inception the PLO was embroiled in factional bickering because its decision-making processes were subject to inter-Arab rivalries, particularly these involving Syria and Egypt and, to a certain degree, Jordan. But Fatah, the leading organization within the PLO, emphasized military action against Israel and managed to rise above the old Arab feuding.[6]

The 1967 War was a disaster for the Arab states as well as for the Palestinians. Another cohort of Palestinian refugees, who went to Jordan and to other Arab states like Syria and Lebanon, were denied the right to return to their homes, while the rest of the Palestinians were destined to stay on their soil and suffer from Israeli occupation. Arab military might was shattered and the leadership disoriented and destroyed, whilst the international community was more sympathetic towards Israel than towards the intransigent regimes, as they were presented in the international press and world public opinion. The Palestinian leadership became disenchanted with the Arab regimes, even when they were supportive, and began to call for Palestinian organizations to be independent of Arab control. They turned from the cause of pan-Arabism and Arab unity to Palestinian nationalism, and the struggle for independence became their main concern.

After the 1967 débâcle, there appeared an urgent need for the reconstruction of Palestinian life. Ideology, armed struggle and diplomatic posture were secondary to the building of an organization that could claim and act on behalf of all Palestinians. The Palestinian leadership concentrated its efforts to gain legitimacy and credibility not only from Palestinians but also from the international community. This involved purchasing arms, raising funds and developing a territorial base that could help in maintaining close contact with the Palestinians on the West Bank and in Gaza, as well as launching military activities against Israel.

Building such an organizational structure was difficult and required strenuous efforts. Struggling to consolidate their power, the leading Palestinian organizations could not afford open confrontation with the small organizations that proliferated during that time. However, the large commando groups contrived, more by persuasion than by sheer force, to coopt these small groups. A tolerance of division and diversity therefore characterized the Palestinian nationalist movement, and a sense of pluralism thrived, to become almost a tradition, though social divisions and fragmented authority could not be completely avoided. But by February 1969, Fatah had succeeded in controlling the PLO and in uniting the fragmented commando movement to a considerable degree.[7]

The PLO has managed to maintain and operate a remarkable infrastructure against all odds, thus catering to the political and existential needs of the dispersed Palestinians.[8] According to Cheryl Rubenberg:

> The PLO's role goes beyond the traditional roles of national lib
> eration movements, for it not only struggles for the attainment
> of the national political rights of the Palestinian people, but it is
> the only instrument for the reconstitution of Palestinian shattered
> society. . . . The PLO has to rehabilitate a nation as well as to struggle
> for its liberation.[9]

Despite the militant elements in the organizational structure of the PLO, it succeeded in building a civilian-institutional infrastructure that tended to the needs of the Palestinian nation in exile. The myriad social institutions and their institutionalization have been crucial in the development of a framework to deal with the internal political processes and strategy formulations.[10] It has provided the PLO with the means and mechanisms for containing factionalism and divisiveness among the resistance groups, and for representing the Palestinians abroad, not to mention the rendering of medicare and social care to the refugee communities in Lebanon and elsewhere.[11]

Though Fatah was the largest, wealthiest and most influential group within the PLO, it could not arbitrarily set PLO policies without coordination with the other smaller groups. It feared fragmentation and could not risk losing its representative and democratic image, and support from Arab states, which prompted it to afford the smaller groups a political leverage far beyond their proportions and capabilities.[12]

Fatah always managed, however, to set objectives geared to promote unity and avoid factionalization.[13] This has made the PLO unique in comparison with other national liberation movements. In 1981, Yasir Arafat, chairman of the PLO Executive Committee, explained this uniqueness:

> Many people think that the cause of Palestine resembles that of Vietnam, Algeria, or even South Africa. But although there is a resemblance in some aspects, there is something entirely unique about our cause. What we have been, and still are, confronted with is not merely foreign invasion, occupation, and even settlement. All this has been experienced by other countries. But no other country has been confronted with a plan to liquidate its national identity, as has happened in the case of the Palestinian people. It goes beyond anything previously recorded in modern history.[14]

This institutionalization of the PLO reflects the political maturity of the Palestinian people and its historic leadership, thus legitimizing its quest for a nationhood and ultimately for statehood. Hence, it becomes important to mention the political institutions of the PLO.

According to the Fundamental Law, the most important political institutions of the PLO are the PNC, the Central Council, and the Executive Committee. Because it has three branches of government, the legislative, the executive, and the judiciary, the PLO has effectively a state infrastructure.[15]

In addition to its political organs, the PLO was able to develop its own regular army and an active military police in Lebanon. A closer look at the formal structure of the major political process organs of the PLO prompts several inferences about the nature of the political process in the PLO and the extent of power sharing and collective decision-making. The basic premise is that over the years the PLO has established a quasi-state form of organization that functions in a democratic way. It is valid to say that the legitimacy of the PLO is derived from the Palestinian people because "the PLO as an umbrella organization subsumes all the various elements of the Palestinian nationalist movement [which] makes authoritarianism an unlikely *modus operandi.*"[16]

Further, the PLO has succeeded in maintaining its legitimacy by integrating the complex positions and attitudes of the various Palestinian social strata. The high level of literacy among Palestinians and their political consciousness, deepened by dispersion, occupation and repression by Israel as well as by authoritarian Arab regimes, gives the Palestinian a unique identity.

In terms of decision-making, the PLO strives towards consensus, although constitutionally, a simple majority will do. Unlike other Arab states, the Chief Executive of the PLO cannot make independent arbitrations or unilateral decisions; he must use the tools of persuasion and bargaining in order to arrive at a balance among the diverse political trends in the PLO. It is fairly clear that authoritarianism could exacerbate factionalism and divisiveness, a trend that could dismantle the PLO and deprive it of its legitimacy.

Of course, one cannot entirely overlook the elements of factionalism in the PLO, based not only on tactics but on ideology, and since Fatah is the predominant faction it can often act unilaterally without deep confrontations and outright contradictions. Chairman Arafat has been a master of diplomacy in containing Palestinian factionalism, and has successfully contrived to use the PLO's political structure to promote his ideas and achieve his pragmatic moves. Of course, he could not have survived débâcles if he had not been backed up by popular mass-based support, in particular from the Palestinians living in the Occupied Territories. This leads to the conclusion that democratic practices are embedded in the pragmatic politics of the PLO. In particular, the PLO's survival has depended heavily on a full synchronization between the "exterior" and "interior" Palestinians, and the *intifada* illustrates this phenomenon best.[17]

In the light of present political realities, one detects a clear transformation in Palestinian politics, especially since the Israeli invasion
of Lebanon in 1982. With the invasion, however, the military and
civilian infrastructures of the Palestinians were almost shattered.

It is evident that three major internal changes within the
Palestinian national movement have been a major catalyst in
changing the strategy of the PLO in its political struggle against
Israel. One of the major changes has been in the role and status of
the formal political organizations, i.e., the commando groups that
compose the PLO. A second major shift was the concentration of
power in Arafat's hands as the undisputed leader of the PLO. A
third major shift was the shift in focus of the national struggle from
the periphery to the center, i.e., the Occupied Territories.[18]

Naturally, the dramatic shifts in PLO politics were not made
in a vacuum, but were a culmination to a particular period of
inter-Arab politics involving especially Jordan and Syria. The focus
of the political struggle shifted to the West Bank and Gaza, since
the PLO's formal institutions and infrastructure had been partially
shattered. The only trump card left for Arafat to play was the West
Bank card, and he succeeded ingeniously in achieving that objective.
His trip to Egypt after the PLO's expulsion from Beirut added a
major component to the success of PLO diplomacy, though there
was a clear demarcation between the Arafat mainstream and the
"rejectionist" opposition composed of the PFLP-General Command
(PFLP-GC) and other groups, which together formed the Palestine
National Salvation Front in March 1985.[19] But in the end its impact
was marginal because it failed to advocate a viable alternative to the
diplomatic posture advocated by Arafat and Fatah.

On the other hand, after Fatah split in 1983, the PFLP and the
DFLP formed a "loyal" opposition camp, critical of Arafat, yet loyal
to the PLO framework. Unlike the National Salvation Front, the two
groups were successful in mobilizing support through the building
of organizational structures in the Occupied Territories and in exile.
The opposition to Arafat hammered on political issues, mainly the
diplomatic strategy of Fatah and the closer relations with Jordan and
Egypt. It was not until the 19th PNC, in 1988, that the traditional
veto power held by the smaller factions was undermined in the
decision-making process. Subsequently, Fatah has dominated the
PLO and confirmed its central role in the PLO's decision-making
process.[20]

According to Emile Sahliyeh:

Although Fatah's moderate leadership demonstrated some willing-ness to give the floating peace plans a chance, it simultaneously continued to pay lip service to the relevance of the strategy of military struggle. The moderate leadership was unwilling to gamble with too many odds working against it. With such mixed feelings and sentiments, the leadership of the PLO moderates approached the Reagan initiative, coordination with Jordan and contact with Egypt, Syria and Israeli peace groups.[21]

The moderates inside the PLO realized that US participation was indispensable for a Middle East settlement in view of its massive assistance to Israel in all realms.[22] Consequently, the moderates tried to improve their situation *vis-à-vis* the United States. In Decem-ber 1988, a US-PLO dialogue was initiated, only to be ruptured as a result of the aborted Abu al-Abbas Tel Aviv beach attack in early 1990. To analyze the evolution of PLO politics further, a closer look at the PNC resolutions will be helpful in order to trace the transformation from "armed struggle" to "peaceful coexistence."

A close analysis of PNC resolutions sheds light on Palestinian democratic and pluralist thinking that had been developing from the 12th PNC, in 1974, onwards. In fact, since 1974, the Palestinians had been moving steadily toward accommodation and compromise. By the 18th PNC, convened in Algiers in April 1987, most of the elements of the peaceful strategy and the acceptance of the two-state solution on the basis of United Nations resolutions were in place.

To illustrate the transition in Palestinian political thought, the PNC sessions since the inception of the PLO should be divided into three distinctive phases:

1. *Liberation and Return* (The First Four PNCs: 1964–1968). Since the destruction of Palestine in 1948, Palestinians have suf-fered homelessness and exile and sought to redress these injustices through the liberation of their occupied homeland and the repatriation of their exiled community.[23] However, the Palestinian National Charter of 1964 and the amended National Charter of 1968 – drawn up in the 4th PNC – and the resolutions of the 2nd and 3rd PNCs, all empha-sized the total liberation of Palestine.[24] Self-reliance along with armed struggle were stipulated in Article 9 of the 1968 National Charter. Moreover, the concept of national unity was reiterated to draw together the different commando groups

within the PLO infrastructure. As a result of the 4th PNC, the newly emerged PLO vigorously stressed the building of sociopolitical and economic institutions that could cater to the needs of a shattered society.[25]

2.   *The Secular Democratic State* (5th–11th PNCs: 1969–1974). During this phase, the Palestinians encountered the problem of how to reconcile their legitimate political rights with the political and demographic realities that had been created after the destruction of Palestine.[26] This phase was characterized by a further dramatic shift in Palestinian objectives, from total liberation to a democratic secular state in which Christians, Jews and Moslems could live harmoniously together. The important concession that must be made by the Israelis: the renouncing of Zionism and the messianic vision of Eretz Israel.

     Thus, the 5th PNC, in 1969, introduced the idea of establishing a "free democratic society in Palestine." However, in the 6th PNC the same concept was reiterated, substituting the word "society" for "state."[27] In fact, in the 11th PNC, the establishment of a "democratic society where all citizens can live in equality, justice, and fraternity," and which would be "opposed to all forms of prejudice on the basis of race, creed and color" was emphasized. This proposal represented historic compromise in which a framework for peace was presented and zero-sum claims were renounced by the Palestinians.

     This official policy of the PLO remained the basic objective until 1974, when the organization made the first gesture toward a two-state solution, at the 12th PNC.[28]

3.   *The Two-State Solution* (12th–19th PNC: 1974–1988). In July 1974, after the October War, new prospects seemed to emerge in the Middle East and hopes for a comprehensive settlement were high. This induced the PLO to embark on a road to a political settlement through pragmatism that culminated in the declaration of a Palestinian state in the Occupied Territories and the ultimate acceptance of a two-state solution. This historic decision was a response to accumulation of vital events such as the Lebanese Civil War, Sadat's visit to Jerusalem, the Camp David Accords, the Egyptian-Israeli

peace treaty, the 1982 Israeli invasion of Lebanon and the *intifada* in the Occupied Territories.

Through these crucial years, the PLO also witnessed internal changes and dramatic events such as the temporary withdrawal of the PFLP from the PLO's Executive Committee, the split of the Abu Musa faction in 1983, and Arafat's controversial trip to Cairo after the PLO's departure from Lebanon. All these incidents were crucial to the fortunes of the Palestinian national movement; however, the Palestinians survived them and the PLO managed to stabilize its profound commitment to the concept of a two-state solution.

One could safely assert that the 12th PNC was the turning point in Palestinian political decision-making and could be considered the earnest beginning for peaceful coexistence and political accommodation. It was in this council that the "ten-point" program was drafted, calling for the establishment of the "people's national, independent, and fighting authority on every part of liberated Palestinian land."[29]

Subsequent PNCs, the 13th, 14th and 15th, emphasized methodically the rights of the Palestinians to establish their independent state under the leadership of the PLO in any part of Palestine.[30] During this period, a broadly based international consensus emerged for the creation of an independent Palestinian state in parts of Palestine as the basis for resolving the Arab-Israeli conflict. The PLO endorsed the resolutions of the 1982 Fez Conference that laid down a practical vision for the resolution of the Arab-Israeli conflict.[31]

The 16th PNC also indicated another shift in PLO policy, that was directed toward accommodation and open dialogue with Jordan and the formation of a confederation. At all events, the confederation plan was continuously reiterated in subsequent PNCs, despite the formal abrogation of this strategy.[32]

From the 12th PNC on, the concept of "armed struggle" became subservient to political diplomacy, but was never ruled out as an option. The strategy set was a political course toward peaceful resolutions of the conflict, through mediation, conciliation, reciprocity and parity.

It was in the 17th PNC (Amman, 1984) that the consensus in PLO debate shifted to majority rule, since the Damascus-based opposition to the mainstream within the PLO had a small base.

The Amman PNC explicitly consecrated the paramountcy of Palestinian aspirations and wishes in the Occupied Territories.[33] Rashid Khalidi sums up the Palestinian desiderata in the following five points: (1) There is a Palestinian people living on its historic land; (2) It has the right to self-determination; (3) It is represented by the PLO; (4) It has the right to an independent state; (5) It wishes to take part in negotiations in the context of an international conference.[34]

The 18th PNC, which was convened in Algiers in April 1988, represented a major PLO triumph over a threat to its unity, national cohesion and legitimacy. According to Muhammad Hallaj, the PNC was significant because:

The return of the opposition to the parliamentary and constitutional structure of the PLO was an admission of the failure of extra-constitutional confrontation and the triumph of democratic dissent within the Palestinian political process. The importance of the reinforcement of the PLO's democratic traditions by the PNC cannot be overestimated.[35]

Hallaj adds:

The re-election of Yasir Arafat to the chairmanship of the Executive Committee happened with the consent of the formerly rebellious opposition, which enhanced the importance of legality and constitutionalism and the principle of the consent of the governed as the basis for legitimacy.[36]

The strategy of Palestinian leadership during this third phase was comprised of three substantial elements: (a) mobilizing and politicizing the Palestinian people behind an organization representing them; (b) maintaining the unity of the Palestinian movement through very difficult times; and (c) achieving a political program based on consensus.[37]

In November 1988, the 19th PNC met in Algiers to adopt a declaration of independence and a political statement. In these documents a clear and concise peace strategy was laid down, along with explicit acceptance of UN resolutions 242 and 338, the recognition of Israel; and the issue of terrorism as an impediment to the United States opening a dialogue with the PLO was addressed. This PNC constituted the most explicit formulation of Palestinian objectives, couched in

unambiguous language, and – explicitly – a comprehensive, peaceful two-state solution of the Palestinian-Israeli conflict.[38]
Undoubtedly, the 19th PNC irrevocably changed the commitment of the PLO from former claims for a state in all Palestine to the objective of a limited one in the West Bank and Gaza. Regardless of the PFLP and DFLP's opposition to the mainstream Fatah in the PLO, George Habash reiterated: "The PFLP and I will remain in the PLO and in all its institutions forever."[39]

The mainstream of Palestinian thinking came to accept a clear, unequivocal and flexible strategy, rejecting past tendencies to adopt the familiar all-or-nothing position. The "no" of the Palestinians with regard to negotiations with Israel and the restoration of their rights in Palestine has been affected by two important developments: (a) the PLO's acceptance of a two-state solution and the relevant UN resolutions, and (b) the willingness of the Palestinians in the Occupied Territories to play a leading role in a process to implement a two-state solution.[40]

In sum, the Palestinian national movement had encountered dramatic shifts in objectives, strategy and political achievements due to changes in the political realities and to pragmatic visions of its leadership that compromised basic principles to reach a political settlement with Israel. Undoubtedly, the radical change from expressive arguments to instrumental ones involved a rather complicated process, culminating in the acceptance of the PLO-Israel accord of 1993, including an interim period of limited autonomy.

The path towards a full normalization of relations is complex and requires perseverance and stamina from both sides. But regardless of the opposition to the Palestinian peace camp, the mainstream had handled flexibility in an ingenious political scheme containing the opposition in a democratic process that emphasizes majority rule.

Notes

1. U.S. National Conference of Catholic Bishops, Statement on the Middle East. "Toward Peace in the Middle East: Perspectives, Principles and Hopes," adopted 6 November 1989, Baltimore, MD, p. 4.
2. Ibid., p. 5.
3. Marie McKarzel, "The Middle East since 1945," *World Review*, Vol. 30, No. 1, *Foreign Affairs* (March 1991) 13–15.

4. Charles Smith, *Palestine and the Arab-Israeli Conflict*, pp. 188–189.
5. Ibid.
6. Helena Cobban, *The Palestinian Liberation Organization: People, Power and Politics* (Cambridge: Cambridge University Press, 1984) p. 35.
7. For the historic evolution of the PLO, see Quandt, Jaber and Lesch, *The Politics of the Palestinian Nationalism* (Berkeley: University of California Press, 1973).
8. Yezid Sayigh, "The Politics of Palestinian Exile," *Third World Quarterly*, Vol. 9, No. 1 (January 1987) 57.
9. Cheryl Rubenberg, *The PLO: Its Institutional Infrastructure* (Massachusetts: Institute of Arab Studies, 1983), p. 1.
10. Sayigh, "The Politics of Palestinian Exile," 59.
11. Aaron David Miller, "The PLO and the Politics of Survival," *The Washington Papers*, 99 (1983) 56.
12. Ibid., 57.
13. Ibid., 59.
14. "A Discussion with Yasir Arafat," *Journal of Palestine Studies*, Vol. 9, No. 4 (1981) 4–5.
15. Sami Musallam, "Al-Bunya al-Tahtiya wa al-Haikal al Moussassati li Munathamat al-Tahrir al-Filastiniyya," *Shu'un Filastinniya*, No. 166–167 (December–January 1987) 103.
16. Rubenberg, *The PLO*, p. 14.
17. See Emile Sahliyeh, *In Search of Leadership: West Bank Politics since 1967* (Washington, D.C.: The Brookings Institution, 1988).
18. Yezid Sayigh, "Struggle Within Struggle Without: The Transformation of PLO Politics since 1982," *International Affairs*, No. 2 (1989) 248.
19. Ibid., 249–250.
20. Ibid., 255; see also, Cobban, *The Palestine Liberation Organization*, pp. 5–17.
21. Emile F. Sahliyeh, *The PLO after Lebanon War* (Boulder, CO and London: Westview Press, 1986), p. 93.
22. Ibid.
23. Muhammad Hallaj, "The Arab-Israeli Conflict: A Palestinian View," *Vierljahtesberichte* (Problems of International Cooperation), No. 99 (March 1985) 32.
24. Muhammad Y. Muslih, "Towards Coexistence: An Analysis of the Resolutions of the Palestinian National Council (PNC), *Journal of Palestine Studies*, Vol. 20, No. 2 (Spring 1990) 8.
25. Ibid., 10.
26. Sa'id Hammoud, "Al-Majalis Al-Wataniyya Al Filastiniyya Wa Al Wihda Al-Wataniyya," *Shu'un Filastiniyya*, No. 18 (February 1973) 80.
27. Hallaj, "The Arab-Israeli Conflict," 32.
28. For the historical background and PLO deliberations on the concept of a "democratic secular state," see Alain Gresh, "Shi'ar al-Dawla al-Dimocratiya" (February 1982) 142–168.

29. Sami Musallam, "Al-Bunya al-Tahtiya," 525–526.
30. Faysal Hourani, "Munathamat al-Tahrir al-Filastiniyya Wa al-Itijah Nahwa al-Taswiya," *Shu'un Filastiniyya*, No. 99 (February 1980) 52–66; Bilal al-Hassan, "Al-Dawra Al-Khamisa 'Ashar Lil Majlis al-Watani al-Filastini: Dawrat al-Tadqiq Fi al-Qarar al-Siyasi," *Shu'un Filastiniyya*, No. 115 (June 1981) 5–13.
31. al-Hassan (June 1981).
32. Hallaj, "The Arab-Israeli Conflict," 33.
33. Rashid Khalidi, "The Palestinian Dilemma: PLO Policy after Lebanon," *Journal of Palestine Studies* (Autumn 1985) 88–91.
34. Khalidi, "The Palestinian Dilemma," 101.
35. Muhammad Hallaj, "PNC 18th," *American-Arab Affairs*, No. 21 (Summer 1987), 44.
36. Hallaj, "PNC 18th"; for further assessment on the 18th PNC, see Farouq al-Qaddumi, "Assessing the 18th PNC," *Journal of Palestine Studies* (Winter 1988).
37. Nadia Hijab, "The Strategy of the Powerless," *Middle East International*, 12 May 1989, 17–18.
38. Rashid Khalidi, "The Resolutions of the 19th PNC," *Journal of Palestine Studies* (Spring 1990) 29–32. See also Matti Steinberg, "Change Despite Duality," *New Outlook*, Vol. 32, No. 1 (1989) 15–17.
39. Maxin Ghillan, "The Palestinians: What has Changed in the PLO," *Israel/Palestine*, November 1988, 2–3.
40. Fouad Moughrabi, Elia T. Zureik, Manuel Hassassian, and Aziz Haidar, "Palestinians on the Peace Process," *Journal of Palestine Studies*, Vol. 31, No. 81 (Autumn 1991) 37.

16

Changes in Israel's Society since the Yom Kippur War

Shmuel N. Eisenstadt

The possibility of making peace is more the outcome of acts of statesmanship than of social processes in Israeli society since the 1973 War. But these developments do provide the background which makes the peace process one possibility – not the only one, and not necessarily a totally irreversible one.

What are these processes? Israeli society has been undergoing some far-reaching changes (very often described as earthquakes) since the Yom Kippur War, indeed ever since the 1967 War. Some of these transformations are well known. The Yom Kippur War itself was often referred to as an earthquake because, for the first time since the establishment of the state, the leadership was found wanting in the crucial arena of security. However, in my opinion there have been at least two events or processes of greater long-term importance since then: the Lebanon War and the *intifada*. I think that these have had a much deeper impact than the Yom Kippur War, although they should be seen against the background of the Yom Kippur War.

The Lebanon war was important because for the first time in the relatively short history of the State of Israel, matters of security, military arrangements, and so on were no longer a matter of consensus. They were opened up to public discourse and to public debate, something the Yom Kippur War did not lead to. The Yom Kippur War led to the questioning of the ability of the leadership. Implicit in this was also the possibility that maybe the famous conception described by the *Agranat Commission* was wrong. (The conception, however, was technical rather than being the basis of the premises of security arrangements or international relations.) The Lebanon War, for good or for bad, opened up war and peace to public discussion and criticism.

This was a new development in the period since the establishment of the State of Israel, although such discussion did exist in the *Yishuv*. The *intifada* had the same impact but in a different way because it shook some of the implicit assumptions about the nature of the Palestinian political will, the Palestinian entity, and possible relations between Israel and the Palestinians. These were implicit rather than explicit assumptions, but implicit assumptions are often stronger and more pervasive, since they are never really examined, just taken for granted. In this way the *intifada* had a very important effect, the culmination of which, in my opinion, has led to the opening up of the arenas of security, international relations, and military relations, to intensive political debate, the like of which has not been known in the State of Israel since its establishment. This was a logical development after what happened following the Yom Kippur War.

This opening up also attests to the fact that, since the 1967 War, the security dimension has been central in the self-consciousness of Israeli society. There is nothing surprising about this but it should be remembered and stressed. It would, however, be wrong to think that, with all its centrality, the security dimension was the only one, and that developments which took place – from 1967, but with intensification after 1973 – were only confined to the security arena. The impact of the processes I mentioned before can only be fully understood if we take into account the wider context of changes and transformations in Israeli society. What are these transformations or processes which have been taking place in Israel within the context of the Yom Kippur, the Lebanon War, and the *intifada*? The first is a continual and intensive change in the self-identity, the symbols of self-consciousness, and the collective self-definition of Israeli society. The second, which I will discuss in greater detail, is the growing discrepancy between what I would like to call the ossification of many of the formal institutions, above all, political institutions and the political elite, and the more dynamic and diversified changes on the ground. Third, there has been a growing openness toward international trends which has had a very important impact on the whole ambience and format of Israeli society. The common denominator of all these processes is that Israeli society has been undergoing a process of changing its own format in a very intensive way, even if it was not always fully conscious of it.

I will now expand briefly on each of these processes. The first is the changes in the collective consciousness, or self-definition, of Israeli society – not only the Jews but also the Arabs, and relations between the two. This process started to some extent after the 1967 War, which reawakened the problem of territorial boundaries (it can be said to have been dormant since the partition decision and the establishment of the State of Israel, but so were many other dimensions of the collective consciousness). Not all of these changes were a direct result of the Six Day War, but the Six Day War and its aftermath provided the framework in which some of them were more fully expressed or visible. One dimension closely related to the Six Day War was the nature of relations between Israel and the Arab countries, between Israel and the Palestinians, and slowly, within this context also, between the Jewish and the Arab populations in Israel. All these problems did exist in a closed framework from 1948 to 1967–68, but they were opened up to public discussion in a mode which was not there before.

The events of 1967 also changed the mode of internal political discourse in Israel. (This is more relevant to the second process mentioned later.) This change can be seen in the fact that the terms Left and Right attained an entirely new connotation, losing whatever social or economic connotation they might have had before, and becoming almost entirely identified with a dovish or hawkish stand with respect to Jewish-Arab relations. This has, in a sense, ossified internal political discourse in Israel on social, economic and other problems to a degree which did not exist before.

It was not only relations with the different parts of the Arab world that affected the self-definition and the self-consciousness, of Israeli society. A parallel complementary development has taken place in the relations between Israeli society and the Jewish community in the Diaspora – a fact perhaps not emphasized often enough. The whole concept of the relationship has changed. If, before 1967, there was a negation of the Diaspora, "*shelilat hagalut*," the situation has changed on both sides. Suddenly Israel has become much more important for many Jewish communities in the Diaspora, even for Jews who have openly said they are not Zionists. The famous French sociologist and great political thinker, Raymond Aron, in a very famous polemic he had with De Gaulle, openly declared that although he had never thought of himself as a Zionist, nor that the creation of the State of Israel was the major historical event of the twentieth century – he could not bear to think of the State of Israel ceasing to exist. The same also happened in the United States, where there was a mutual change in the relationship. The modes of interaction and terms of power between Jewish communities abroad and in Israel have changed, naturally resulting in changes in the historical self-perception of Israeli society, its self-definition in terms of Jewish history and cultural heritage. Within this framework two major changes have taken place, namely, the importance of the ethnic and the religious components in the collective self-definition of Israel. This in itself is more or less well known, but I would like to emphasize something that is often overlooked, namely that all these components – the ethnic, the religious, the Israeli-Arab relations, and relations with the Diaspora – were foci of struggle, intensive discourse, and intensive disagreements within Israeli society. One result of this is that there has been a growing sort of pluralization and diversification in discourse. Many things have become open to discussion, and the self-assurance with respect to the former collective identity, which existed until 1967, has to some extent been shattered, resulting in potentially constructive but also destructive possibilities. This is then, the first series of processes.

The second series deals with a sort of discrepancy between the relative ossification of many political and institutional frameworks, and what is actually happening in many sectors of Israeli society. The famous *"mahapach,"* or change of government, in 1977, was due not only – I would claim not even possibly – to the outcomes of the Yom Kippur War, but rather to the fact that many sectors of Israeli society have reached maturity in this changed society, for example, new immigrants, younger generations and professional groups, to name a few. These groups have all felt excluded from the political process, which they see as ossified and incapable of facing new problems. The Yom Kippur War was an illustration of this inability, but it goes much deeper than that. For many years, especially during periods under national unity governments, there was a feeling that the political structure was stagnating, while at the same time there developed in many sectors of society new developments on the ground. And there were many such developments which somehow could not find their expression in the major central institutional frameworks. The other trend which was very strong might be traced to the recent influx of Russian immigrants, which has had a great psychological impact in opening up new possibilities. In addition there was the growing international orientation of Israeli society – not only talk about internationalization and the necessity of becoming part of a wider world, but also a growing professionalization which could be seen in many sectors: many more Israeli tourists going abroad, many more goods imported. Israel somehow became much more attuned or sensitive, you might say, to a growing emphasis on the different opportunities of life, or of what has sometimes been coined as consumer and commodity capitalism. All these developments have had a great impact on Israeli daily life, on the feeling of Israelis, and their aspirations. The common denominator of all this is that Israeli society since 1967, and more intensely after 1973, underwent a great change. From an ideological, creative society – it was very creative in institutional terms, although relatively closed and homogeneic in its ideology – it became much less ideological and much more open. This entailed more struggles and more confrontations, but also growing opportunities for new types of discourse and new group life. People sought new possibilities, veering between the possibilities of growing creativity, perhaps not that ideological, and of a greater emphasis on a better, more peaceful life.

All these processes are still there but nothing has been resolved. It is the nature of such a processes that it cannot be fully resolved, because it is very dynamic. This dynamic process could give rise to many struggles and intolerances, to stagnation and to stalemate. It could, however, also provide a background for more constructive developments. As mentioned earlier, which of these will take place depends not only on these general processes but also very much on the combination of such general processes with different acts of statesmanship and the reconstructing of institutions. The peace process is one possibility within this broader framework, and I think it is mainly within such a framework that we can understand both the possibilities offered by, as well as the fragility of, the peace process that we are now witnessing.

Part IV

Toward Regional Peace

This section, "Toward Regional Peace," looks at the potential for extending the Israel-PLO agreement throughout the Middle East in regard to the involvement of other regional and outside forces and issues. Two Arab states bordering Israel – Syria and Jordan – also must conclude agreements. Syria's military power and Jordan's intimate relationship to the Palestinians pose particular problems. The parts played by Russia, Europe, and the potentially ominous issue of arms control can be important factors in the success or failure of finding negotiated solutions to conflicts which have led to war and international crisis more often than any other global problem.

Professor Moshe Ma'oz, in "Syria, Israel and the Peace Process," discusses the complex territorial and political issues standing between Damascus and Jerusalem. While the future of the Golan Heights, captured from Syria by Israel in 1967, is the most salient issue, the questions of the extent of peace Syria is willing to offer and security arrangements are equally important – and extraordinarily sensitive.

Jordan's long and close relationship with the Palestine question is outlined by Nasser Eddin Nashashibi, in "Palestine and Jordan," and he stresses the future importance of a Jordanian role, along with King Hussein's eagerness to play that part. Dr. Asher Susser, in "Jordan and the Palestinian Question: Coming Full Circle," stresses that Jordan has no choice – given its proximity and Palestinian majority – but to continue its intimate involvement in the issue.

Itzhak Minerbi points out, in "The European Community and the Middle East," that Europe's principal role in the Middle East has been in terms of economic interchange and arms' supplies. He notes that the Middle East has also posed a serious challenge to European unity on a number of occasions but that a consensus now exists for a more even-handed stand on the region's issues.

Vladimir Titorenko, in "Disarmament and Security in the Middle East," surveys the vicious circle created by the regional arms race – mutual trust is difficult without controls on weaponry, but reducing military spending or imports requires a settlement of political issues. The threat of proliferation of nuclear and chemical weapons as well as missiles could make the area the center of a world crisis.

Evgeniy Bazhanov, in "Russia's Middle East Policy under Gorbachev and Yeltsin," shows how Moscow's post-Communist strategy has developed in the region. It is far more cooperative with the West but still based on distinctive Russian interests.

Prof. Yair Evron discusses the new goals and interests of the United States in "The United States and the Middle East in the Post Cold-War Era."

Professor Yehoshafat Harkabi, in "World Order and the Arab-Israeli Conflict," concludes with reflections on the link between global politics and regional problems.

17

Syria, Israel and the Peace Process

Moshe Ma'oz

Syrian-Israeli relations are pivotal to the Middle East peace process; no comprehensive, stable, and durable peace can be achieved without a political settlement between the two countries. In many respects, the course of events since 1973 has transformed the Arab-Israeli conflict – which started largely as a result of the Arab-Jewish dispute in Palestine going back to the 1880s – into a Syrian-Israeli confrontation.

Egypt, the veteran leader of the all-Arab campaign against Israel, signed the 1978 Camp David Accords and the 1979 peace treaty with Israel; since then it has maintained peaceful relations with the Jewish state. With Jordan, there has been de facto peaceful coexistence since 1967. Iraq, officially at war with Israel since 1948, has played no more than a marginal role in the military struggle against it. Following the destruction of its military machine in 1991, Iraq is not expected, in the near future, to play a major role in any new Arab-Israeli confrontation.

Thus, during the last decade Syria and Israel have become the major protagonists in the Middle East conflict, as well as the main rivals not only with respect to the Golan Heights but also over influence in Lebanon and the fate of the Palestinians. Indeed, Israel and Syria each control large sections of the Palestinian people (Syria also has certain Palestinian guerrilla organizations under its control) and both are thus able greatly to affect the settlement of the Palestinian problem – the core of the Arab-Israeli conflict as well as of the current peace process.

What then are the positions of Damascus and Jerusalem in this process, notably concerning the Golan and the Palestinians, and what are the prospects for a durable settlement of the Syrian-Israeli conflict?

Israel accepted UN Resolution 242 of 22 November 1967, which called for "withdrawal of Israel armed forces from territories occupied in the recent conflict" and "termination of all claims or states of belligerency and respect for and acknowledgement of the sovereignty, territorial integrity and political independence of every state in the area and their right to live in peace within secure and recognized boundaries, free from threats or acts of force."[1]

Furthermore, earlier the Israeli cabinet had unanimously adopted (on 19 June 1967) a resolution to the effect that "Israel offers to conclude a peace treaty with Syria on the basis of the international boundary and Israel's security needs," namely, "demilitarization of the Syrian Heights . . . and an absolute guarantee of the free flow of the River Jordan's sources into Israel."[2]

This decision was abolished in 1968. After the advent to power of the Likud Party in 1977, Menachem Begin, the new prime minister, stated that "Israel will remain in the Golan Heights but in the framework of a peace treaty we will be ready to withdraw our forces from their present line to a [new] line that will be . . . a permanent boundary."[3] The guidelines of Begin's new government also pointed out Israel's readiness to participate, without preconditions, in the Geneva peace conference on the basis of UN Resolutions 242 and 338 (of 1973).[4]

Yet in view of the belligerent position of Syria and Israel's security needs, Israeli leaders, both before and after 1977, periodically called for the retention of the Golan Heights under Israeli control. In December 1981 the Israeli Knesset passed the Golan Heights Law which applied Israeli law, jurisdiction, and administration to the area. Half a year later, in June 1982, the Israeli army invaded Lebanon with the declared aim of destroying the PLO's military infrastructure. The IDF also attacked Syrian troops – without provocation on their part – and temporarily established positions some twenty-five miles west of Damascus.

Subsequently, Israel's hostile attitude toward Syria intensified in reaction to the Damascus-sponsored war of attrition against Israeli troops in Lebanon during 1983–85 and the Syrian attempt to blow up an El Al plane at London's Heathrow airport in 1986.

Both Likud and Labor leaders (not to mention quarters further to the right) continued during the late 1980s and early 1990s to assert that Israel should not return the Golan to Syria even in exchange for peace. Yitzhak Rabin, for example, while Israel's defense minister, declared in June 1988 that he did not regard Syria under Asad as a partner for peace. The issue of peace for territories was therefore irrelevant as far as Syria was concerned.[5] Following Syrian-Egyptian reconciliation in 1989 – which could be interpreted as signaling a new, flexible Syrian attitude toward Israel – Rabin stated: "We don't see a change in the Syrian position."[6]

In fact, however, the Syrian position regarding Israel has significantly changed since 1967. Following the Six Day War, Syria adopted an extremely militant position, rejecting even the resolutions of the Arab summit at Khartoum (29 August – 1 September 1967) which agreed on the following principles: "No peace with Israel, no recognition of Israel, no negotiations with it."[7] The Syrian regime's official organ, *Al-Ba'th*, stated on 31 August 1967: "The Israeli enemy will be liquidated only by means of force."[8] Obviously, Syria rejected UN Resolution 242 of November 1967.

However, following his ascent to power in 1970, Hafez al-Asad, now Syria's president, accepted the resolution, in March 1972, on condition that Israel withdrew completely from all occupied Arab territories and that the rights of the Palestinians be guaranteed.[9]

To be sure, Asad did not relinquish the military option as the major component of his struggle against Israel; but unlike his predecessor, Salah Jadid, Asad also regarded diplomacy and political maneuvering as important ingredients of an overall strategy toward Israel, to use his own words, to "facilitate the military campaign . . . to gain time or to acquire the sympathy of international public opinion."[10]

Accordingly, Asad developed and employed Syria's military power with massive Soviet help, while simultaneously – notably at periods of military weakness – adopting diplomatic action, mostly toward the United States, in his confrontation with Israel. Thus, for example, he joined Anwar Sadat in launching the October 1973 War against Israel but, having been defeated, he accepted UN Resolution 338 of 22 October 1973, calling for a cease-fire and the implementation of UN Resolution 242. Subsequently, Syria initiated a war of attrition against Israel's army, yet simultaneously conducted a diplomatic campaign against Israel – trying to utilize Henry Kissinger's mediation efforts to secure a satisfactory disengagement agreement in the Golan (May 1974).[11]

Significantly, following this agreement, Asad for the first time entertained the idea of signing a peace agreement with Israel within a comprehensive political settlement of the Arab-Israeli dispute based on Resolutions 242 and 338. In fact he suggested a non-belligerency agreement with no diplomatic relations. This remained predicated, however, on Israel's full withdrawal from all occupied territories and on the rights of the Palestinian people being safeguarded through the establishment of a Palestinian state in the West Bank and Gaza.[12]

To be sure, Asad's peace overture was primarily directed toward winning over American public opinion, and gaining the Nixon administration's support for an Israeli withdrawal from the Golan, Sinai, the West Bank, and Gaza and – if possible – to push a wedge between the United States and Israel. To these ends, Asad renewed diplomatic relations with the United States (June 1974) and even indicated his preparedness to integrate, possibly alongside Sadat, into an American-sponsored Middle East peace process.

However, in the face of the combined Israeli-Egyptian-American positions, Asad's bold diplomatic efforts failed. Israel, for its part, was unwilling to make further withdrawals from the Golan (beyond that of 1974) or to recognize the "national rights" of the Palestinians. Golda Meir, then Israel's prime minister, declared early in March 1974 that the Golan was an inseparable part of Israel. The Israeli government was prepared for further partial withdrawals from Sinai (following those of 1974) as part of another Egyptian-Israeli agreement, but would keep the Golan and thus further widen the split between Sadat and Asad. As it turned out, Asad's pleas and pressures notwithstanding, Sadat was prepared to accept separate partial deals with Israel, and his policy was supported by Kissinger's step-by-step diplomacy, to the dismay of Syria and the U.S.S.R., which advocated an overall Arab-Israeli settlement.[13]

Having failed to recover the Golan by (in his own words) "political action," Asad harshly criticized Sadat for his "total submission to Israel's demands [and for causing] a breach in Arab solidarity,"[14] severely denounced Israel as a "racist fascist state," and threatened it with "another October War."[15] Simultaneously, the Twelfth National Congress of the Ba'th Party (July 1975) stated that, following the recovery of the 1967 territories, Syria would continue the struggle against Israel "toward liberating all the Palestinian lands."[16] Along with these statements, Asad embarked on an ambitious strategy aimed at establishing a northern and eastern front against Israel to consist of Syria, Iraq, Jordan, Lebanon, and the PLO.

But only Jordan was inclined to work toward military, political, and economic integration with Syria (and that, too, only for a limited span of time), whereas Iraq rejected Asad's approach, arguing that Syria continued to adhere to UN Resolutions 242 and 338, i.e., to a political rather than a military solution.

Indeed, in 1976–77 Asad renewed his diplomatic initiative toward Israel on lines similar to his 1974–75 venture. Syria was again exposed to a potential Israeli threat following Damascus's intervention in the Lebanese civil war and the deployment of its troops near the Lebanese-Israeli border. To neutralize this threat, Syria, utilizing American auspices, reached the tacit "red line" agreement with Israel in southern Lebanon (spring 1976),[17] which acknowledged the interests of both sides there.

Subsequently (late 1976 and early 1977) Asad suggested to the Carter administration resuming the Geneva negotiations for a peaceful solution to the Arab-Israeli conflict. He stated that he was willing to sign a "peace agreement" (though in fact, a closer look shows that he meant no more than a nonbelligerency agreement) provided Israel withdrew from all territories occupied in 1967 and agreed to the creation of a Palestinian state in the West Bank and Gaza. Asad also implied that the United States should have the major role in mediating such a settlement.[18]

However, once again Asad's overture was foiled by the combined policies of Israel, Egypt, and the United States. Like the Labor coalition government before it, the Likud government in Israel continued to take its stand firmly on a separate settlement with Egypt, with no linkage whatsoever with either the Syrian or Palestinian issue. For various reasons, Egyptian President Sadat also kept believing that a comprehensive Arab-Israeli settlement was not feasible and thus opted for the more limited objective of recovering Sinai from Israel. Finally, in November 1977, he made his historic trip to Jerusalem, which led to the 1978 Camp David Accords and the 1979 Egyptian-Israeli peace treaty. Both were facilitated by U.S. President Jimmy Carter, who had thus retreated from his previous support for a comprehensive settlement, to the deep frustration of Asad.[19]

Under these circumstances, Asad almost entirely abandoned his diplomatic efforts. For the next decade he concentrated his energies and skills on building, with the massive help of the Soviet Union, a military option *vis-à-vis* Israel. The underlying concept was Asad's doctrine of strategic balance and military parity with

Israel, essentially aimed at the following goals: to build a strong and credible military machine capable both of deterring Israel from attacking Syria and of effectively defending Damascus should such an attack occur all the same; to use his armed strength at the appropriate time to launch a limited or all-out war against Israel, primarily in order to recover the Golan Heights; and to negotiate a comprehensive political settlement with Israel from a position of military strength.[20]

Asad's need to strengthen his military power *vis-à-vis* Israel became a great deal more urgent during the early 1980s. Since the Likud government had come to power, Israel had increasingly supported the Christian Maronites' opposition to Syrian control of Lebanon. In June 1982, it invaded southern Lebanon, attacked Syrian troops, and advanced along the Beirut–Damascus highway in the direction of Damascus.

Iraq, Syria's rival as well as potential military ally, had been engaged in a bloody war against Iran since 1980, thus indirectly strengthening Israel's hand *vis-à-vis* Damascus. Egypt did not exercise any tangible pressure on Israel to withdraw from Lebanon; and the Reagan administration, for its part, "opted to back the Israeli action, at least insofar as it was aimed at effecting a pro-Western order in Lebanon."[21] In reacting to the growing Israeli menace, Asad not only engineered a war of attrition by proxy against Israeli troops in Lebanon, but also substantially enlarged and modernized his armed forces and his weapon systems in a further attempt to attain strategic parity with Israel.

To be sure, despite his vast efforts Syria had not been able to achieve a strategic balance with Israel, although presumably succeeding in reaching a quantitative military parity with it. Following their buildup, the Syrian armed forces could possibly deter Israel from attacking Syria, or else effectively defend Damascus against an Israeli offensive. They are presumably also capable of grabbing parts of the Golan in a surprise assault, although they are likely to be defeated in a resultant all-out war with Israel, owing to its qualitative superiority.

So far, Syria has thus been unable to counterbalance Israel's strategic superiority and is unlikely to do so in the near future. Among the reasons for Syria's failure to attain strategic parity with Israel were the severe economic difficulties it ran into in the 1980s, caused largely by the huge military buildup (which absorbed some 65 percent of the yearly budget), by the costly military involvement in Lebanon, by mismanagement and corruption in various public sectors, as well as by the decrease in Arab aid and international credits. The prolonged economic crisis, which led to high inflation and created great poverty, forced the government to make major cuts in defense spending, including a reduction in the size of the army.[22]

This has been one of the main factors which prompted Asad, since 1988, to revert again to diplomacy and to seek to integrate Syria into the Middle East peace process. The other main factor which influenced Asad's decision to seek a political settlement was the crucial change in Moscow's policy toward Damascus and toward the Arab-Israeli conflict. True, following the conclusion of the 1980 Soviet-Syrian Treaty of Friendship and Cooperation and particularly during 1982–84, the Soviet Union supplied Syria with huge quantities of weapons, including sophisticated long-range missiles. But other than Yuri Andropov (1982–84), Soviet leaders, notably Mikhail Gorbachev, have made a point of supplying weapons calculated to strengthen Syria's defensive rather than its offensive capabilities. For example, the Soviets did not equip the Syrian army with the accurate long-range SS-23 ground-to-ground missiles, despite repeated requests from Damascus to do so. In recent years, Moscow has apparently reduced the shipment of arms to Syria and requested payments in hard currency for its arms.[23]

In addition, Syria did not, during the early 1980s, consistently enjoy Soviet military and political backing even when confronted with an Israeli threat, notably during the 1982 war in Lebanon. Most crucially, following the advent of Gorbachev in 1985, Soviet policy toward the Syrian-Israeli (as well as toward the Palestinian-Israeli) conflict dramatically changed: during a visit by Asad to Moscow in April 1987, Gorbachev told him bluntly, "The reliance on military force in settling the Arab-Israeli conflict has completely lost its credibility." The Soviet leader also pointed out that Moscow would no longer support Syria's doctrine of strategic parity with Israel, and urged Asad to seek a political settlement to the conflict; Gorbachev offered Soviet help in doing so.[24] Subsequently, Gorbachev continued to send messages to Damascus through the new Soviet ambassador, Aleksandr Zotov (appointed in early 1989), again urging Asad to relinquish "illusions about a military option against Israel."[25]

Beginning in mid-1988, Asad realized that Syria did not possess a military option for an all-out war against Israel. The change in

Soviet policy was not the only reason. Another was that the end of the Iran–Iraq war (more or less in Baghdad's favor) exposed Syria – which had supported Iran – to a new Iraqi threat, whether on its eastern borders or by means of Iraqi-sponsored subversive activities in Lebanon. It also led to Syria's growing isolation in the Arab world.

Consequently, Damascus could not rely on military backing from Iraq (let alone from Egypt) in case of war with Israel. The constraint to adopt diplomatic action thus became more severe. Yet, in order to revert to diplomacy, Damascus first needed to mend fences with Egypt – the major Arab power and the champion of a diplomatic breakthrough with Israel – as well as with the United States.

The latter was seen in Damascus as potentially helpful in working for a favorable political settlement with Israel, but its hostile attitude toward Damascus had to be first essentially changed. For in October and November 1986, the United States had recalled its ambassador from Damascus, Britain had severed diplomatic relations, and both the European Community and the United States had adopted sanctions against Syria because of its involvement in the bombing attempt of an El Al plane in London on 17 April 1986.[26]

At the end of 1988, after a decade of Syrian hostility toward Egypt over the Egyptian-Israeli peace treaty, Damascus started to emit conciliatory signals in the direction of Cairo. In December 1988, Asad publicly stated that he "acknowledged the importance of Egypt in the Arab arena" and that Syrian-Egyptian cooperation had always been compatible with the interests of the Arab world.[27]

In May 1989, after a ten-year absence, Egypt was readmitted to the Arab League. Syria no longer objected, and in late December 1989 full diplomatic relations between Syria and Egypt were restored. In mid-July 1990, Asad paid his first official visit to Egypt in thirteen years, thus acknowledging that Sadat's diplomatic-peaceful approach had the advantage over his own belligerent-rejectionist policy toward Israel. On his departure from Cairo, Asad stated: "We are ready to join the peace process . . . we accept UN Resolutions 242 and 338 and we still call for a just and comprehensive peace."[28] Asad had made similar statements earlier that year in his meetings with American senators, and particularly in his talks with former President Carter in Damascus in March 1990.[29]

Indeed, alongside its new conciliatory approach to Egypt, Syria was seeking a rapprochement with the United States. Under the Reagan administration, Washington had developed an antagonistic attitude toward Damascus on account of its alleged involvement in anti-American "state terrorism," notably in the 1983 attack on the U.S. Marine compound in Lebanon and the bombing of Pan-American flight 103 in 1988. But toward the end of the Reagan administration (i.e., at the same time as the change in Asad's approach), the United States itself became interested in improving relations with Syria, partly because of its major role in releas-ing American hostages and partly because of Damascus's poten-tial capability of restoring order and stability in Lebanon. The United States and Syria began to cooperate on these two issues, thereby noticeably enhancing their relationship, particularly during the Bush administration. Yet for the time being they remained in disagreement regarding the settlement of the Arab-Israeli dispute: whereas the United States initially advocated a step-by-step process under its sponsorship, starting with Israeli-Palestinian negotiations, Syria insisted on convening a conference of Israel and all Arab states under UN auspices, with the participation of the U.S.S.R., then still Syria's major ally. By 1990 and particularly following the Iraqi invasion of Kuwait, however, Damascus significantly changed its stand, moving closer to the American position.

To be sure, Asad and other Syrian leaders continued until 1990 to publicly depict Israel as an aggressive, racist state, a neo-Crusader entity, alien to the region, that should be fought.[30] But this harsh ideological position notwithstanding, Asad has made major attempts – much bolder than in 1974–75 and 1976–77 – to use diplomacy in the confrontation with Israel, notably through combining American support and coordination with other Arab states. He was prompted to do so because, beginning in 1989, Syria's chances for diplomatic gains have greatly improved, while simultaneously, as we have seen, its military option has significantly diminished.

The Iraqi menace was ended by the destruction of Baghdad's military machine in the 1990–91 Gulf War, but this also eliminated for quite some time Syria's potential strategic depth or backing in case of war with Israel. On the other hand, the U.S. victories in the Cold War and in the Gulf have demonstrated its global military superiority and its readiness to use military power in order to assist its allies in the Middle East – whether Kuwait, Israel, or others – against external aggression. America's new predominance, no longer challenged by Moscow, has increased Syria's political and economic dependence on the United States while diminishing

Israel's status as a strategic asset for the United States. Washington has thus assumed a role as the major broker for a Syrian-Israeli settlement.

Unlike the Israeli government, Asad adjusted his policies to these new global and regional realities even before the Iraqi invasion of Kuwait in August 1990. Yet this invasion offered him a unique opportunity to emerge from his predicaments and to solidify his new orientations. By joining the American-led campaign against Iraq, Syria was able to contribute (however symbolically) to countering the Iraqi menace, consolidate its indirect control over Lebanon, end its regional isolation, erase its image as a "terrorist state" in the West, and turn itself into a respectable member of the American-Arab coalition. Subsequently, Syria expected to be rewarded by the United States, mainly through support for its attitudes in the newly-launched Arab-Israeli peace process.

Washington, for its part, valued Damascus at that juncture not only for its contribution to Lebanon's stability and for adding to the Arab legitimation for the American campaign against Iraq, but also for its potentially crucial role in the peace process. This new American-Syrian bond of mutual interests was demonstrated by Secretary of State James Baker's visit to Damascus in September 1990 and by Asad's meeting with President George Bush in Geneva in November 1990 – his first meeting with an American president in thirteen years.

Following the Gulf War, Asad responded in July 1991 to the American-engineered Arab-Israeli peace process by adopting new, flexible positions more or less in line with the American terms. These represented a major departure from Syria's previous conditions. For example, Syria had previously demanded a full-fledged international conference under UN sponsorship, to meet only after an advance commitment by Israel to withdraw from all occupied territories including East Jerusalem. Furthermore, at such a conference, whose resolutions would be binding, the Arabs were to negotiate with Israel jointly rather than separately, and indirectly rather than directly; the Palestinian people were to be represented by the PLO and be entitled to establish an independent state in the occupied territories including East Jerusalem.

Under the new American terms, Syria now agreed to convene a regional conference under U.S. and Soviet sponsorship, with only a passive UN observer, and, following the opening of the conference, to conduct direct negotiations with Israel. Syria also dropped the demands that Israel must commit itself in advance to withdraw from the occupied territories or that the PLO must represent the Palestinians. Nor did Damascus now insist on the establishment of an independent Palestinian state, demanding only that the "Palestinian problem" must be "resolved."[31]

To be sure, these new positions, which various U.S. government officials and other observers depicted as a diplomatic breakthrough, primarily manifested Syrian concessions on procedural issues, though they also touched on certain matters of substance. Yet on the most essential points, Syria has not changed its positions: it has continued to demand the withdrawal of Israel from the entire Golan Heights, as well as from southern Lebanon, the Gaza Strip, and the West Bank including East Jerusalem. Syrian Vice President Abd al-Halim Khaddam stated, for example, on 5 October 1991: "Not a single Arab participating in the peace process can sell out one inch of the occupied territories or a single right of the national Palestinian rights." The Syrian Foreign Minister Faruk al-Shar'a, in his militant anti-Israeli speech at the opening of the Madrid peace conference (31 October 1991), made certain statements that were reminiscent of passages broadcast in a Radio Damascus commentary on 8 October 1991: "Syria and all the Arabs adhere to the Golan Heights, Jerusalem, the West Bank and Gaza. We will not bargain over our territories or relinquish our rights."[32]

In return for these territories Syrian leaders offered until 1992 a "peace agreement" with Israel, which in fact was devoid of full recognition of Israel and was certainly open to interpretation as no more than a nonbelligerency agreement. Indeed, in July 1991, in an interview with an American journalist, Asad evaded the question whether or not he accepted "the existence of a Jewish state in the Middle East."[33] Other Syrian officials repeatedly insisted that peace with Israel should include neither full diplomatic relations nor economic cooperation, cultural ties, and so on. Accordingly, Syria refused to attend the "third round" of the peace negotiations designed to discuss these latter issues. And when, for example, the Syrian vice-president was asked in October 1991 about Damascus's position on Israeli attempts to attend a meeting in Turkey on regional water problems, he said: "Israel has no right to a single drop of water in the region. It is absolutely unacceptable for Israel to be a party to any arrangements on water or any other issues in the region."[34]

Possibly Syria's stiff refusal to recognize Israel's legitimacy and to sign a full peace treaty with it represented a bargaining position in the negotiation process; and once Israel commits itself to withdraw from all occupied territories and concedes the national rights of the Palestinians, Asad would agree to sign a full peace treaty with Israel, as Sadat did in 1979. Yet it would appear that Asad, while determined to recover the entire Golan – just as Sadat recovered the Sinai – would, unlike Sadat, also insist on a clear-cut settlement of the Palestinian issue in one form or another.

The majority of Israelis have been reluctant to give up the Golan, whether from strategic considerations, psychological motives, or both. Unlike Sinai, a vast desert distant from Israel's population centers, the Golan is a small plateau of some five hundred square miles. Topographically and strategically, it controls northern Galilee and the Sea of Galilee, and had been used, before the 1967 War, to shell Israeli villages. Given Syria's aggressive record and its image of brutality, it is no wonder that public opinion polls since 1967 have periodically shown that some 90 percent of Israeli Jews wish to retain the Golan.[35]

Nevertheless, since the end of the Gulf War and the beginning of the peace process, more Israelis have been ready to give up part of the Golan in return for real peace with Syria – 28 percent or 33 percent (respectively, in two polls) – as against a majority of 57 percent or 65 percent who opposed any territorial concessions to Syria.[36] Significantly, according to yet another poll (October 1991), 55 percent of Likud members were prepared to give up part of the Golan – provided it is demilitarized – for peace with Syria, compared to 42 percent who were against.[37]

It would indeed appear that whereas more Likud members were prepared to make some territorial concessions in a demilitarized Golan (but not in the West Bank, which they regard as part of the Land of Israel), more Laborites refused for security reasons to give up even part of the Golan (but have been prepared to withdraw from the bulk of the West Bank and Gaza). Indeed, while serving as defense minister and Labor leader Yitzhak Rabin declared in June 1990 that he would rather retain the Golan even if this prevented peace with Syria than make peace with Syria and relinquish the Golan.[38]

Nevertheless, once the peace process started, the Labor Party late in 1991 adopted a new platform on the Golan that stated somewhat ambiguously:

The peace treaty with Syria will be based on Security Council Resolutions 242 and 338, whose meaning is the principle of territorial compromise within a framework of a full and viable peace, in which the security needs of Israel will be provided for . . . in any peace agreement with Syria and in the [accompanying] security arrangements Israel's presence and control, both [through] settlement and militarily, in the Golan Heights . . . will continue.[39]

As for the Israeli government, its official position regarding the Golan had not changed since Israel launched its May 1989 peace initiative "based on Resolutions 242 and 338." It calls for "the establishment of peaceful relations [with] those Arab states which still maintain a state of war with [Israel]" but neither mentioned Syria specifically nor suggested the application of Resolutions 242 and 338 to the Golan Heights.[40] Indeed, Prime Minister Yitzhak Shamir and other government ministers repeatedly stated their opposition to returning the Golan Heights to Syria in return for peace.

In March 1991, for example, Shamir declared: "The Syrians will tell us that they want the Golan Heights and we shall tell them – No! . . . Undoubtedly the Golan Heights is part of Israel . . . this is the government's position . . . [UN] Resolution 242 has nothing to do with the Golan."[41] At the end of July 1991, following Syria's positive reply to President Bush's peace initiative, Israeli Defense Minister Moshe Arens asserted that there would be no negotiation with Syria over the Golan.[42]

As it were, the position of the new Israeli Labor government was not initially different from that of its predecessor. Following the Israeli elections on 23 June, Rabin even stressed the need to strengthen the Israeli presence in the Golan.[43]

Furthermore, Rabin also announced that he would first work toward implementing Palestinian autonomy "within six to nine months," and leave the Syrian-Golan issue for the final stages of negotiations.[44] By analyzing such a statement Rabin possibly believed that realizing the Palestinian autonomy would be more acceptable to the Israeli public than relinquishing the Golan. And apart from his difficulties in simultaneously negotiating on two crucial issues, it can be assumed that by pressing first on the Palestinian track, Rabin possibly also intended to put pressure on Asad to meet Israel's terms regarding the peace process, or be left behind.

Asad apparently reacted by unleashing in July 1992 further

Hizbullah terrorist/guerrilla attacks against Israeli targets, and ordering in mid-August a test firing of an advanced Scud-C missile. General Mordechai Gur, Israel's deputy defense minister, threatened to storm Damascus should Syria launch missiles against Israel, while Rabin expressed his skepticism regarding Asad's peace intentions.[45] Subsequently, however, with the mediation of Baker and Mubarak both Rabin and Asad adopted more positive attitudes toward the Israeli-Syrian negotiation. (President Bush apparently promised Prime Minister Rabin in August 1992 to support the loan guarantees to Israel and to maintain its qualitative military superiority.)[46]

Recognizing now that Syria could undermine the Israeli-Palestinian track, Rabin sought to improve the atmosphere with Damascus. He mentioned the possibility of an interim settlement with Syria whereby Israel would give up a few kilometers in the Golan. Furthermore, Israel's newly-appointed chief negotiator with the Syrian delegation, Prof. Itamar Rabinovich, announced for the first time on 24 August 1992 that Israel considered UN resolution 242 to be applicable also to the negotiations with Syria. Bushra Kanafani, the spokesperson for the Syrian delegation, praised the new Israeli approach as "constructive" and reflecting a fresh "political mentality."[47]

Asad himself responded positively to the new Israeli line by speaking for the first time in Damascus on 9 September 1992 about his concept of peace: "The peace of the brave, the peace of knights, real peace, a peace that lives, endures and guarantees the interests of all." But he added that in return for a peace settlement Syria demanded to have "each centimeter of the Golan." Syria's minister of foreign affairs, Faruq al-Shara made a further significant step when he announced for the first time in New York on 23 September 1992 that Syria was prepared to sign "a total peace" with Israel in return for Israel's withdrawal from the occupied Arab lands.[48]

Prime Minister Rabin considered Asad's statement as "important progress" but was not yet ready to accept the Syrian terms and to change his concept of territorial compromise. In his address to a special meeting of the Knesset Rabin said (amidst strong vocal protests from right-wing MKs): "Our intention is indeed to exhaust that chance, not on the assumption that in return for peace we give everything; certainly, the precedent of the peace with Egypt should not be repeated. The government has a mandate and it will conduct the negotiations in order to achieve full peace, while maintaining as much as possible, the territorial security assets."[49]

In short, Rabin summarized his position in two sentences: "We shall not enter into any territorial discussion with the Syrians before they will say in a loud voice to us and to the people in Syria that peace for them means embassies, open borders and normalization. Peace with Syria must stand on its own feet and must not be conditioned on agreements with other states [parties] with whom we negotiate."

Rabin's new strategy can be assessed as showing his belief that a strategic change toward Israel had occurred in Damascus. Asad realized that Syria had been unable to defeat Israel militarily and he was now ready to strike a political deal, possibly a peace agreement with Israel. True, Rabin was not convinced that Damascus had undergone an ideological transformation and a change of heart ("peace does not mean love for the other nation"). But he demanded that Asad provide proofs that he seriously sought peace: "I do not have x-rays to examine a person's intentions. I judge on the basis of moves, deeds and expressions, and this component is greatly missing on the part of Syria."[50]

Whether or not Rabin's terms were realistic or perhaps constituted a bargaining position, Asad refused to elaborate further on the Syrian notion of "total peace," or to meet with Rabin. He continued to insist on a prior Israeli commitment to total withdrawal from the Golan, as well as on the "comprehensiveness" of the peace agreement, relating to the all-Arab conflict with Israel.

It is very likely that Asad has been already prepared to accept in principle Rabin's terms for peace and normalization and implement them in the course of time, provided Israel agreed to his terms for peace. For although peace and normalization with Israel certainly has not been compatible with the Ba'thist pan-Arab tenets nor with his own ideological beliefs, Asad has recognized that he would not have a better alternative. Yet in order to convince his own people, long indoctrinated on anti-Israeli lines, to accept Israel he would need to demonstrate to them that he made Israel withdraw from all occupied Arab lands, notably the entire Golan, and that he was the only Arab leader since 1948 capable of obtaining national rights for the Palestinians.

Apart from his ideological motives, Asad also had strategic considerations behind his peace terms: on the one hand, he sought to push back the Israeli forces from their Golan positions some 35 miles from Damascus, down to the international boundary along the Hula and Jordan valleys; and on the other hand, he has sought not only to maintain his control over Lebanon, but also to extend his influence to a Palestinian entity or state (and possibly also in Jordan). Consequently, he could not afford to commit to peace and normalization with Israel before he could be sure to achieve these strategic and ideological objectives. If he did and Israel then refused to withdraw from the entire Golan and settle the Palestinian problem, Asad's credibility and prestige as well as Syria's ideological and strategic positions could be seriously damaged.

The sixth round of Israeli-Arab peace talks, from 24 August to 24 September 1992, brought for the first time significant progress, but not yet a breakthrough, in the peace-making process between Syria and Israel. Shifting its emphasis from the Palestinian track (which proved to be greatly obstructed) to the Syrian one, Rabin said: "Syria is a clear address, with a householder who is capable of taking decisions."[51]

Israel has confirmed that UN resolution 242 applies also to the Golan. But it has demanded from Syria to first clarify its ideas on the nature of peace or "total peace" before Israel details the extent of its withdrawal in the Golan. Syria had made more concessions than Israel in comparison to its previous positions: it has accepted the simultaneity of Israel's withdrawal and its implementation of peace, mutual security arrangements with Israel, and the term "peace agreement" – *Itifaqiyal Salam* – as a final product of the negotiation.

Syrian leaders have also hinted that they envisaged a "full peace," possibly entailing diplomatic relations and gradual normalization. But Syria has also insisted on a prior Israel commitment to total withdrawal from the Golan before it would officially specify the components of full peace. Damascus has repeatedly demanded also that the peace should be "just and comprehensive," and include the Lebanese, Jordanian and especially Palestinian fronts.[52]

Both Syria and Israel continued their efforts to win the support of the world community, notably the United States, for their respective positions. Asad signalled to President Bush and subsequently also to Clinton that Syria is the key for peace or war in the Middle East and that in addition to joining the American-led coalition in the Gulf War, Damascus had made several important concessions in the peace process, in accordance with the United States' requests, and it now expected American support for its position; otherwise, the peace process would be undermined and Syria might use its alliance with Iran to destabilize the Middle East.

On the whole, despite the continuous American military and financial assistance to Israel (which Damascus criticized), Syria considered President Bush's policy as empathetic, if not sympathetic. But following the Clinton victory in the November 1992 elections, Syrian leaders and media expressed concerns regarding his Middle East policy, apparently in view of the new president's record as a supporter of democratic Israel and his aversion toward dictatorships and "terrorist states" such as Syria. Syria's chief negotiator Mr. Allaf complained, for example, that "it seems that Israel, thinking that the Clinton administration is likely to be inclined to satisfy its ambitious endeavors, would bring about a standstill until the new administration takes office."[53] Allaf accused Israel of "attacking Lebanon [Hizbullah targets] without justification or provocation." Israel by contrast blamed Syria for encouraging Hizbullah's guerrilla actions against Israel in order to remind Clinton that Asad was the "Arab master of war-and-peace decisions."[54]

Thus, by the end of 1992, following the Clinton victory and two more rounds – seven and eight – of the Arab-Israeli peace talks, the Syrian-Israeli negotiations were in a state of deadlock, despite the significant progress achieved since August 1992. While Israel had stated that UN resolution 242 was applicable to the Golan Heights and gave priority to the negotiation with Syria, Syria had declared its readiness for "total" peace and to a "peace agreement" with Israel and made other positive gestures such as permitting Syrian Jews to emigrate. Both Syria and Israel had agreed on the need for mutual security, and managed also to contain the eruption of the serious fire exchanges between Hizbullah and Israeli forces on the Lebanese-Israel border. But on the core issues – the Syrian definition of peace and the extent of Israeli withdrawal – the serious gap still remained.

The Clinton administration began its term on 20 January and the new Secretary of State, Warren Christopher, was soon assigned to "revitalize" the peace process, suspended for several months because of divergent positions of the participants and their inclination to wait for the new American administration. On 17 December 1993, following the kidnapping and killing of an Israel police officer inside Israel by a Palestinian Hamas group, Israel deported some 400 Hamas leaders and activists to South Lebanon. This Israeli action triggered widespread international criticism and intense Palestinian violence in the occupied territories, and led to a long delay in the resumption of the peace talks.

Significantly, in contrast to the PLO position, Syrian Foreign Minister Faraq al-Shara, after his meeting with Christopher, said on 21 February 1993 that Syria no longer would link the exiled Palestinians' return to the renewal of the peace negotiations, because a peace settlement was more important. Lebanon's Foreign Minister Farrs Buwayz, apparently under Syrian directives, expressed a similar position, while Lebanese Prime Minister Rafiq al-Hariri, had stated a month earlier that his government was willing to conclude a peace treaty with Israel.[55]

In early May 1993 Asad gave an exclusive and important interview to Patrick Seale for *al-Wasat*, an Arabic weekly published in London. Expressing his doubts that the Israeli government wished to make peace, and reiterating Syrian principles for a comprehensive peace, Asad made several significant comments, such as, "During the past two years [there has been] a great support for peace efforts in Israel, and certainly it will have an influence on Israeli rulers." Asked by Seale whether he agrees to Israel's existence in the region, Asad answered that he supported the Palestinian and Arab "new position that Palestine consists of both the Arabs and the Israelis."

Asad also remarked that there could be varying speeds in the different tracks of negotiations that might produce agreements at different times; but these agreements should be subject to a comprehensive settlement or "the collective interests of all" [Arabs] – to be approved by Syria.[56]

Asad's messages were possibly directed to give the impression that Syria would not object to separate bilateral agreements between other Arab delegations and Israel, on condition that they did not harm Syrian interests and met the goal of a comprehensive settlement. In addition to his attempt to win (or regain) American support to his position, Asad endeavored: (a) To throw "the ball into the Israeli court," by manifesting a flexible new position; (b) to prevent a separate deal between Israel and the Palestinians (or Jordan) thus leaving Syria in the cold; (c) to assure the PLO that Syria would not sign a separate agreement with Israel, leaving them behind.[57]

Apparently to indicate Israel's strong inclination to conclude a peace agreement with Syria, both Prime Minister Rabin and Foreign Minister Peres conveyed their optimism about an imminent peace with Syria. In an April 1993 interview Rabin said, "there is a risk in descending from the Golan like the risk in the [Israeli] withdrawal from all Sinai."[58] If Rabin's statement was correctly reported it indeed represented for the first time a signal that he was considering a total withdrawal from the Golan Heights in return for a bilateral full peace agreement with Syria. To corroborate this assumption, it should be pointed out that around the same time Rabin changed his previous motto "Withdrawal on the Golan, not *from* the Golan" to a more flexible one, namely: the extent (or "depth") of Israeli withdrawal will depend on the extent ("depth") of the Syrian peace. This assertion could be interpreted as readiness for full Israeli withdrawal from the Golan in return for a full peace and normalization with Syria (but with no linkage to other Arab parties).[59]

Nevertheless, by mid-July 1993 neither Syria nor Israel were ready to say the magic words "peace and normalization" or "total withdrawal," respectively, although Damascus continued to send more positive signals of its readiness to sign a peace agreement compatible with Israeli expectations. Jerusalem, however, did not show any inclination to give up the Golan in its entirety, and renewed its previous attempts at maneuvering Syria into accepting Israeli terms for peace, namely: withdrawal from the major part of the Golan, but not from the entire region; and delinking the Golan-Syrian issue from the Palestinian-Israeli settlement. Rabin possibly expected that he could achieve these aims by resuming his initial policy of summer 1992: to first implement Palestinian autonomy or self-rule in Gaza and the West Bank, deferring settlement with Syria to a point when Israel would negotiate from an advantageous position.

Presumably Rabin resorted to his initial strategy toward Syria not only out of personal conviction and deep concern lest the majority of the Israeli Jews refuse to relinquish the entire Golan area for peace with Syria; the secret negotiations held in Oslo during that period between Israeli and PLO representatives, made Rabin again prefer the Palestinian over the Syrian track.

Apparently in reaction to Rabin's refusal to give up the entire Golan for peace, Asad resorted again to his old tactics of exerting military pressure on Israel through southern Lebanon. During the first two weeks of July 1993, the Syria-directed Hizbullah and Syrian-controlled Jibril group (Popular Front for Liberation of Palestine – General Command) launched several attacks, including firing Katyusha rockets, on Israeli targets in southern Lebanon and northern Israel, killing five soldiers and wounding eight. Israel responded with a large-scale artillery and air bombardment against terrorist/guerrilla positions and villages in southern Lebanon. In this operation (*"Din ve-Heshbon"*) which lasted seven days, some 50 to 70 terrorists and 114 civilians were reportedly killed, 400 to 500 wounded, and several hundred thousands of Lebanese villagers temporarily fled their homes.

With American mediation an understanding was reached in early August between Syria-Lebanon and Israel whereby Damascus and Beirut undertook to prevent the launching of Katyusha rockets from Lebanon into Israel[60] (although not against the Israeli-held security zone in southern Lebanon). This new Syrian-Israeli understanding demonstrated not only that Damascus was capable of curbing the Hizbullah and was holding the key for stability in the region; it also indicated that Asad was not interested in a military showdown, but rather in a political settlement, with Israel. As Rabin admitted in late August: "Today there is a greater chance for the achievement of stability in Lebanon, as well as progress toward peace with Syria." Asad himself gave earlier yet another signal of his peace strategy. In a written message to the Syrian army on its anniversary in early August Asad said: "We are in the battle for peace and we conduct it in the same capability that we have conducted the military battles. Our positions in the peace battle will not be less courageous than these in the battlefield." (At the same time however – in August 1993 – Syria continued to receive Scud-C missiles from North Korea, while Asad reportedly depicted Israel as "the enemy" and the United States as "the friend of our enemy").[61]

As it turned out, an Israeli-PLO breakthrough happened in Oslo on 19 August, whereas the Syrian-Israeli negotiations would not produce any substantial results for many more months. It was only on 16 January 1994, during the Clinton–Asad summit, that significant progress, perhaps even a breakthrough, occurred in the Syrian-Israeli peace negotiations. During the press conference that followed the summit, Asad for the first time spoke about "normal [or regular] peaceful relations" [*alakat sihm adiyya*], "real and durable peace" and "respectable peace." Asad also referred to the joint efforts (with the United States) "to put an end to the Arab-Israeli conflict and reach a comprehensive and true peace that will enable the peoples of the region to concentrate on their growth and progress [in] a new era of security and stability." Finally – in response to a question – he said that "we are ready to sign peace now."

Clinton's understanding or interpretation of Asad's message regarding the nature of peace went beyond the public statements of the Syrian leader himself. When asked: "Do you feel that you have a firm commitment from President Asad to normalize relations with Israel . . . open borders, free trade and diplomatic relations [?]" Clinton responded: "The short answer is yes. I believe that President Asad has made a clear, forthright and very important statement on normal relations. Now, in order to achieve those relations, a peace agreement has to be negotiated in good faith and carried out. But this is an important statement – the first time that there has been a clear expression that there will be a possibility of that sort of relationships."

In addition, Clinton not only stressed that "Syria is the key to the achievement of an enduring and comprehensive peace," but also supported Asad's notion "that there still would have to be a comprehensive peace in which the issues affecting Lebanon, the issues affecting Jordan and the issues relating to the PLO would – in addition to the Syrian issues – all be resolved."

Apparently Clinton was not only expressing his own personal commitment to Middle East peace but was also deeply impressed with Asad's commitment to peace with Israel. (Vice President Gore depicted it as a huge "breakthrough".) Placing Asad at the core of the peace process and helping him to put the onus for new movement on Rabin, Clinton expected Israel in particular to now take "crucial decisions" on the "question of relating withdrawal to peace and security."[62] In this respect the U.S. now urged Israel to discuss during the renewed talks with Syria the withdrawal issue which in fact represented paragraph five in the Syrian working paper of August 1992.[63]

Rabin indeed realized after the Geneva summit that even though Asad's remarks had not included the "magic words" that he had expected, they certainly satisfied Clinton. Yet, the Israeli government needed not only to please Washington, but to avoid antagonizing the Israeli public, while striking a hard bargain with Syria.

Possibly with these aims in mind, Rabin suggested to the Knesset on 18 January 1994, through Deputy Defense Minister, Motta Gur, that "should the territorial price demanded from us in the Golan Heights be significant, the government will bring the subject to a referendum." By this suggestion Rabin has sought first to neutralize domestic opposition to and prepare the public for a substantial withdrawal on the Golan, and perhaps even from the Golan. Secondly, he has sought to throw back the ball into Asad's court and induce him to make peace gestures that the Israeli public could not refuse, thereby helping Rabin to gain domestic support for his Syrian policy.[64]

Notes

1. C. H. Dodd and M. Sales (eds), *Israel and the Arab World* (London, 1970), p. 183.
2. R. Pedhazur, *Ha'aretz*, 3 May, 11 August 1991. Cf. G. Rafael, *Destination Peace* (New York: Council on Foreign Relations, 1981), p. 177.
3. Cited in I. Rabinovich, "Israel, Syria and Jordan," paper presented at the Council of Foreign Relations, New York, October 1989; cf. A. Drysdale and R. A. Hinnebusch, *Syria and the Middle East Peace Process* (New York: Council on Foreign Relations, 1991), p. 114.
4. Y. Nedava (ed.), *The Arab-Israeli Conflict* (Ramat Gan: Revivim, 1983), p. 273. (Hebrew).
5. *Ha'aretz*, 8 June 1988.
6. *New York Times*, 29 December 1989.
7. Dodd and Sales, *Israel*, p. 174.
8. Ibid., pp. 175–176.
9. Damascus Radio, 8 March 1972.
10. Interview with *al-Nahar* (Lebanon), 17 March 1971.
11. For details, see M. Ma'oz, *Asad – The Sphinx of Damascus: A Political Biography* (London and New York: Weidenfeld and Nicolson, 1988), pp. 94–97.
12. Ibid., pp. 97ff.
13. Ibid., pp. 102–103; W. B. Quandt, *Decade of Decisions* (Berkeley: University of California Press, 1977), pp. 261ff.
14. Damascus Radio, 6 October 1975; *Newsweek*, 22 September 1975.
15. Ma'oz, *Sphinx of Damascus*, p. 104.
16. Drysdale and Hinnebusch, *Syria*, p. 112; Ma'oz, *Sphinx of Damascus*, pp. 105–106.
17. I. Rabinovich, *The War for Lebanon* (Ithaca: Cornell University Press, 1984), pp. 49, 106.
18. Asad's interviews with the *Washington Post*, 2 December 1976 and with *Time*, 17 January 1977. Further details in Ma'oz, *Sphinx of Damascus*, pp. 138ff.; Drysdale and Hinnebusch, *Syria*, pp. 114–115.
19. For an excellent study on this issue, see W. B. Quandt, *Camp David, Peace Making and Politics* (Washington, D.C.: The Brookings Institution, 1986).
20. For a more detailed discussion, see Ma'oz, *Sphinx of Damascus*, pp. 146–148, 177ff.

21. H. Cobban, *The Superpowers and the Syrian-Israeli Conflict* (Washington, D.C.: CSIS, 1991), p. 38.
22. For details, see Drysdale and Hinnebusch, *Syria*, pp. 44ff.; *International Herald Tribune*, 7 August 1984; D. Hopwood, *Syria 1945–1986* (London: Unwin Hyman, 1988), pp. 112–114; *Washington Post*, 15 November 1986; *Al-Dustur*, 31 March 1986; *Jerusalem Post*, 29 January 1987; A. Cowell, "Trouble in Damascus," *New York Times Magazine*, 1 April 1990.
23. Cobban, *Superpowers*, pp. 52ff.; Drysdale and Hinnebusch, *Syria*, pp. 166–167; see also E. Karsh, *The Soviet Union and Syria* (London, 1988), pp. 81ff.
24. Karsh, *Soviet Union*, p. 92; Cobban, *Superpowers*, pp. 57–58.
25. *Al-Qabas* (Kuwait), 27 January 1989, quoted in *The Middle East Journal*, Summer 1989, p. 502; see also Drysdale and Hinnebusch, *Syria*, pp. 166–167.
26. *Middle East Journal*, Spring 1987, p. 277.
27. *Ha'aretz*, 23 December 1988; *Middle East Journal*, Spring 1989, p. 286.
28. *New York Times*, 17 July 1990 and 15 July 1990.
29. *Ha'aretz*, 19 March 1990.
30. Asad's speech, Damascus Radio, 8 March, 1988; Asad's interview with *Newsweek*, 3 April 1989; Asad's speech, Damascus Radio, 8 March 1990.
31. Cf. *New York Times*, 17 July 1991; interview with Syria's foreign minister, Faruk al-Shar'a, *Newsweek*, 1 July 1991; *New York Times*, 19 April 1991; *Pravda*, 17 July 1991, quoted in *The Soviet Union and the Middle East* (Hebrew University) 16, 7 (1991): 1–2; *Al-Ba'th*, 25 December 1991.
32. Quoted in *FBIS*, 10 October 1991, p. 27.
33. In an interview with Lally Weymouth, *Los Angeles Times*, 29 July 1991. Syrian Foreign Minister al-Shar'a, in his Madrid speech, also rejected the notion of Jewish nationhood, speaking of Jews as merely belonging to a religion rather than forming a nation.
34. *FBIS*, 10 October 1991; *al-Hayat*, 28 August 1991.
35. Poll-taker Hanoch Smith, *New York Times*, 24 March 1991.
36. *FBIS*, 25 July 1991, pp. 29–30, quoting *Jerusalem Post*, 22 July and *Hadashot*, 24 July 1991.
37. Israel Radio, 5 October 1991.
38. *Yediot Aharonot*, 17 June 1990.
39. *Spectrum* (Labor Party monthly), December 1991, p. 11.
40. For its full text, see the *Jerusalem Post*, 15 May 1989.
41. *Yediot Aharonot*, 19 March 1991; Drysdale and Hinnebusch, *Syria*, p. 205; cf. Shamir's conversation with the Golan settlers, Israel Radio, 7 August 1990.
42. Israel Radio, 28 July 1991, quoted in *FBIS*, 29 July 1991; cf. Drysdale and Hinnebusch, *Syria*, pp. 205–206; *New York Times*, 17 July 1991.
43. See, e.g., *Ha'aretz*, 5 July 1992.

44. *Financial Times*, 25 June 1992; *Ha'aretz* (Tel Aviv) 3 July and 23 August 1992.
45. *Ma'ariv* (Tel Aviv), 14 August 1992; *Ha'aretz* (Tel Aviv), 23 August 1992.
46. *Ha'aretz*, 23 August 1992; *Peacewatch*, No. 39, 21 August 1992. Cf. Quandt, *Peace Process*, p. 407.
47. *Ha'aretz* (Tel Aviv), 25 August 1992.
48. See respectively, *Yediot Aharonot* (Tel Aviv), 10 and 24 September 1992; *Peacewatch*, No. 40, 14 September 1992; *al-Safir* (Lebanon), 24 September 1992. Cf. interview with Usama al-Bay, Mubarak's chief adviser; *Yediot Aharonot*, 30 August 1992; *al-Wasal* (London), 18 September 1992.
49. See respectively, *Yediot Aharonot* (Tel Aviv), 10 September 1992; *Ha'aretz* (Tel Aviv), 10, 13 and 15 September 1992; *Peacewatch*, No. 40, 14 September 1992; No. 43, 25 September 1992; *Ma'ariv* (Tel Aviv) 11, 22 & 27 September 1992.
50. Citations from *Ma'ariv* (Tel Aviv), 22 & 27 September 1992; *al-Hamishmar* (Tel Aviv), 23 September 1992.
51. *Ma'ariv* (Tel Aviv), 27 September 1992; Cf. *Yediot Aharonot* (Tel Aviv), 8 December 1992.
52. Cf. "Reported Text of Syria's Proposed Formal Statement of Principles October 26, 1992," *FBIS*, 28 October 1992; *al-Wasal* (London), 18 September 1992; *al-Hayat* (Beirut), 26 July 1992.
53. Interview of Muaffaq Allaf to *al-Quds al-Arabi* (London), 17 November 1992. See also Khaddam's interview, Radio Monte Carlo, 10 November 1992; *Tishrin* (Damascus), 9 November 1992.
54. See respectively, Allaf's interview 16 November 1992; R. Satloff, "The Arab-Israeli Talks: Pause for November 3," *Peacewatch*, No. 45, 29 October 1992. See also, "Signals from Two Old Foes," *Time*, 30 November 1992, pp. 30–33; *Washington Post*, 19 November 1992.
55. *Middle East Journal*, Summer 1993, pp. 479–483; *Middle East International*, 5 March 1993, p. 8.
56. *Al-Wasal* (London) No. 67, 10 May 1993, pp. 12–20; *Ha'aretz* (Tel Aviv) 24 May 1993. Cf. E. Ya'ari, "The Problem with Asad," *The Jerusalem Report*, 6 May 1993, p. 31; *Yediot Aharonot* (Tel Aviv) 12 May 1993. Cf. *FBIS* 10–16 May 1993, pp. 45–52.
57. "It is a known fact that the rulers in Tel Aviv topped by Yitzhak Rabin are relentlessly seeking to divide the ranks of Arab negotiators . . . Syria could have reached long ago a bilateral agreement with Israel . . . [but] Syria has repeatedly said that it is concerned with Jerusalem, the West Bank and South Lebanon in the same way it is concerned with the Golan." See respectively, Damascus Radio, 1 May and 18 March 1993; Asad's interview; *al-Wasal*, 10 May 1993.
58. *Ma'ariv* (Tel Aviv), 25 April 1993. See also *Yediot Aharonot* (Tel Aviv), 8 December 1992 and 4 May 1993; *FBIS*, 19 January 1993.
59. Rabin's interview, *Yediot Aharonot*, 4 May 1993. Cf. Y. Marcus, "Return

of Golan: Rabin's Victory, Likud's Loss," *Ha'aretz* (Tel Aviv), 30 April 1993; Rabin to Israel Radio, 4 June 1993.

60. See Z. Schiff, "Asad Bohen et Rabin," *Ha'aretz* (Tel Aviv), 16 July 1993; also *Ha'aretz* 2, 4 and 8 August 1993; *Near East Report* (Washington, D.C.), 19 July 1993. Cf. T. W. Seelye, "Syria and the Peace Process," *Middle East Policy*, Vol. II, No. 2, 2 November 1993, p. 109.

61. See respectively, *Near East Report*, 23 August 1993, *Ha'aretz* (Tel Aviv), 4 August 1993. Cf. *idem*, 2 and 10 August 1993.

62. For the full Arabic text of the Clinton-Asad press conference, see *al-Quds* (Jerusalem), 16 January 1994. See also *Ma'ariv* and *Ha'aretz* (Tel Aviv), 17 January 1994; R. Satloff, "Asad's Geneva Success," *Policywatch* (The Washington Institute) No. 111, 19 January 1994; *New York Times* & *Washington Post*, 17 January 1994.

63. On this working paper and Israel's reaction see *al-Wasal* (London), 18 September 1992; *Ha'aretz* (Tel Aviv), 6 July and 21 November 1993.

64. See respectively *Ha'aretz* (Tel Aviv), 18 January 1994; *Al-Hamishmar* (Tel Aviv), 20 January 1994; *Ma'ariv* (Tel Aviv), 29 January 1994; see also *New East Report*, 24 January 1994.

18

Palestine and Jordan

Nasser Eddin Nashashibi

Jordan to me is another Palestine! I have worked in it. I have lived in the palaces of its king and founder, the late Abdullah al-Hussein. I have contributed to the shaping of its history – political and social. I have been honored with its highest rewards and decorations. Some of my books are about Jordan, and some of my best friends are Jordanians.

Jordan was and still is a poor country. When the United Nations General Assembly was discussing the division of Palestine in November 1947 – under the assumption that the Arab part would be annexed to Jordan – the Foreign Minister of Pakistan, Sir Zafrulla Khan, spoke against such a solution. "If we add zero to zero, the result would only be zero," he said, adding that "annexing the rocky, poor part of Palestine to the Jordan desert would not solve anything."

In 1989 serious riots broke out in the southern part of the kingdom over price increases which were imposed in accordance with an agreement with the International Monetary Fund. The economy is poor – no oil and no real income from tourism. Some minerals, like potash and phosphate, are all that can be exported.

A brief study of the contemporary history of Jordan emphasizes the fact that the country was always an Arab country, linked to the western side of the River – culturally and politically. The Arabs conquered the area in the seventh century; the Ottomans took control of it in the sixteenth century, and in 1920 Britain imposed the Mandate on both sides of the Jordan, i.e., on Palestine and Transjordan, until 1946, when an independent kingdom was born with King Abdullah as its monarch.

All through the years of that British Mandate over Palestine and

Transjordan, and through all the disturbances, events, bloodshed and continuous visits by investigating British commissions to Palestine, the attitude of a major Palestinian political party was always decided by an invisible Jordanian shadow – King Abdullah.

Let me explain. To a well-known Palestinian leader, Haj Amin al-Husseini, the arch-enemy of the Palestinian cause – after the Zionists and the British – was Abdullah of Jordan. Ever since the 1920s, the Mufti, or "Haj Amin," refused every political solution to the Palestinian problem which was suggested – whether it involved the division of Palestine or keeping the status quo, pending better circumstances – because of the shadow of Abdullah of Jordan. The Mufti feared that any such solution would divide Palestine and result in the annexation of the Arab part to the Hashemite regime, with the cooperation of Abdullah's main Palestine ally and friend, Ragheb al-Nashashibi – who was, at the same time, as head of the National Defense Party and mayor of Jerusalem, the Mufti's main political enemy.

Thus, the Arab Higher Committee of Palestine refused the recommendation of the Peel Commission of 1937; refused the recommendations of the 1939 White Paper; refused the recommendations of the Anglo-American Commission of 1946, and refused the final decisions of the United Nations Committee of 1947 – all because the Mufti felt that such solutions to the Palestinian problem would mean that the Arabs would lose half of Palestine and that the other half would be left to Abdullah and his Palestinian allies, the Nashashibis.

Although this fact was well known to Abdullah and to the Nashashibis, that knowledge could not prevent the continuing bloodshed and hostilities from the beginning of the 1930s until the creation of Israel.

I can thus say with full confidence that Jordan and its rulers were – indirectly – the main factor in shaping the future of Palestine for a period of thirty years.

It may be true to say that Abdullah's ambition was mainly directed toward regaining the throne of Damascus, which his brother, King Faisal Ibn al-Husseini, had lost to the French in 1920 after the battle of Maysaloon. Because of that life-long ambition, Abdullah wanted to get part or all of Palestine under his control and was willing to offer the Jews a sort of autonomy within his kingdom. Damascus was his ultimate target but Palestine was his starting point toward realizing that goal.

On 1 December 1948, King Abdullah convened a conference of his Palestinian supporters in Jericho and had himself declared King of Palestine. The conference passed a resolution which – in my opinion – was prepared for the delegates in advance. It reads as follows:

1.   The Conference thanks the Arab states for services rendered to Palestine.
2.   It proclaims the unity between Transjordan and Palestine as a step toward complete Arab unity.
3.   It proclaims King Abdullah to be the legitimate king of all Palestine and salutes, with gratitude, his great and courageous army.
4.   It requests His Majesty to take steps to enable the Palestinians to choose their legal representatives.

On the same day, a delegation from the conference crossed the frontier and went to meet Abdullah to hand him a copy of the resolution. I was with them. Abdullah waited for us at his palace at "Shuna" near Jericho. He addressed the delegates as follows:

> "I consider your resolution as a blessing from Almighty God. . . . In the present circumstances there is no room for rhetoric but for thought and discipline. . . . I hope and believe that your resolutions will undoubtably help to take Palestine out of its present dilemma . . . "

The unification of the West Bank and Jordan dealt a fatal blow to the Mufti's "Arab Government of All Palestine," which he had created in Gaza. The absorption of a part of Palestine into Abdullah's kingdom was the culmination of Abdullah's efforts since the early 1930s.

Less than two years later, Abdullah was assassinated at the door to the Al-Aqsa Mosque in Jerusalem. I still remember that, at 11:48 on Friday, 25 July 1951, King Abdullah fell dead next to me.

It is also correct to say that the Palestinian problem and the Palestinians had a great influence on many different decisions and steps taken by Jordanian rulers. In 1991 Jordan refused to join the Western-led military coalition against the invasion of Kuwait by Iraq – which cost Jordan dearly in money and support from the oil-rich Gulf states – because of the overwhelming and nearly unanimous support of the Palestinian people, in and outside of Jordan, for Saddam Hussein of Iraq.

Jordan, like all other Arab states, depends entirely on imported food, and agricultural development in Jordan has not kept pace with the growth of the population. The essential issue in such agricultural development is water and water resources, which are, in turn, affected by political considerations and the relations with neighboring countries, like Israel.

Furthermore, the Gulf oil industry's recession and the Gulf War led to the dismissal of half a million Palestinians, who moved to Jordan, adding to its economic problems and threatening it with grave unemployment. Jordan – for the time being – remains dependent on financial subsidies from the United States, Europe and the rich Arab oil states. Figures show that, for example, in 1987 Jordan received a total of $450 million in financial aid. But the fact remains that Jordan's economic prospects, at the present, are bleak, unless the miracle of peace solves the tragedy of the Palestinians and the needs of the Jordanians.

Future mutual agreements between Israel and Jordan on the issues of water, agriculture, tourism, trade and security measures – together with a possible agreement on the building of the "Great Canal" connecting the Red and the Dead Seas – are all necessary ingredients to cement the peace.

Three times, in 1948, 1967 and 1991, the only refuge the Palestinians found after their tragic exodus was Jordan. No other Arab country treated the Palestinian refugees with full consideration for their pride and dignity. No other Arab country granted the Palestinians full citizenship and full rights.

And now, when the PLO talks about some sort of confederation with Jordan, King Hussein – as he told me personally – says: "Yes, I have no objection to such a link with the Palestinians, provided three conditions are taken into consideration:

1. We have to wait and see what sort of a Palestinian entity or government is created on the West Bank.
2. Such a confederation would not be, in any future development, an application of the "Jordan option" (substituting Jordan for any Palestinian entity).
3. A referendum should be held in Jordan and among the Palestinians about such a confederation."

In August 1988 Abdullah's grandson, King Hussein – whose reign was marked by continuous wars and challenges, not only from Israel but also from Egypt's Nasser, Iraq's Kassem, the rulers of Syria and, lately, the Kuwaitis and Saudis – severed all juridical and administrative ties with the occupied West Bank, thereby undoing what his grandfather had accomplished forty years earlier and enabling the Palestine National Council to declare the state of Palestine, in November 1988.

Earlier, at the Arab Summit Conference in Rabat in 1974, the PLO had been designated as the sole and legal representative of the Palestinians.

Yet at the 1991 Madrid Conference, Jordan was the only legal and official umbrella under which the Palestinians could take their seat. Forgetting everything about the Jordanian-Palestinian civil war of September 1970 and the war of words between Amman and the Palestinians, a new chapter in the relationship between the two was opened.

There is no need to go back to each step in the past two years and enumerate the services rendered by Jordan to the "Peace Process" and especially to the Palestinian party in the Peace Conference. Yet Jordan, like most of the Arabs, was, at the end of the first ten days of September 1993, confronted with the results of the secret Oslo talks between Israel and the Palestinians, which led to the famous agreement. After a period of hesitation and astonishment, the King publicly accepted the Oslo agreement – probably due to Jordan's economic needs and pressure from the United States.

Political and economic cooperation between the state of Jordan and the Palestinians will continue, but I do not think that the future road of such cooperation between East Jordan and West Jordan will be as smooth as it used to be in the past.

I also predict that political and economic cooperation between Jordan and Israel will continue and will develop further.

In his office, Foreign Minister Shimon Peres told me that the future solution to the Arab-Israeli conflict will depend on two "pillars":

1.   A political confederation between Jordan and any Palestinian entity in the West Bank.
2.   An economic confederation between Israel, Jordan and the Palestinians.

At that meeting I took the liberty of telling him we should not be flattered, distracted, or deceived by the success that Israel achieved by signing the agreement with the PLO on 13 September 1933.

In our contemporary history, many peace treaties and many peace agreements died because they could not be successfully implemented and could not achieve a badly needed period of initial success.

Whether with the PLO, with Jordan, or with any other Arab country, the good peace is the just peace. And the just peace is the one which takes into consideration all the national and legitimate rights of all the parties. We must not forget that the high hopes expressed in the Rhodes Armistice Agreements of 1949 failed to be realized! We must not forget that the treaty initiated in the early 1950s between Jordan and Israel also died! We must not forget that the 1983 peace treaty between Lebanon and Israel was stillborn. And lastly, we must not forget that all the secret contacts between Israel and the late King Abdullah of Jordan had no result except Abdullah's assassination at the door of Al-Aqsa Mosque in Jerusalem. The peace we need is a just and comprehensive peace which possesses the requirements of life.

There should be no mistake by any body or party in underestimating the real geopolitical value of a neighborly state such as Jordan. Jordan is not merely a buffer state between Israel and the Arab world. It is a state with a special role to play in the area, and it is the only state able to play such a role. Nor is Israel unaware of that role – and Amman should be encouraged to play it.

19

Jordan and the Palestinian Question: Coming Full Circle

Asher Susser

The pressure of events of recent times has put the Jordanians on the defensive and in an undesirable situation. Jordan in its relations with the Palestinians has come full circle in the sense that at the end of 1993 the Jordanians found themselves pretty much where they were facing the Rabat resolutions in 1974, albeit now in somewhat more difficult circumstances. What the Rabat resolutions only suggested, the Israeli-PLO agreement is beginning to put into practice, and that makes things a lot more difficult from the Jordanian point of view.

Jordan's relation to Palestine, and Jordan's relation to the Palestinian question, is unique. In that respect, Jordan is not an ordinary confrontation state. Jordan was born out of the Palestine question. The Palestine question gave rise to three political entities, the Israeli, the Palestinian, and the Jordanian, and Jordan was locked into the politics and the fate of Palestine from the day it was founded in 1921.

For Jordan the Palestine question is existential. It is neither a border matter nor simply a question of historical rights in the conflict with Israel.

King Abdullah was never satisfied with his little desert emirate, and always sought a role of dominance in Palestine, and it was Abdullah who said that, in reference to Palestine, he wanted to be the rider, not the ridden.

After the 1949 armistice negotiations with Israel, Jordan became in its own view the inheritor of Palestine. Jordan sought to absorb the Palestinians and the Palestinian entity into the Jordanian kingdom and to Jordanize both the Palestinians, and the Palestinian question. The Jordanians granted citizenship to all Palestinians, refugees and non-refugees alike. Jordan settled refugees and Jordan encouraged or at least acquiesced in the emigration of Palestinians from the West Bank to the East Bank. Jordan opposed the formation of any independent Palestinian power base west of the river. And Jordan sought to create a Jordanian-Palestinian two-bank entity in which clearly the East Bank was preferred politically and economically.

Therefore, for Jordan in the late 1950s, what was called in the parlance of Arab relations of those days, "the revival of the Palestinian entity" – "*ihya al-Kiyan al-Falastini*" was very unwelcome. Jordan sought to block the establishment of the PLO, then acquiesced in its establishment, but prevented it from taking root in the West Bank. In the years preceding the Six Day War, the political clash between Jordan and the PLO, then under the leadership of Ahmed Shukayri, was not over influence in the West Bank, but, in the view of both protagonists, over the political fate of the Jordanian-Palestinian entity on both banks of the river.

If the Jordanians had been absolutely convinced that whatever happened in the West Bank had no implications for the East Bank, they would have been far less involved, and even today would be less concerned about events in the West Bank. But because the Jordanians have believed for a very long time, and apparently still believe, that whatever happens in the West Bank has far-reaching ramifications for the East Bank, the struggle is not really over the future of the West Bank.

The struggle is really over the relationship between the East Bank and the West Bank, and Palestinian or Jordanian predominance in this special relationship. For Jordan, 1967 was therefore a watershed because Jordan, by losing the West Bank, lost control of the Palestinian destiny, their manipulative control over the Palestinian national movement. From then on, there was a freezing of the Jordanization of the Palestinians, the re-Palestinization of the Arab-Israeli conflict, and the re-emergence of the Palestinians as determiners of their own future with the PLO as their legitimate representative. The Jordanians sought but failed to prevent these processes after the Six Day War. The overview of the Jordanian interest in this question must relate to two factors in particular. One is geography: the proximity of Jordan to Palestine. When Hussein says they are the closest to Palestine, this means many things, but at least, geographically, it is certainly true.

Demographically, about 50 percent of the population of the East Bank today are of Palestinian extraction. Many people say 60 percent and 70 percent – the percentage often rises in accord with the political views of the person talking, but, to the best of our knowledge, it is somewhere in the vicinity of 50 percent. No one knows exactly; it is very difficult to make these calculations, but 60 percent and above are exaggerations.

What are the possible implications for the Hashemite kingdom of Jordan of the exercise by the Palestinians of their right to self-determination?

There are more Palestinians on the East Bank than there are on the West Bank. There cannot be any solution to the Palestinian question that does not have ramifications for the East Bank. Therefore, any settlement based on Palestinian rights to self-determination raises questions and anxieties in Jordan about the future status of the Palestinians in Jordan. To whom do the Palestinians in Jordan owe their political allegiance? To the PLO, their sole legitimate representative, or to the king?

In recent years, the slogan that the Jordanians use in reference to the Palestinian question has changed. In the 1960s, when the Jordanians wanted to prevent the establishment of the PLO, they used to say that Jordan is Palestine, and Palestine is Jordan. The logic of that statement was that if Jordan is Palestine and Palestine is Jordan, Jordan is the inheritor of Palestine.

If Jordan is the inheritor of Palestine, there is no need for the PLO to represent the Palestinians; Jordan represents the Palestinians. But since the elevation of the Palestinians through the PLO to political prominence, the Jordanians have changed that slogan and it is now, Jordan is Jordan, and Palestine is Palestine. That is, leave the East Bank to us Jordanians! This is our political patrimony, and it is that which we wish to protect.

There has been a gradual evolution of Jordan's vision of the Palestinian settlement. The early 1970s were times of great change in this respect, and the 1973 War was definitely a turning point in regard to the status of the PLO in the eyes of the Arab world. And it was in Hussein's federation plan of 1972 that the historical change was made, not in the disengagement of 1988.

When Hussein launched that federation plan in 1972, for the first time he recognized the Palestinian people as deserving a separate political entity, linked in a federation with Jordan as an entity unto themselves. That was the first and the most important change. The rest were tactical maneuvers around the question of the federative or confederative relationship.

But what the Jordanians tried to do after concluding that federation was perhaps the best solution, was to portray themselves as the guarantors of Palestinian self-determination. That is, if the Palestinians wanted self-determination, they would achieve it via Jordan through the federation. The federation and the notion of Palestinian self-determination became in the eyes of the Jordanians an instrument against the PLO. That was the initial objective. But in that, they failed, as they did in many other of the competitions with the PLO.

They failed in the aftermath of the Yom Kippur War in their effort to prevent the recognition by the Arab world of the PLO as the sole legitimate representative of the Palestinians. Jordan accepted the Rabat resolutions, unwillingly, grudgingly, and hoping at some time in the future perhaps to overturn them. But they accepted the political reality for lack of any better choice. The Jordanians continued, after the Rabat resolutions, to try and separate the PLO and Palestinian self-determination, linking self-determination to the people in the West Bank and Gaza. The people in the West Bank and Gaza were the true Palestinians, as far as the Jordanians were concerned.

From the late 1970s and early 1980s onward, the Jordanians changed their tactics. After the war in Lebanon, the PLO was weak and Jordan then tried, via agreements with Arafat, to subordinate the PLO to Jordan's peace-making strategy. That failed too.

There was an agreement between Arafat and Hussein in February 1985 but it only papered over the differences and didn't really solve very much. And the ties between Hussein and Arafat were suspended shortly thereafter. For Hussein, there was a triangle of representation, as far as the Palestinian question was concerned: Jordan, the PLO, and the people in the West Bank and Gaza. Hussein sought all along to change the balance within that triangle in favor of Jordan on the one hand, and the people in the West Bank and Gaza on the other, trying to reduce the role of the PLO as much as possible.

Then came the *intifada*. The *intifada* set back this Jordanian concept considerably. For the *intifada*, at least in its initial phases, tipped the scales in the PLO's favor against Jordan. If the war in Lebanon had tipped the scales in Jordan's favor, and against the PLO, the *intifada* reversed the order. And this was the background to the disengagement decision of 1988.

Yet the disengagement was not an abdication of the Jordanians from the Palestinian question. For those geographic and demographic reasons mentioned before, even if Jordan wished to, it could not withdraw from the Palestinian question.

Therefore, the disengagement was not a Jordanian withdrawal, rather, it was a concession to the Palestinians, and to the PLO in particular, in an effort to create a balanced partnership between Jordan and the PLO on the basis of some kind of mutual trust.

Jordan was opposed to Israeli-Palestinian bilateral negotiations that would leave Jordan out of the picture. And the Jordanians were absolutely convinced that if they did not come together with the PLO, they themselves would be excluded from the process. Jordan had access to the process only if it joined together with the PLO. That was the logic of Jordan's emphasis on the international conference; not only to bring the PLO in, but to keep Jordan in the picture as well. Jordan could not afford exclusion.

And Jordan faces a dilemma from which there is no easy solution or exit. In the aftermath of 1967, pan-Arabism declined as a major force in the Arab world. The Arab world came to terms with separate states. On the one hand, for the Jordanians this was a blessing because the Arab world came to terms with Jordan as a state, as well. But what this also meant was that the Arab world recognized the Palestinians' right to their own state. And Jordan, in order to preserve its own inter-Arab legitimacy, had no choice but to acquiesce in an Arab consensus on Palestine which in the long term could be detrimental, or even dangerous, as far as Jordanian interests are concerned.

The other problem that the Jordanians face is that they do not control the regional context in which they operate. The regional context changes from time to time, and the Jordanians can only react to a regional context created by others. This sometimes works in Jordan's favor, and sometimes works against Jordan's best interests. It worked in Jordan's favor, strangely enough, in the aftermath of the Gulf War, which severely weakened the stature of the PLO regionally, internationally, and financially because of Arab states' sanctions against the organization.

These factors are the backdrop to Jordan and the Palestinians, predominantly from the West Bank and backed by the PLO, creating a joint delegation to the Madrid conference. This was exactly what the Jordanians really wanted from their disengagement announcement:

to create a partnership with the Palestinians, preferably the West Bankers, with the PLO shunted aside to as great an extent as possible. Therefore, the Madrid formula for Jordan was more than an umbrella. It was the fulfillment of a Jordanian strategic objective.

One thing the Jordanians and the West Bankers did not have in this triangular relationship was the inter-Arab and Palestinian legitimacy to substitute for the PLO. Neither Jordan could do so, nor could the people in the West Bank and Gaza. And it is this that has brought the Jordanians back full circle, not to the federation plan of 1972, as Hussein would have liked, but to the Rabat resolutions of 1974.

In this light, one can understand Jordanian anxiety over the PLO-Israeli agreement. The PLO-Israeli agreement runs counter to almost everything the Jordanians have been trying to do for 20 years, and certainly what the Jordanians were trying to do in the framework of the Madrid process. This accounts for the combination of absolute rage and anxiety.

For decades, Israel had a special attitude toward Jordan. Israel saw Jordan as an essential component of a stable Middle East. And the reason why Jordan was so important for Israel, from the 1930s until the present, was the inability of Israel and the Zionist movement to come to terms with the Palestinian nationalist movement. This necessitated some kind of special association with Jordan. But when Israel comes to terms with the PLO, the Jordanians may very well ask themselves where this leaves them in Israel's strategic vision of the region. There were reports of meetings between King Hussein and Yitzhak Rabin in the aftermath of the agreement, in which the Jordanians were asking for reassurance. Whether these meetings took place, the Jordanians, in one way or another, were certainly seeking reassurance from Israel about Jordan's fate in the future.

What is to be Jordan's fate? What does a Palestinian state in the West Bank and Gaza mean for the Palestinians on the East Bank? These are open questions, and indeed, existential ones from the Jordanian point of view.

Interestingly enough, shortly after the Israel-PLO agreement, King Hussein published one of his speeches as a reaction to this quandary – the speech he made at the Rabat conference in 1974 against acceptance of the PLO as the sole legitimate representative. This was a reflection of the King's anxiety and the need of Jordan to acquiesce in an agreement that it certainly did not like, as much as it did not like the Rabat resolutions of 1974. But just as the Jordanians in 1974 fought against the recognition of the PLO but accepted the reality that was imposed upon them, very much the same is true today concerning the 1993 agreement.

What then is the attitude of the Jordanians toward the Palestinians at present? The King still emphasizes that Jordan is the closest to Palestine, that the Hashemites have a special status in Jerusalem, and that there is a need for some kind of association in the future between Jordan and a Palestinian state. At the same time, there is a warning directed to the PLO, that anyone who meddles with national unity on the East Bank will become the enemy of the King for all time to come. There is a fear that Palestinians may at some time in the future meddle in the unity of Jordanians of different extractions and, therefore, cause serious political difficulty in Jordan.

Jordan still favors the idea of confederation, but the Jordanians have not committed themselves to the formula of confederation because they do not know what it means. They are waiting to see what kind of Palestinian entity or state emerges before they make any decisions. For if a confederation means a Palestinian takeover of the East Bank, the Jordanians would not enter such an association. If, on the other hand, it means an instrument whereby Jordan can maintain a measure of influence over the Palestinians, that would be an acceptable outcome.

20

The European Community and the Middle East

S. Itzhak Minerbi

Since 1973 the member states of the European Community, now numbering 12 – they were only nine in 1973 – has held a position that is generally anti-Israeli and pro-Palestinian.[1] Even on such a sensitive matter as the proliferation of nuclear weapons, the Europeans were much less cautious than the Soviet Union. The Soviet Union had a much more conservative policy in the Middle East insofar as this issue was concerned, while some countries such as France, Italy, Belgium, and probably the Federal Republic of Germany, contributed to the proliferation of nuclear weapons in Iran and Iraq.

What were the motives of the Europeans in acting in this way? First, it was an exercise to find a common denominator in a foreign policy matter – and the Middle East seemed very appropriate for this purpose – to help build their own political unity.

Second, the major reason was Europe's need to ensure the flow of oil from its main suppliers in the Middle East. During the 1970s the annual reports of the European Commission show a terrible worry about oil supply. Somebody adds to this "at a reasonable price," but generally this was not the case; they wanted to ensure the physical supply at any price. We know today, according to statistics of Lloyds of London and other companies, that never during the oil crisis of 1973 was a single barrel of crude oil lacking in Europe, and the physical supply was always ensured.

There is naturally a very great economic interest at stake in the Middle East in the sale of goods, armaments, public works, and so on. There was a feeling also that in any case, Israel was well-protected by the United States and, since Israel was perceived as a mini-power in the regional sphere, there was no worry for Israel's survival. There was also a successful propaganda of demonization of Israel[2] – compared for many years to the Nazis – and this became some years later a media success for the *intifada*.

This may be seen in several events during the period. The first event was on 16 October 1973, when OAPEC – which is the Arab part of OPEC – decided to boycott the United States and Holland simultaneously. The immediate reaction of the then-nine members of the European Communities was to split; no more European solidarity. No more common policy. No more united stand. France and Great Britain immediately declared that they would not share oil reserves with other member states of the Community hit by the boycott. Thus, the first consequence was to split this newly created European Community.

Moreover, there were traumatic effects, such as horses being ridden down Avenue Louise in Brussels on a Sunday morning or the fan of a football team who came from Naples to Rome by taxi because cars could not drive on a Sunday. The impact was so great that on 6 November 1973, the nine members made a declaration urging the parties to "return immediately to the positions they occupied on 22 October", which in practical terms would have meant that the Israeli forces should withdraw from Egypt immediately; and the nine also thought that an eventual peace treaty between Israel and the neighboring countries should be based on the principle of "the need of Israel to end the territorial occupation," without any price in exchange for it, nothing. For the first time they spoke about the legitimate rights of the Palestinians, a phrase which then became a very common feature in many international statements.[3]

Thus the victory of the Arab countries, using oil as a weapon, proved that European solidarity could be shaken. They imposed their view of what they called "the legitimate rights of the Palestinians." They imposed, at least in a declarative way, only on Israel the obligation to do something, namely, to withdraw from all territories without any recompense. This declaration was immediately labeled in Israel by Abba Eban as a slogan which should be called "oil for Europe," and not "peace for the Middle East".

Some months later the Euro-Arab dialogue was established,[4] and immediately there was an obstacle. The Rabat conference in 1974 decided that the PLO must be involved. As a matter of fact, in about 20 years of life – 19 to be precise – this dialogue brought neither concrete results nor political advantage to either party. But it did go on for many years.

In 1978 there was the first Camp David agreement between Israel and Egypt, and this was very badly received in the Palestinian camp, and likewise so in the European camp. It seemed a prelude to a pax Americana from which the Europeans felt excluded.

After the signature of the treaty in 1979, came the famous Venice declaration of 13 June 1980, in which the Middle Eastern policy of the European Communities was established for many years to come – as a matter of fact, till up to 1993. It spoke again of the legitimate rights of the Palestinians; of the necessity for international guarantees; of the PLO, which must participate in the negotiations and the Palestinian right to self-determination; and of the Israelis, who should put an end to the territorial occupation. This Venice declaration was Europe's answer to the fantastic breakthrough of the Egypt-Israel treaty, which they practically snubbed.[5] The Euro-Arab dialogue was also frozen for a long period because Egypt was suspended from membership in the Arab League. For all these reasons, the peace treaty was very badly received in Europe. This was also a part of the very complex relations that the European Communities have with the United States. On the one hand, they could not forget that it was the United States, after the Second World War, whose Marshall Plan laid the basis for European integration. On the other hand, today Europeans regard the United States as a competitor in trade matters, and a hate-love relation characterizes U.S.-European relations. This was particularly true as regards the Middle East because France and Great Britain were so important in this arena before World War II. Their importance has steadily declined, and they feel this has been due to the U.S. presence.

During the 1982 Lebanese war, I was in Brussels as Israel's ambassador, and I was called by Mr. Tindermanns, the then-president of the council of ministers, to protest against the fact that Israel had stopped a ship full of humanitarian aid supplies sent by the European Communities to Lebanon, and therefore the ship never arrived.

I had some inside information about this ship. The ship was never prepared by the Commission. The ship never did leave any European port. The ship was simply non-existent. A protest was lodged by an official group of countries about something which never happened. This is the level of information fed to the president of the council of ministers at that time by the European Commission.

But the real crisis came with the Gulf War; the crisis in 1990, and the war in 1991. Again, as happened many times in the past, the Europeans had terrible difficulty in finding a common denominator for their policy. France was, as usual, going its own way. President Mitterrand, on 24 September 1990, in his speech at the United Nations General Assembly, presented a plan proposing that free elections be held in Kuwait, "free elections" which in this case only means to put a pro-Iraqi government into power. The Kuwait issue was also to be linked with the Palestinian issue.

To officially link the Kuwait issue with the Palestinian problem, as Saddam wanted, was not a very friendly act to Israel or the United States. The Catholic Church did something very similar; they never approved the war against Saddam Hussein, and even after the war, on 6 March 1991, there was a Synod of Middle Eastern bishops in Rome where the Pope himself linked the Kuwait issue to the Palestinian issue and declared that the war was inhuman and unjust.

French President Mitterrand said, with a great pathos, "It would be enough that Iraq expresses its intention to withdraw its troops, that it frees the hostages, and everything becomes possible."[6] So a simple declaration would have been enough. Even on the eve of the war, on 14 January 1991, France again went to the Security Council separately from the other member states of the Community, in order to advance again its own solution. The *Economist* wrote at that time that the Gulf had shown how slim were the European Community's prospects of becoming a new Western power; that it could only try to coordinate.[7]

Before the 1991 Madrid conference, the troika formed by the three ministers of foreign affairs, who were the current, previous and future chairmen of the European Council of Ministers, met Israel's Foreign Minister David Levy, and there was, according to the press, a seat found for the European Community in Madrid on condition that Israel would be included in the European Economic Area which was formed between EFTA countries and Europe. Not only did the Europeans participate in the Madrid conference, they also chaired one of the five committees of the multilateral negotiations, the Committee on Regional Economic Cooperation. This is significant because Europe has extensive experience in economic integration and can provide technical advice, as well as funds. The Europeans decided, at least in principle, to provide 500 million ECUs, half in grants and half by the European Investment Bank, to the Palestinian autonomy in order to assist in the first phase.[8]

The Israeli approach has also changed toward Europe. Instead of saying, "Hands off and please don't intervene in the Middle East, because any way you intervene, you are against us," Israeli Foreign Minister Shimon Peres has said that "the building of a Middle East of tolerance, economic cooperation and peace will have to take the form of a joint venture between the United States and the European Communities, because we need both."[9]

Notes

1. On the relations between Israel and the European Community see: Minerbi, Sergio Itzhak, "1992–The Year of the European Community," *Encyclopedia Judaica Yearbook, 1990/91*, Encyclopedia Judaica, Jerusalem, 1991; S. I. Minerbi, "Europe 1992 and the State of Israel," *The Jerusalem Journal of International Relations*, Vol. 12, No. 3, 1990; S. I. Minerbi, "Europe and the Middle East: An Israeli Perspective," *The Jerusalem Journal of International Relations*, Vol. 10, No. 3, 1988.
2. See Sergio Minerbi, *Mentir avec les images* (Brussels: Musin, 1985).
3. See Ilan Greilsammer, and Joseph Weiler, *Europe's Middle East Dilemma* (Boulder: Westview Press, 1987).
4. See Bichara Khader, *L'Europe et le monde arabe* (Paris: Publisud, 1992).
5. See S. I. Minerbi, "Israel et l'Europe," *Politique Etrangère*, No. 2, 1981.
6. See "Mitterand à l'assemblée generale des Nations Unies le 24 septembre 1990," *Le Monde*, 26 September 1990.
7. See *The Economist*, 19 January 1991.
8. See *Agence Europe*, 2 October 1993.
9. See *Agence Europe*, 3 September 1993.

21

Disarmament and Security in the Middle East

Vladimir Titorenko

The course of the peace process, especially in its multilateral track, has demonstrated once again the importance of disarmament and arms control in the Middle East. Previous sessions of the Multilateral Group on Arms Control (MGACRS), as well as some workshops on these issues, vividly showed to regional and outside parties in the Arab-Israeli talks the existence of a big gap in the approaches of different sides of the Middle East conflict and the serious impact of the problem on the global political atmosphere. The end of the Cold War did not result in the solution of the region's problems.

The Middle East now stands immediately after Europe in the size of armed forces and military arsenals, as well as in the qualitative and technological sophistication of weapons.

All this pushes toward the conclusion that any large-scale military conflict in the region can cross borders and bring the inevitable involvement of world powers.

The negative side of this problem consists of several factors, which turn the Middle East into the most explosive part of our planet:

1. In comparison with Europe and the U.S.-Soviet military situation – where there are rather effective mechanisms for arms control and settlement of disputes, as well as a whole system to prevent and manage crises – the Middle East lacks any regional cooperation in the fields of arms control, security measures and mutual trust.
2. Despite the peace process, there is still a potential for a dangerous confrontation between the Arabs and Israel, which

involves almost all world big powers; deep psychological gaps; and no effective disarmament process.

3. There are other conflicts in the region and sporadic outbreaks of local or bilateral disputes, including the Persian Gulf, the Lebanese civil war, Arab-Iranian disputes, Egyptian-Sudanese problems, Saudi-Yemeni border questions, etc., as well as conflicts with neighbors of the region – the problem of Kurdistan, Syrian-Turkish and Iraqi-Turkish disputes.

4. There is a lack of stability inside many Middle East countries, often related to the growing influence of radical Islamic trends (Egypt, Algeria, the Sudan, Tunis, Jordan, Palestinian territories and even Gulf emirates). The process of an Islamic fundamentalist consolidation of power on a regional level could result in the establishment of a whole network or empire of extremist regimes. With modern military equipment, such an alliance could deal a heavy blow to the interests of moderate forces in the Middle East, as well as undermining the interests of many world powers.

5. There is a general spirit of dissatisfaction in the Arab world with the U.S. monopoly in the role of sole superpower, and strong criticism of UN policy in the region, which is considered by many Arabs as a cover for the U.S. double-standard behavior in the region, or even as providing an international umbrella for interference in their domestic affairs. In this regard, one can understand why UN actions against Iraq and Libya are painfully perceived by some Arabs. In such an atmosphere of despair, many countries of the Middle East see only one alternative – building up their military machines as the only means to withstand outside pressures.

6. Unlike many other regions, the majority of Middle East countries have enough financial resources to buy new weapons. Besides, they have a rather high scientific and technical potential to develop their own military production and even conduct research on sophisticated missile, nuclear and chemical technologies. Some countries of the region have approached the level where the use of space becomes possible.

7. The democratic institutions in the overwhelming majority of Middle Eastern States are very weak and the ruling elites keep strong armed forces as the pillar of their stability. In exchange for military support in internal affairs, regimes have

to satisfy demands for weapon modernization and high levels of spending on the armed forces.

All parties in the Arab-Israeli conflict have extremely large armed forces with huge military arsenals. In the zone of direct confrontation, alone, there are 2 million soldiers, 16,000 tanks, 2,250 combat aircraft and 8,000 units of field artillery. Enormous efforts must be made to reach regional agreement on mutual reduction of such armed forces. As an example in this field we can use only the experience of Central Europe. But in the Middle East this formula cannot be fully applied: conditions are different and the confrontation has another historical background. Just copying previous experience can bring more damage than success. Both sides of the conflict have to start a very long, hard process of setting up a mechanism through which they can hold negotiations, using the MGACRS and bilateral tracks. But any serious talks here are almost impossible until political peace accords between Arabs and Israel are signed and security measures for mutual coexistence are reached.

It seems that every big country of the region is trying to guarantee its national security by means of strengthening military power instead of proposing some kind of regional system of collective security based on certain joint mechanisms. Such an approach stimulates the arms race, especially in strategic kinds of weapons, and this can only increase the level of confrontation. Slow progress in the multilateral part of the peace process, especially in MGACRS, continuation of tension around Iraq and Libya, Arab concerns about future Iranian policy in the Gulf, and setbacks in achieving Arab solidarity, all make the Middle East arms race uncontrolled and unpredictable. Ambitions to become a regional leader push many countries toward access to weapons of mass destruction and missile technologies. This undermines the global system of non-proliferation of nuclear weapons and weakens control over transfer of missile technologies while the Arab-Israeli dispute and other regional conflicts are still not resolved.

Instead of preventive diplomacy, outside powers might have to act to save the world from the consequences of a possible use of weapons of mass destruction. This problem is very delicate and demands the most cautious treatment from both inside and outside. Some countries of the region allegedly have nuclear and chemical warheads, or are very close to it. In any case, military nuclear and chemical programs can be quickly developed by many states in the Middle East. Things become more complicated because of modern means of delivery, like middle-range and long-range missiles, possessed by the armed forces of every big Middle East country.

"Outsiders" who want to earn money by exporting modern technologies make their own negative contribution to this problem. By selling technical documents or even certain components, they accelerate the process of turning the region into a warehouse of nuclear, chemical, and missile weapons. Under the specific conditions of the Middle East – where distances between the capitals of Arab states and Israel are very short – any attack with weapons of mass destruction will mean a catastrophe for the region and its neighboring areas, including south-eastern Europe, the Balkans and the Caucasus. Experience during the Gulf War demonstrated the vulnerability of every country in the Middle East if an aggressor uses missiles. This limits the strategic value of territory and complicates the solution of disputes. In order to solve the problem there is one thing to be done – prohibition and elimination of all kinds of weapons of mass destruction and the means for their delivery. Movement in this direction can be started with certain control mechanisms and a joint obligation of non-use of weapons of mass destruction.

It is also clear that this is not only the problem of Arabs and Israel. Countries like Iran and Pakistan cannot be ignored. There may be a need to include in MGACRS all neighboring countries with the potential to possess weapons of mass destruction (Iran, Iraq, Libya and Pakistan). Solving the problem also requires some measures from non-regional countries, especially industrially developed nations, in order to prevent any leakage of components and technologies that could be used in the Middle East for military nuclear and chemical programs, as well as for the production of middle-range and long-range missiles. Disarmament in the region must be supported by a parallel installation of security measures. The experience of Russian-American cooperation in this field, as well as all joint actions of the "nuclear club" and many international efforts, could be very helpful, if applied in a regional package.

Arms sales in the Middle East, especially after the end of the Cold War and Gulf crisis, prove only one thing: all big powers and large weapons-exporters, whether they like it or not, increase the level of possible military conflicts, even if they are sincerely devoted to the idea of a peaceful Middle East settlement and stability in the region. Political declarations do not coincide with economic interests, especially when taking into account the huge profits of military sales. Competition in this field is very natural, so it is difficult to say which country is more responsible for increasing the level of armament and growing confrontation. It is very naive to think that complete cessation of arms supplies in the Middle East can open the way to disarmament. Every country has the right to self-defense, and if this cannot be provided by its own means, weapons are bought on foreign markets.

But certain reasonable limits should be set in order to cut down extreme ambitions toward military superiority. Some kind of code of rules among arms suppliers, limiting access to offensive and the most sophisticated kinds of weapons, becomes a vital necessity. If we want to put an end to the escalation of the arms race in the Middle East, any attempts to illegally obtain military equipment subject to sales' prohibition, should be severely punished by some kind of international body established for this purpose. But such a policy cannot be allowed to undermine the legitimate security needs of any country or impose any unilateral discrimination.

The growing capacity of military industries in the Middle East also poses some additional barriers on the way toward disarmament in the region. While Iraq's military production was destroyed during the Gulf War, Israel and Egypt hold leading positions there. These two countries have reached a rather high technological level in this field, although their production units cannot provide self-sufficiency in defense demands. But no one can exclude the possibility that, in a few years, the military industries of Israel and Egypt will become absolutely independent on foreign technologies and components imported from outside, thus giving new impetus to the Middle East arms race. They have already produced airplanes, anti-aircraft systems, missiles, tanks, armored vehicles, laser equipment, etc. Their products bring good profits from export to other regions: from Africa to Latin America. It is no secret that some countries of the Middle East are looking for cooperation between themselves in joint military production, or are trying to establish such ties with outside partners. All this creates a certain imbalance between countries of the region, which stimulates those who are lagging behind and depend on foreign weapons to narrow the gap either by introducing their own military production or by increasing military imports. Competition in this field is very dangerous, and it is not clear how to find a just and practical solution to the problem. There are no serious regulations on this issue on the international level, so the problem of setting certain rules here is very difficult. But certainly for a comprehensive solution of Arab-Israeli disputes, some agreements concerning local military industries will be needed.

Foreign military presence, de facto and de jure, in the Middle East brings additional elements of tension. (I'm speaking about the foreign navies' presence in the Gulf, in the Red Sea or Eastern Mediterranean, military facilities and installations in Israel, Egypt, Iraq, Kuwait, Bahrain and Saudi Arabia.) This, of course, can be justified by some emergency situations, but it is also clear that foreign troops cannot provide normal peace. Maybe the time has come to lay down ideas regulating international or multinational military participation in peace-keeping operations to guarantee security in the post-crisis coexistence between Arabs and Israel. We have a rather positive example of multilateral forces' activities in Sinai on the Egypt-Israel border, but, of course, something more wide-scale for the Golan Heights, South Lebanon, West Bank, Gaza Strip and maybe Jordan will be necessary.

I can see here different formulas: UN forces, multinational forces, mixed national forces (for example, Syrian-Israeli or Israeli-Lebanese) or a combination of multinational and mixed national troops. Perhaps the effectiveness of their function in the zone of future peace between Arabs and Israel will serve as an example for alternatives to foreign military presence in other parts of the region. I do believe that no country, even the great military powers of the world, can alone provide lasting security in the Middle East; at the same time, regional parties can do what seems to be impossible now in this field.

No military coalition or union in the Middle East has proved to be effective in crisis situations. Arab collective security within the framework of the Arab League failed in confrontation with Israel, as well as in many disputes among the Arabs themselves. Any other multilateral or bilateral military alliances in the region existed for a very short time and then ex-allies became enemies. The 1990–91 Gulf crisis showed this once again.

The radical solution of the security problem in the Middle East may lie in radically new approaches to the issue. It seems to me that a security system based on the principles of equal guarantees to every country without any discrimination can serve as a solid pillar of peace and stability. In this respect, although it may sound crazy now, I would like to propose the idea of turning the Arab defense pact, signed in 1945, into a Middle East treaty of mutual defense and security, with Israeli participation, and open for neighboring countries like Iran and Turkey. Perhaps the Arab League will be transformed into the Middle East League after some time.

All talks on disarmament in the Middle East have tended to remain in the theoretical sphere, despite several rounds of MGACRS. The Arab side is pressing for something to be done about the nuclear potential of Israel, while Israel is calling on the Arabs to start with the reduction of conventional weapons and armed forces. This means that the concepts of both sides are based on the balance of power and not on the balance of interests and mutual trust. The lack of mutual trust prevents any serious talks on disarmament and any substantive progress in this area.

It seems now that Israel and the Arabs are ready only for some kind of control system, consisting of mechanisms to watch each other's military activities. But the end of the Arab-Israel political conflict will inevitably make issues of military aspects of peace a top priority for a final settlement. This will raise many questions: Why do huge arms supplies continue to be provided to the region? Why does a country develop a military industrial machine? Why does a country seek military superiority over its neighbors? It is time, within the framework of a political settlement of the Middle East conflict, to start a real disarmament process. The arms race will only bring further escalation of confrontation which could undermine peace efforts on other tracks of Arab-Israeli negotiations.

— 22 —

Russia's Middle East Policy under Gorbachev and Yeltsin

Evgeniy Bazhanov

A distinct Russian policy in the Middle East exists, even though not everyone in the Soviet Union has liked what Mikhail Gorbachev or Boris Yeltsin have done there. These two leaders' departure from traditional Soviet behavior in that part of the world has been too drastic, too fast for people in Russia to comprehend and to appreciate the transformation.

Let us examine the evolution of the Kremlin's strategies in the Middle East, starting from Mr Gorbachev's advent to power in 1985, and up to 1993. From the very beginning, Gorbachev proclaimed his desire to slow down the arms race, to relax international tensions, to seek political solutions to outstanding problems, and to develop peaceful cooperation with the West. Displaying much more honesty and flexibility than his predecessors in promoting these goals, the new Soviet leader, nevertheless, adhered to the basic tenets of the traditional Communist view of the contemporary world. Gorbachev believed that the U.S.S.R. and its "socialist camp," notwithstanding their obvious shortcomings and mistakes, were "the forces of progress" and their international activities were sound and correct.

In the Kremlin's eyes the Middle East remained a very important center of "the anti-imperialist liberation movement." At the same time, the United States was turning that rich, strategically located region into a springboard for aggression against the U.S.S.R. and its allies. So, Gorbachev did not hesitate in continuing the former policies of supporting old friends and rebuffing the Americans and their allies in the Middle East.

Much as in the past, the Kremlin poured military and economic aid into Syria, the PLO, Iraq, and South Yemen, and trained their "cadres," including guerrilla fighters. Moscow did not stop denunciations of Washington's militarist activities in the area, nor of the White House's attempts "to split the Arabs" and promote "the erroneous separatist Camp David process." Soviet leaders did not change their essentially hostile attitude to Israel, blaming it for violating Palestinians' rights and for new "aggressive Zionist designs."

Simultaneously, Gorbachev energetically pushed for "a just solution of the Israeli-Arab conflict" through convening an international conference. With time, though, changes in Soviet policies were becoming increasingly profound as the phenomenon of Gorbachev's "new thinking" spread over all aspects of international relations. A number of factors were influencing Soviet behavior.

First, Moscow's positions were changing as a result of improvements in Soviet-American relations, and in the overall international situation. Progress in curtailing the arms race made the Soviets more flexible and receptive to the ideas of opponents in the Middle East. The Kremlin started to take into account the opposing side's legitimate interests and concerns. As the global Soviet-American confrontation softened, the Middle East's strategic value as a front of the Cold War correspondingly diminished.

Secondly, along with Soviet society's ideological transformation, a new appraisal of Middle Eastern societies emerged. Some of the old Arab friends were found to be repressive, undemocratic regimes with terrorist tendencies in the international arena. The Soviet Communist Party's attempts to plant socialism on Arab soil were recognized as futile and detrimental to the development of Middle Eastern states. It was acknowledged that Moscow's economic aid to such regimes was a total loss, a burden that the faltering Soviet economy could not sustain.

In contrast, strategists in the Kremlin came to realize that moderate and conservative Arab regimes could become good political and lucrative economic partners of the Soviet Union. It was likewise realized that rapprochement with Israel was both necessary for a Middle East political settlement and desirable for economic reasons and for building the West's confidence in the U.S.S.R.

Consequently, Soviet behavior in the Middle East was drastically altered. By the end of the 1980s it clearly aimed for accommodation with former adversaries, resolution of regional conflicts, attainment of a stable peace, and development of mutually beneficial

economic links. New features of Soviet behavior in the region
emerged:

- Close cooperation with the United States. The two sides consulted, coordinated efforts, and made joint moves on the Israeli-
  Arab conflict, the Iraq-Iran war, the Kuwait crisis, and all other
  major problems of the region.
- Rapprochement with Egypt, Jordan, and Arab regimes of the
  Persian Gulf. The Kremlin renounced all previous misgivings
  about moderates and conservatives in the Arab world, sharing
  their political views on settling the dispute with Israel and
  on countermeasures against aggressive Iraq. The U.S.S.R. was
  eager to engage in profitable economic exchanges with oil-rich
  and affluent Arab countries.
- Distancing from radicals, who refused to compromise with
  Israel and engaged in terrorism. Moscow argued with its traditional friends, refusing to back them and directly opposing
  client-states, as in the case of Iraq's invasion of Kuwait. Economic and other forms of aid were noticeably reduced. As
  a result, friends of the U.S.S.R. had to adjust policies. Syria
  became more open to the West, South Yemen moved to reunify
  with North Yemen, the PLO plunged into internal crises, and
  Iraq shifted to more extremist positions. All of them complained
  about the Soviet "betrayal and cowardliness."
- Fast progress was made toward accommodation with Israel.
  Early in 1986, Gorbachev declared that Moscow recognized
  Israel's right to exist and to have security guarantees. The
  Soviet leader promised to establish diplomatic relations with
  Israel as soon as there was progress in settling the conflict. In
  1989, the U.S.S.R. and Israel exchanged consular offices.
- The Soviet Union was becoming increasingly instrumental in
  bringing the opposing sides in the Israeli-Arab conflict to the
  negotiating table. Top Soviet diplomats held frequent consulta-
  tions with both sides. The thrust of the Soviet position was to
  implement UN Security Council resolutions 242 and 338 and
  to guarantee Israel's security in exchange for territory and a
  solution of the Palestinian problem. By the summer of 1991,
  progress in the Middle East was evident, thanks, to a large
  extent, to combined U.S.-Soviet efforts.
- In 1988 the Iran-Iraq war finally ended, in part due to the
  two superpowers' actions. If in the past their mutual rivalry

had broadened and aggravated the conflict, by the late 1980s Moscow and Washington urged and pressured the belligerents to restore peace. The superpowers had helped to adopt the UN Security Council Resolution 598, which was accepted by the warring parties.

- The U.S.S.R. promptly condemned its client state Iraq's 1990 invasion of Kuwait and joined the U.S. in an arms embargo. Though Gorbachev preferred diplomatic measures to resolve the crisis, Moscow nevertheless approved an early resort to military action, sponsored by Washington. In this first post-Cold War crisis, the Kremlin could not have acted differently: support of Iraq would have ruined "new thinking" and would have pitted Moscow against most of the international community. The line chosen by Gorbachev not only strengthened Soviet-American ties but it also opened a way to normalize relations between Gulf states and the Soviet Union. Saudi Arabia, United Arab Emirates, Bahrein and others renounced the thesis of the Soviet threat, exchanged embassies with the U.S.S.R., and extended $2 billion in loans to the Soviet Union.

However, Gorbachev's Persian Gulf policy became the target of a broad conservative assault inside the U.S.S.R. The Soviet president was attacked for "betrayal of old friends," "assisting American hegemonistic ambitions," and "undermining Soviet economic interests in Iraq and other Middle Eastern countries." All other aspects of Gorbachev's Middle East policies as well as the whole strategy of new thinking were also condemned. Anti-Western paranoia reached its peak by the middle of 1991 and contributed to the Communist coup attempt in August.

After the defeat of the coup, the political atmosphere in the Kremlin and in the U.S.S.R. as a whole abruptly changed. When the doors of the Central Committee of the U.S.S.R. Communist Party were closed, the way was open for fundamental change in foreign policy. With anti-Communist feelings running high, the Kremlin turned its back on the Stalinist regimes in North Korea and Cuba, froze ties with foreign Communist parties, and concentrated on bringing Soviet policies in line with those of Western democracies.

In the Middle East, the new Foreign Minister B. Pankin finally established diplomatic relations with Israel, and the Soviet Union co-chaired the Madrid conference. But by that time foreign policy was hobbled by internal problems as senior staff members of the Foreign Ministry recalled Pankin from the conference, angrily demanding that he forget about Middle East peace and concentrate on saving the Soviet diplomatic establishment from collapse.

Neither the Soviet Foreign Ministry nor the U.S.S.R. itself were saved. A new state – Russia – appeared on the world map. For a number of reasons, this new state could not immediately define or implement a comprehensive long-term strategy in world affairs, including the Middle East.

First, the state was so young that it had not yet devised a new constitution and did not have a clear picture of its borders, armed forces, and many other essential aspects of a sovereign state.

Second, there was the chaos in Moscow's relations with the former republics of the U.S.S.R. It could not be guaranteed that the situation in the defunct Soviet empire would not follow the fate of Yugoslavia.

Third, the pattern of Russian foreign policy was further blurred by the profound internal crisis. More often than not, what Moscow did in foreign affairs was a reaction to internal pressures and emergencies.

Fourth, Russia was divided into two opposing camps on the issue of foreign policy. While the first, headed by Yeltsin, tried to make Russia "rejoin the family of civilized Western nations," the second preached hatred toward the West and advocated a highly nationalistic, Communist-type policy, similar to the one practiced under Stalin and Brezhnev.

The fifth factor complicating the creation of a well-defined foreign policy was the collapse of the system of decision-making. The new system was disastrously bad. Presidency, Parliament, Council of Ministers, Defense Ministry – each seemed to have its own foreign policy, different from that of the Foreign Ministry.

The Ministry did try to work out a coherent strategy and even issued a foreign policy doctrine by the end of 1992. It was aimed at making Russia a close partner and then an ally of the West. In the Middle East three basic goals of Russia were underlined: *security* (not to allow local conflicts and the subversive activities of some Middle Eastern forces to further undermine stability in Russia and adjacent areas); *economy* (to sell products in Middle Eastern markets and to attract local capital and technology for the modernization of Russia); *great power ambitions* (to play a significant role in the region, to be respected there).

In real life, goals set in the Foreign Ministry doctrine are not easily achieved, nor was the Middle East the first priority on the Russian diplomatic agenda. Initially Russia was not adequately active in the area; its role visibly diminished and was overshadowed by the vigorous advance of the United States on all fronts – political, military, economic. Moscow lost much of its influence among former radical friends in the Arab world. Among new friends – Israel, moderate and conservative Arab regimes – it gained a reputation as a non-threatening country, which, however, was not a reliable economic partner or strong political force. Moscow behaved well on the whole, but was not any longer an impressive player in regional affairs.

Gradually, however, Russia tried harder to regain its role and status in the region. Moscow's policies were getting tougher as well, due to the pressures from pro-communist and nationalist opposition. The opposition, uniting parliamentarians, former Communist party officials, army and security officers, the military-industrial complex, and experts on Arab affairs, to a large degree ignored Yeltsin's policy and pursued its own diplomacy in the Middle East: anti-American, anti-Israel, anti-Jewish, pro-terrorist and pro-radical. The opposition's activities stretched from publishing extremist tabloids to selling weapons and personally fighting on the side of radical Arabs.

Let us now examine concrete directions of Russian policies in the Middle East in 1992–93.

Russian-American Interactions: Rivalry and even competition between Moscow and Washington in the Middle East does not exist. The two countries closely cooperate concerning sanctions against Iraq and other violations of international law, pushing forward the Israeli-Arab negotiation process. The U.S. is the clear leader, and Russia plays a supportive role. The Russian government was among the first to express understanding of American bombings of Iraq in January 1993. Foreign Minister Kozyrev participated in the 13 September 1993 signing ceremony for the Israel-PLO agreement. Russian conservatives noisily disagreed with the Iraq bombings. Parliament condemned the action and promised to make Yeltsin veto any further U.S. moves against Saddam in the UN. A majority of deputies constantly demanded tough anti-American actions in the Middle East.

"The Old Friends" of the U.S.S.R.: Initially the Yeltsin government virtually abandoned "old friends" like Iraq, Syria, South Yemen, the PLO and Libya. Negative feelings were enhanced by these states'

behavior of cursing post-communist Russia for "bowing" to the U.S., "playing games" with Israel, stopping aid, and for its internal democratization. Later both Moscow and its former clients began to reconsider their extreme stands. In the Russian government it was argued that these regimes had been created and nurtured with Soviet help. Moscow had to take responsibility for their behavior. A continuing relationship was necessary to induce "the old friends" to settle regional conflicts and not to interfere with "hot spots" on the territory of the former Soviet Union. At the same time it called for revision or cancellation of obsolete friendship and alliance treaties with them. Moscow also wants very much to collect debts from "the old friends" in the Middle East, constituting half of the foreign debt owed to the former U.S.S.R. Attempts to get this money back so far have not been very successful (partly due to the low professionalism of Russian officials).

Israel: The Russian government puts an emphasis on development of relations with Israel for several reasons. It realizes that without normal links with Israel it is impossible to influence the peace process. Russia would also like to use Israeli experience in agriculture and technology. Since many Israeli citizens have a Russian background, this could offer an opportunity for close economic and cultural cooperation. Finally, a good rapport with Israel is an important factor in maintaining good relations with leading Western political and economic circles. There is also a religious factor; Russians' desire to have an access to the Holy Land.

There are, however, some circumstances restricting the faster development of Russian-Israeli cooperation: disagreement of Moscow with certain aspects of the Israeli stand on the Middle Eastern settlement; Arab pressures on Russia; anti-Israel sentiments of conservative political and military circles in Russia, stemming from Cold War thinking; and persistent anti-Semitism. On the whole, nevertheless, bilateral cooperation has continued to develop.

Moderate and Conservative Arabs: Moscow considers Egypt and Saudi Arabia, as well as smaller moderate and conservative Arab regimes, to be important partners. Egypt is attractive as an influential leader of the Arab world with a great economic and political potential. The heritage of Soviet-Egyptian partnership from the 1950s–1960s is also a favorable factor. Saudi Arabia and other Persian Gulf states are needed as investors and as outlets of arms sales for cash. Russia shares the moderate and conservative regimes' views on the settlement of regional conflicts and establishment of a security system.

Israeli-Arab Settlement: Russia was less prominent than the U.S. in bringing Israel and the PLO to Washington in September 1993. However, the formula of the Israel-PLO agreement was close to the one advocated by Moscow all along. Without Russian participation, the PLO and its Arab supporters might not have consented to the agreement, which was heartily welcomed by the Russian government and democratic press. Moscow has vowed to work with Syria and Lebanon to push further the Israeli-Arab settlement process. On some points, the Russian government is closer to the Arab's stand (for example, on the status of Jerusalem). At the same time Russia intends to exert influence on the Palestinians, encouraging them to stick to political methods rather than to military or terrorist ones.

Other Conflicts: Moscow has demonstrated its interest in suppressing and preventing other conflicts in the Middle East, including inter-Arab disputes and tensions between Iran and its Arab neighbors. Domestic critics, however, have claimed that the Russian government did not do enough, especially ignoring the potentially dangerous Kurdish problem. In the past the U.S.S.R. had very close ties with Kurds, and now Americans and other Western nations have become champions of the Kurdish cause.

Terrorism: The Kremlin not only discontinued any support of terrorism, but it was increasingly cooperative in fighting this evil. Russia, through various channels (diplomatic, security, immigration, military), coordinated efforts with other governments to fight terrorism and exchanged information. Public statements were made by Russian officials condemning certain Middle Eastern organizations like "Hizbullah." Russia characterized as legitimate and understandable Israel's concern about terrorist attacks and desire to counter them. At the same time Moscow stressed that there was an urgent need to eliminate one of the basic causes of terrorism in the Middle East, namely the Israeli-Arab confrontation. The Russian government also tried to restrain an excessive response to terrorist groups, jeopardizing other nations' sovereignty. Even such a balanced stand on Moscow's part did not satisfy radical Arab regimes and, of course, those directly involved in terrorist activities. Simultaneously, warm ties continued between terrorists and Russian extremists.

The Deterrence of Threats from the South: According to the Russian foreign policy doctrine, participation in the settlement of Middle

East conflicts and anti-terrorist activities is directly connected with the security of Russia. Instability could spread to former parts of the U.S.S.R. and to Russian territory. Moscow is aware of attempts by some forces in the Middle East to gain predominant influence and even to undermine stability and peace in Russia and its vicinity. Russian authorities carefully watch growing interactions between the former Soviet republics of Turkmenistan, Tadjikistan and Azerbaijan with Iran. Activities of a political-religious nature between Saudi Arabia and Moslem minorities of Russia in the Volga basin (Bashkiria, Tataria) are scrutinized. Russia notes the fact that numerous and influential ethnic minorities live in the Middle East, whose roots go back to the southern regions of Russia and to former Soviet States. Moscow does not wish to be pushed out of these areas. Even more worrisome for Russia is any penetration of political extremists and religious fundamentalists from the Middle Eastern countries into the highly explosive area of the Caucasus mountains near the Black Sea. The Russian Foreign Ministry's doctrine stipulates that penetration "must be rebuffed." The cooperation of the West and Turkey is solicited.

Arms Control: Russia considers the Middle East arms race to be excessive and dangerous, contributing to regional tensions. Moscow calls upon local states to join the nuclear non-proliferation treaty and the convention banning chemical weapons. Russia stands for reduction of arms levels of confronting states and for balancing their military potential. As a way to exchange information and to monitor military activities, Russia has proposed to establish a center for reducing military threats in the Middle East. Russia favors limiting both imports of weapons by local states and their production in the area.

Arms Sales: Russia, however, sells and intends to continue sales of weapons to the Middle East for three reasons: (1) commercial motives; Russia badly needs money and must help its military-industrial complex to adjust gradually to new circumstances; (2) a need to maintain the regional military balance important for peace and stability; and (3) an interest in restoring good relations with "the old friends" and strengthening ties with new partners, to deter interference with our "hot spots" by some Middle Eastern states. It is argued in Russia that when we stop exporting arms, the vacuum will immediately be filled by other producers, including the U.S. As a result of all the factors mentioned, Moscow will continue to be an arms supplier to the Middle East, but with restraint, following international agreements and common sense. Our actual levels of arms exports are much lower than in the past. Thus, between 1985 and 1988 Moscow supplied Syria with $7.8 billion worth of weapons. Between 1989 and 1992 the figure dropped to $500 million. Sales to Iraq went down from $7.8 billion in 1985–88 to zero nowadays. It is only Iran which today gets over $1 billion worth of weapons. In most cases the clients pay cash. Criticism of Russian exports, sometimes unfounded, is being heard from military-industrial complex lobbies in the West. Export controls are very weak in Russia these days, and various private or even state companies – for commercial and political reasons – violate laws, government obligations and regulations.

Security Arrangements: The Russian Foreign Ministry considers it important to strive for the establishment of a comprehensive security system in the Middle East not only in order to strengthen peace between Israel and its Arab neighbors, but also to defuse such problems as inter-Arab or internal crises, religious fundamentalism, terrorism, and proliferation of chemical or nuclear weapons. Support is given to the specific idea, already advanced in the area, of a Persian Gulf security system. Russia is even ready to join the arrangements, considering that it is necessary for this system to be open to every nation. Another Russian idea is to launch in the Middle East a process similar to the Conference on Security and Cooperation in Europe.

Economic Cooperation: The Russian government has a great interest in attracting investments and technology from such countries as Israel, Saudi Arabia, Kuwait, Iran, United Arab Emirates and others. A possibility being contemplated is to work closer with, or even to join, the Organization of Petroleum Producing Countries (though obstacles on the way are serious). Economic cooperation by Russia with the Middle East so far has not been really successful. In addition to mistakes by the government, there are objective difficulties: a chaotic Russian economy and political instability. It must be noted here that the dissolved Russian parliament castigated Yeltsin's administration for losing billions of dollars because of the trade embargo against Iraq, Libya, etc.

Great Power Ambitions: Even the most democratically minded, liberal Russian politicians and officials support the idea of maintaining (or restoring) Russia's great power role. For the pro-Communist and nationalist opposition, the loss of Russia's great power status is central in their attacks against Yeltsin.

Analyzing Russian behavior, moves and statements in the Middle East, it is important to bear in mind the great power motives of Moscow. These motives are enhanced by the interest of a number of Arab nations to have Russia in the region as a key player, in order to counterbalance the U.S.

23

The United States and the Middle East in the Post Cold-War Era

Yair Evron

The debate about the role of leaders in the shaping of history will never be satisfactorily settled. It is worthwhile, when analyzing any single historical event, to look at both "fundamental" causes and the role of decision makers in the formulation of foreign policy.[1] Some leaders have tremendous impact on the direction of international relations, but so do changes in the international system's structure, as well as changes in the structure of the regional system.

In this case, the subject is the potential advantage to peace and stability in the Arab-Israeli domain resulting from the end of competitive bipolarity and the Cold War. A subsidiary yet central question is the U.S. role in enhancing regional stability.[2]

Let us first consider the impact of the end of competitive bipolarity in the Middle East on regional peace and stability. During the Cold War and its projection into the Middle East, the superpowers were involved in sharp competition in the region. The intensity of the competition as well as other variations in their behavior, however, were dependent on the issues at hand. Here one has to make a distinction between three categories: conflict resolution, conflict management, and crisis management.

The competition between the two superpowers made it very difficult to achieve conflict resolution – the achievement of formal peace treaties – between Israel and its Arab neighbors for several reasons.[3] First, the superpowers (primarily the Soviet Union, but occasionally also the United States) used regional conflicts to enhance their own political objectives.[4]

Secondly, even when they were prepared to contribute to the

resolution of the conflict, their respective commitments to their allies were stronger than their readiness to cooperate. They were more inclined to back their allies' objectives rather than agree on joint policies.

Thirdly, in the late 1960s and early 1970s, when the Soviet Union became ready to cooperate with the United States in resolving the conflict, it demanded in return American recognition of the "equal" position that the Soviet Union sought in the Middle East. This was unacceptable to the United States. Thus, competitive bipolarity made cooperative superpower policy difficult to sustain in the Arab-Israeli region.

The same factors also made it difficult for the superpowers to contribute to conflict management, that is, strategic stability and avoidance of regional wars. Here, however, the historical record is more complex and presents composite situations. Thus, on the negative side, the political competition between the superpowers spilled over into regional conflicts and aggravated them.[5] Furthermore, the arms race that has for so long characterized the Middle East has partly been fed by the suppliers, primarily the superpowers.

Finally, as in the category of conflict resolution, the Soviet Union encouraged regional powers to adopt intransigent policies that might ultimately have led to crisis behavior and even military escalation. On the positive side, however, by and large, the two superpowers did not directly encourage military escalation among the regional powers; they usually advised their respective allies to adopt cautious strategies.[6] During specific periods they also tried to limit the transfer of specific weapons systems, by themselves or other suppliers, to the regional allies, with the objective of lowering the risks of military escalation.[7] Altogether, however, the ability of the superpowers to constrain their respective allies and preempt escalation into general war was limited. Whenever the regional powers considered that their vital national interests compelled them to resort to war, they followed their own security logic.[8]

It was, however, during major military crises that the superpowers did intervene in order to manage and stabilize the situation. Already in 1956, Washington and Moscow had intervened to terminate the British-French-Israeli operation against Egypt. In the event, it was American pressure that determined the outcome of that intervention; the Soviet role was secondary. Yet the broad outlines of a pattern of behavior that later became very central had already begun to emerge. Much more important were the superpowers' interventions during the 1967 War, the 1969–70 War of Attrition, the 1973 War, and the Lebanon War of 1982. In all these wars, the superpowers in fact cooperated to terminate the military crisis and stabilize the situation. They did this because of their mutual fear of becoming involved in an unintended escalation between themselves, possibly leading to a nuclear crisis.

It was, then, the combination of three different types of behavior in the areas of conflict resolution, conflict management, and crisis management (I once termed the last two "controlled competition")[9] that characterized competitive bipolarity in the Middle East. The end of bipolarity brought with it a paradoxical situation. The ability of the United States, as the remaining superpower, to considerably enhance processes of conflict resolution (in the limited sense of facilitating the diplomatic peace process) has greatly increased. This is mainly because the Arab states opposed to peace can no longer rely on the Soviet Union to back them in a military operation. Also, the United States, and the West in general, control the economic resources that can aid Arab states in their development. (Needless to say, without an Israeli readiness to adopt moderate policies, the change in the Arab states' policies would not have lasted.) As a correlate, conflict management in the Arab-Israeli region has also benefited. On the other hand, it is possible that, in the absence of formal peace between Israel and its Arab neighbors, the ability of the United States to terminate major regional military escalations might be more limited than during bipolarity, when the superpowers cooperated in crisis management.

The conclusion that emerges from this brief analysis is that the new structure of the international system and its projection into the Middle East make conflict resolution (in the said narrow sense of achieving formal peace treaties) easier to achieve, but at the same time might make war termination more difficult.

Although the pattern of bipolarity and its projected "controlled competition" into the Middle East have had an important impact on interstate relations in the region, the policies of the regional powers were ultimately more decisive in shaping the structure of the Middle Eastern state system. Indeed, as mentioned, the interaction between superpower policies and regional interactions is central to the understanding of regional interstate events. We shall, therefore, consider changes in the structure of the regional powers' relationship, and then the possible link between these changes and the current situation, in which the United States has become the dominant external power in the region.

Relations among the leading Arab states have been characterized over long periods by competition for influence. Thus, during the 1940s and 1950s Egypt and Iraq led respective coalitions that competed, especially in the Fertile Crescent.[10] This situation was partly renewed in the first half of the 1960s, though coalition formation during that period was more complex. The competition subsided to an extent from 1967 to 1973, when the Arab world was focused on the devastating outcomes of the 1967 War. During the 1970s the competition became much more diffuse and the Arab state-system overall quite fragmented, with no strong coalitions being formed and Arab solidarity (where it existed) suffering erosion. The Egypt-Israel peace treaty of 1979, and the lengthy Iraq-Iran war that ended only in 1988, increased this fragmentation.

The pattern of competition resulted from genuine regional causes, namely the ambitions of regional powers. However, at times these patterns reflected the effects of the Cold War on the region. Altogether, the combination of competitive bipolarity, the Arab-Israeli conflict, and inter-Arab state competition led to overall increased instability. These conditions were certainly not conducive to conflict resolution or conflict management.

After being formally ostracized by the Arab world because of its peace with Israel, Egypt began to reemerge as a key power in the second half of the 1980s.[11] By the late 1980s, Egypt, Iraq, Jordan and North Yemen had formed the Arab Cooperation Council (AAC), which, in cooperation with the Gulf Cooperation Council (GCC), comprising the Arab Gulf states, formed a central bloc. It did not lack its own internal conflicts of interest and differed from the coalitions of the 1940s and 1950s, which were more coherent and were led by hegemonic powers. Nevertheless, the members of this bloc did cooperate on many issues, and they were not divided by international orientation: its members were either oriented toward the West or were neutral and searching for accommodation with it.

The Gulf crisis and war tore this bloc apart and renewed the old pattern of competition between Egypt and Iraq. This time, however, more of the Arab states sided with Egypt or remained neutral and, with the defeat of Iraq, the central bloc reemerged as the main alliance in the Arab world. As already mentioned, this bloc is not a coherent one and many disagreements exist among its members. Moreover, Egypt, the main Arab power, does not enjoy the role of hegemonic leader of the bloc, nor does it seek such a role (as Nasser did in the 1950s and 1960s). However, it is not likely that major conflicts verging on diplomatic crises or even military escalation would take place among its members. The members are more likely to try and coordinate their policies on major issues and resolve their differences by diplomacy.

This new structure of inter-Arab relations appears to complement the new position enjoyed by the United States in the Middle East. The latter is better able to pursue policies of conflict management and conflict resolution in the Arab-Israeli zone now that there is only one friendly Arab bloc that is not plagued by deep divisions and bitter rivalry. Indeed, if past competition had continued, nothing short of joint superpower policies might have enhanced conflict resolution and conflict management in the Arab-Israel region.

In my view, power relationships and "high politics," on the level both of the external powers and of regional interstate politics, are the determining factors in increasing stability.[12] In the present context, one can refer to a concert of parties, a system of coordination among the main international powers, with the United States at their head.[13] The main West European powers, Russia, Japan, and possibly China, might participate in such a system; therefore it would contain elements of both unipolarity and multipolarity. This system would be loose and its membership might vary with respect to different issues. Furthermore, the coordination would not be projected into all the regional subsystems of global international relations.

As far as the Middle East is concerned, it is likely that the United States will continue to play a special role. The elements of unipolarity would, therefore, be more significant and the role of other global powers limited. However, some coordination of policies among the leading global powers would be conducive to stability in several ways. First, it would give international backing to unilateral American political and strategic initiatives. Secondly, it might be important in at least two specific areas: economic aid for development projects linked to the peace process; and the application of various arms control and confidence- and security-building measures.

The fit between the current set of interstate relations in the Middle East and the unique position that the United States now holds there is conducive to the peace process and to the introduction of other security measures designed to increase stability in the area. The vital interests the U.S. has in the Middle East, and the image of its readiness to resort even to force to defend these interests, as demonstrated in the Gulf War, have contributed considerably to the peace process.

It is likely that this image of American determination will continue to influence regional decision makers, even as the Clinton administration devotes most of its energy and resources to domestic issues and appears to refrain from foreign policy activism as much as possible. The administration would probably be prepared to become involved in guaranteeing some aspects of the peace treaties, primarily between Israel and Syria, even through military commitments. These might involve the positioning of American forces on the Golan when it is demilitarized as part of a comprehensive peace settlement.

Beyond that, once the peace process reaches its positive conclusion, the broad strategic situation in the Middle East should alter significantly. There will then be an enhanced need for considering different regional approaches to security. In all of them, the United States should, and probably will, play an important role. Regional security might be approached through the application of various regional confidence- and security-building measures, such as a regional crisis management center, agreements to control and monitor regional military capabilities and exercises, agreements on nonproliferation of weapons of mass destruction, and so on.

Another approach, which might be unconnected, or an addition to the above elements, would involve the creation of various types of mutual security agreements. These might include the establishment of an Israeli-Jordanian-Palestinian security zone,[14] and/or of a strategic axis in which Egypt, Israel, Turkey, and possibly other Arab states would take part. In all of these arrangements the United States might play different sorts of roles, from active participant to benign guarantor.

The changes in the regional structure of interstate relations since the late 1980s, and especially since the Gulf War, have resulted in the emergence of a central bloc in the Arab world that marks a departure from, first, the traditional pattern of coalition formation in the Arab world and the competition for hegemony by ambitious Arab regimes, and secondly, the deep fragmentation among Arab states that characterized the Middle East during parts of the 1970s and 1980s. This overall change, coupled as it is with the process of the political legitimization of Israel among most Arab elites and a corresponding moderation of policy toward Israel, accords with the emergence of the United States as the dominant external power in the region and the decline of Soviet influence.

Whereas competitive bipolarity made conflict resolution in the Middle East more difficult, unipolarity – or a possible mixed system of unipolarity and some elements of a concert of powers – could enhance both conflict resolution and management.

Notes

1. And see, on this distinction, the chapter by Shimon Shamir in this volume.
2. I agree with the analysis and predictions concerning future American policy in the Middle East presented by Joseph Sisco in this volume.
3. Conflict Resolution usually comprises more ambitious objectives than formal peace agreements. Basic among them is accommodation between societies erstwhile in conflict, and inter-societal connections. Close economic relations is one important dimension of conflict resolution, as well as positive changes in mutual images between nations.
4. The literature on the superpowers' relations in the Middle East is of course considerable. On the roots and early phases of their competition, see for example, John D. Campbell, *Defense of the Middle East* (revised edition) (New York: Praeger, 1960); Nadav Safran, *From War to War: The Arab-Israeli Confrontation 1948–1967* (New York: Pegasus, 1969); Jacob C. Hurewits (ed.), *Soviet-American Rivalry in the Middle East* (New York: Praeger, 1969). On the superpowers' competition in general, see *inter alia*: Peter Mangold, *Superpowers Intervention in the Middle East* (London: Croom Helm, 1978); Yair Evron, *The Middle East: Nations, Superpowers and Wars* (New York: Praeger, and London: Croom Helm, 1973); William Quandt, *Decade of Decisions* (Los Angeles: University of California Press, 1979).
5. This had begun already in the early 1950s with several American and British efforts to organize the Middle East in a defence alliance connected with the West. The creation of the Baghdad Pact in February 1955, culminating these efforts, led to the worsening of inter-Arab states' competition and ultimately was one of the reasons for the Egyptian decision to seek Soviet arms. The Egyptian-Czech (in fact Egyptian-Soviet) arms deal of 1955 led on its own part to tremendous concern inside Israel and contributed eventually to Israel's decision to participate in the 1956 war against Egypt. On these developments, see Nadav Safran, op. cit., Yair Evron, op. cit. On the Suez campaign of 1956, see *inter alia*, Hugh Thomas, *The Suez Affair* (London, 1967).

On Israel's security policy during that period, see *inter alia* Mordechai Bar-On, *The Gates of Gaza: Defense and Foreign Policy 1955–1957* (in Hebrew) (Tel Aviv: Am Oved, 1992).

Throughout the Cold War, large segments of the decision making elites in Washington and in Moscow, respectively, perceived Middle Eastern states' relations through the prism of global rivalry. This led to many misperceptions concerning regional developments. Thus, many policy decisions taken by regional states were seen as resulting not from regional causes but rather from initiatives taken by the respective superpowers.

In addition, both superpowers utilized at times the Arab-Israeli conflict as an instrument for the enhancement of their respective objectives. The Soviet Union, for example, utilized Arab defeats in 1967 in order to increase its influence in Egypt and Syria, while the United States during 1970–73 backed Israel's intransigent policy *vis-à-vis* Egypt in order to compel Egypt to abandon its dependence on the Soviet Union and turn to the United States. On American policy during that period, see Quandt, op. cit., Henry Kissinger, *White House Years* (Boston: Little Brown, 1979) and *Years of Upheaval* (Boston: Little Brown, 1982).

6. Soviet behavior during the 1967 crisis encouraged Egypt to adopt an inflexible position but preferred no war to war. See *inter alia*, Safran, op. cit., Evron, op. cit., Walter Laqueur, *The Road to War 1967: The Origins of the Arab-Israeli Conflict* (London: Weidenfeld and Nicolson, 1968).

7. On Soviet limitations on the supply of some specific weapons systems to Egypt, see for example, Jon David Glassman, *Arms for the Arabs* (Baltimore: Johns Hopkins University Press, 1975). The United States refrained from supplying any arms to Israel until the early 1960s. After the 1967 War, American arms began to flow to Israel but, even then, the United States imposed, at different times, limitations on the supply of some specific weapons systems to Israel.

8. See Yair Evron, "Superpowers Military Intervention in the Middle East," in Milton Leitenberge and Gabriel Sheffer (eds), *Great Power Intervention in the Middle East* (New York: Pergamon Press, 1979).

9. Ibid.

10. On the patterns of coalition formation among the Arab states, see *inter alia*, Stephen M. Walt, *The Origins of Alliances* (Ithaca: Cornell University Press, 1987); Yair Evron and Ya'acov Bar-Siman-Tov, "Coalitions in the Arab World," *The Jerusalem Journal of International Relations*, Summer 1976.

11. On developments in the Arab world during the 1980s, see *inter alia*, the annual volumes of the Middle East Contemporary Survey (MECS) (New York: Homes and Meier); Bruce Maddy Weitzman, "The Inter-Arab System and the Gulf War: Continuity and Change," *Occasional Papers Series* (The Carter Center of Emory University, 1992).

12. The literature on realism in international politics is of course enormous. For a pessimistic realist approach to European security after the end of the Cold War, see John Mearsheimer, "Back to the Future: Instability in Europe after the Cold War," *International Security*, Summer 1990. A general realist approach to international events following the end of the Cold War is included in Henry Kissinger, "Balance of Power Sustained," in *Rethinking American Security*, (New York and London: W. W. Norton, 1992). On the liberal approach to international politics, see *inter alia*, Michael Doyle, "An International Liberal Community," in Graham Allison and Gregory Treverton (eds), *Rethinking America's Security*; Francis Fukuyama, "The End of History?," *National Interest*, Summer 1990.

13. A set of arguments as to why unipolarity characterizes current international politics following the end of the Cold War and the disintegration of the Soviet bloc and of the Soviet Union is included in Charles Krauthammer, "The Unipolar Moment," in *Rethinking American Security*, ibid. On the idea of a "concert" of powers which might emerge following the end of competitive bipolarity, see *inter alia*, Richard Rosencrance, "A New Concert of Powers," *Foreign Affairs*, Vol. 71, No. 2, Spring 1992.

14. See Yair Evron, "Israeli-Palestinian-Jordanian Security Relations: The Idea of a 'Security Zone,'" *Occasional Papers Series*, No. 3, 1990, American Academy of Arts and Sciences.

24

World Order and the Arab-Israeli Conflict

Yehoshafat Harkabi

I consider the achievement of reaching the Israel-PLO agreement on principles a very important event in the annals of the Arab-Israeli conflict. It is a sea change, and it didn't come about only because of a change in understanding. It seems to me that what brought it about is much more serious: an important change in substance in the parties' position. If we compare what leaders said before and what they are saying nowadays, we can evaluate how important and serious is the change. Many of the leaders on both sides have now to eat crow; Israelis and Arabs and, I would say, others – interlocutors, observers and commentators on the Arab-Israeli conflict.

The question arises: How did they reach such a change? The significance of the agreement is that it involved concessions on both sides. It seems to me that one of the elements is that both sides had the audacity to take a train without knowing exactly the destination of that train. Until now, that was an important bone of contention which foreclosed any agreement on the Arab-Israeli conflict.

In order to describe how wide the change is, let me describe the positions before. Previously neither side felt urgency in settling the Arab-Israeli conflict. Furthermore, both sides – and especially the previous government in Israel – considered the Arab-Israeli conflict as a war of attrition. You simply had to wait until the other side was exhausted and then he would agree to your terms. That was the position among Palestinians and Mr. Shamir made no bones that that was his position, that negotiations would go on and on for years; there was no urgency in reaching a settlement.

Now suddenly there is a change and it is the realization of the leaders from both sides that they are standing on the brink of an abyss and cannot wait. Only thus did they become ready to offer the big concessions needed on principle to reach the settlement. There is, however, a problem here. So long as they have not formulated the final settlement, all kinds of obstacles await us, once it becomes clearer to both sides that the price of the settlement is much higher than they envisaged.

Of course, there is also a possibility that what has been achieved may be called a positive Gordian knot. Usually, when we describe a Gordian knot we describe it in negative terms or, in colloquial Hebrew, you call it a *"plonter."* Now what has happened is that both sides are in a *"plonter."* But these are positive Gordian knots for they will force them to continue on the route that they have started.

What brought the change and how did it come? World order is a neutral term. It does not mean that the world is orderly or tidy. In each period, there was a world order, and world order is simply the characterization, our conceptualization of the character of the world: How do the political entities that compose the world behave?

I believe that part of the difference was caused by leaders finding themselves in a world order which negated their previous positions and obliged them to make the change. In this present world order, competition is no longer primarily over territory and power but over economy and commerce. That has brought about a certain decline in the war system. In most countries now there is a tendency to cut the armies' powers, to stop military industry. There is not one international war nowadays, though, of course, there are some internal wars, and it's very difficult to intervene there and stop them. But on an international scale, war has stopped being a solution to problems.

In addition, however, order is very patchy. There is world order, but within it there are many islands of different orders. Part of the world is marginalized. As the main transactions are commercial, not all the world takes part in those transactions. They are between the more developed countries and within the developed bloc. And therefore what we see is marginalization of part of the world. Furthermore, it's easier to intervene in an inter-state war than in an internal war where you have to enter every village. The agenda of leaders is overburdened with their own internal problems and not much time and attention is left to deal with other parts of the world. Consequently it is a very heterogeneous world order.

There is also fear of being marginalized. Arab intellectuals always repeat the theme of the marginalization of the Middle East. And they are afraid of it. But this situation also creates a productive feeling that we cannot rely on others; we have to do it ourselves in reaching an agreement. There is a great divergence of opinion between us but we must bridge the gap and start making progress without knowing what is our final destination.

The intellectuals understood, too, that postponing a settlement of the conflict is impossible. The Middle East is going to be in grave danger if we wait. It seems to me that Arafat was very alive to that factor of threat, to himself and to his movement, from Hamas. If Hamas should take over, it will become a conflict to the bitter end because of the involvement of the religious element. You cannot compromise on religious views, especially when you believe that God is on your side and you will prevail in the end, and that victory is bound to be yours.

There are other elements in understanding that there *is* a possibility that those directly involved in the conflict will be marginalized, that people will say: "We are sick and tired of the Jews and Arabs. Let us leave them to their devices: it's impossible to bring them to their senses." I believe that this was an important element in the consciousness of both sides, a feeling that there is no time to lose. Hoping for a long attrition in which the other side will get tired is an illusion. And thus they came to reach that agreement, without knowing what the final settlement will be. I don't believe that there are many such agreements in history.

Despite these very real factors and perceptions, I do believe that the international community is worried about the Arab-Israeli conflict. I doubt that this conflict could be marginalized, despite the parties' fear, because of the arsenals in this area; and the fear that its conflict could spread into a big conflagration all over the Middle East and beyond. Consequently, there is an international willingness to help the diplomatic settlement.

It will take a lot of effort by both sides to redefine their national ideologies and to rewrite the history of the Arab-Israeli conflict. Each side will have to admit that it caused a lot of suffering to the other side and atone for it. This intellectual redefinition, along with the required political changes and compromises, can bring the Middle East toward a period of renaissance and great prosperity.

Contributors

Evgeniy Bazhanov is deputy director of the Russian Foreign Ministry's Diplomatic Academy for Research and International Relations and director of the Institute of International Studies in Moscow.

Yossi Beilin, a scholar who has taught at Tel Aviv University, is presently a member of Knesset, serving as Israel's Deputy Minister of Foreign Affairs. His record of public service includes appointments as government secretary, Foreign Ministry director-general for political affairs and Deputy Minister of Finance.

Gabriel Ben-Dor teaches political science at the University of Haifa and is a former rector. He is the author of *State and Conflict in the Middle East* and co-author of *Confidence Building in the Middle East* and *Conflict Management in the Middle East*.

Shmuel N. Eisenstadt is professor emeritus of sociology at the Hebrew University of Jerusalem. A member of the Israeli Academy of Sciences and Humanities and a foreign honorary fellow of the American Academy of Arts and Sciences. He has also been awarded the International Balzan Prize in sociology, the McIver award of the American Sociological Association and the Israel Prize in his field.

Yair Evron lectures on international politics and strategic studies at Tel Aviv University and is also head of the university's graduate program for security studies. He has published extensively on international politics in the Middle East and his most recent books are *War and Intervention in Lebanon: The Israeli-Syrian Deterrence Dialogue* and *Israel's Nuclear Dilemma* (forthcoming).

Joseph Ginat is professor of social and cultural anthropology and head of the Jewish-Arab Center at the University of Haifa. He served as adviser to the cabinet and the Prime Minister on Arab Affairs and as personal adviser to Moshe Dayan, and he was formerly head of the Israeli Academic Center in Cairo.

Yehoshafat Harkabi, professor emeritus of International Relations and Middle Eastern Studies at the Hebrew University, presently teaches strategy at the Israeli Defense College. In the 1950s he served as Chief of Military Intelligence. He has published many books on the Arab-Israeli conflict and strategy. In 1993 he was awarded the Israel Prize in International Relations and Strategic Studies.

Manuel Hassassian, professor of political science at Bethlehem University, is also dean of the Faculty of Arts and chairman of the Humanities Department. He is a research fellow of the Truman Institute and is a member of the editorial board of the *Journal of the Arab Political Science Association.*

Yair Hirschfeld is senior lecturer on Middle Eastern History at the University of Haifa. A member of Shimon Peres' "Hundred-Day Team" (responsible for planning Israel's policies in the West Bank and Gaza), Dr. Hirschfeld was also responsible for opening the Oslo channel for peace negotiations and was a member of the Israeli delegation to Oslo in 1993.

Moshe Ma'oz is head of the Truman Institute and professor of Middle Eastern and Islamic Studies at the Hebrew University. He served as deputy adviser to the Prime Minister on Arab Affairs and as adviser to Ezer Weizman, when he was Minister of Defense.

Zeev Maoz is professor of political science at the University of Haifa and director of the Center for Policy and Security Studies. Specializing in international conflict and strategic studies, his books include *Paradoxes of War* and *National Choices and International Prophesies.*

Yoram Meital lectures at the Department of History of the Middle East at the University of Haifa. With numerous publications to his credit, he has recently completed a manuscript, *Egypt's Road for Peace with Israel: 1967 to 1977.*

Itzhak Minerbi is professor of political science at the University of Haifa and senior researcher at the Davis Institute for International Relations, Jerusalem. Former Assistant Director-General for Economic Affairs at the Foreign Ministry, Minervi also served as Israel's ambassador to the Côte d'Ivoire, Belgium and Luxemburg, and as head of the Israeli mission to the EEC.

Nasser Eddin Nashashibi, a former high-ranking officer and private adviser at the Hashemite Court of King Abdullah of Jordan, has also served as Director-General of the Jordanian Broadcasting Service, as

Arab League Ambassador for Special Missions, and as Chief Editor of *Al-Qumirriyah* daily in Cairo.

Barry Rubin, who teaches at Tel Aviv and Hebrew universities, is a fellow at the Truman Institute and the University of Haifa's Jewish-Arab Center. His most recent books include *Cauldron of Turmoil: America in the Middle East* and *Revolution Until Victory?: The Politics and History of the PLO.*

Amnon Sella, who teaches Russian Studies and International Relations at Hebrew University and is the head of the Leonard Davis Institute for International Relations, served as advisor to the strategy division in the Foreign Ministry. His most recent book is *The Value of Life in Soviet Warfare.*

Shimon Shamir, a professor of Modern Middle Eastern History at Tel Aviv University, is also head of the university's Tami Steinmetz Center for Peace Research. Founder and first director of the Israeli Academic Center in Cairo, Shamir also served as Israel's third ambassador to Egypt.

Moshe Shemesh is a senior lecturer in the Department of History at Ben-Gurion University and a senior research associate at the Ben-Gurion Research Center at Sde Boker. His publications include *The Palestinian Entity 1959–1974: Arab Politics and the PLO.*

Joseph Sisco represented the United States in the UN Security Council and held the positions of assistant and under secretaries in the administrations of Presidents Ford, Nixon, Johnson and Kennedy. He is now president of the American University in Washington D.C. and is on the advisory board of the Center for Strategic Studies.

Matti Steinberg, a lecturer at the Hebrew University, specializes in Arab and Palestinian attitudes toward Israel. Among his publications are *The Palestinian Covenant – The Test of Time and Practice* (with Y. Harkabi) and *The Arab World in the 1980s.*

Asher Susser, senior lecturer in the Department of Middle Eastern and African History at Tel Aviv University, is also head of the university's Dayan Center for Middle Eastern and African Studies. He specializes in the political history of Jordan and the Palestinians. His most recent books are *On Both Banks of the River* and *At the Core of the Conflict: The Intifada* (in Hebrew).

Abraham Tamir (General Ret.), throughout a distinguished career, has been instrumental in developing the Israel Defense Forces and the infrastructure for Israel's national security. He has also played a major role in the peace process with Israel's Arab neighbors and in developing Israel's relations with countries throughout the world. The many prominent positions that he has held in the IDF and the Ministry of Defense include Chief of Operations, Chief of Strategic Planning (a branch which he established), National Security Advisor, and Director-General of the Prime Minister's office and the Foreign Ministry.

Vladimir Titorenko is a diplomat and a graduate of the Moscow Institute of International Relations. In recent years he has served in the Russian Ministry of Foreign Affairs, dealing with Middle East affairs and the peace process.

President Ezer Weizman, founder and former Chief of Staff of the Israeli air force, also served as Minister of Defense and Minister for Arab Affairs. He participated in the peace process with Egypt as a member of the negotiating team at the Camp David talks.

Index

Note: For a name starting with al- or el- see its second part.

From war to peace